"Katherine is truly gifted! Her magical techniques ⸱ changing . . . especially if your heart is blocked to recei⸱ and wisdom can assist anyone wanting to find 'The One.' Her processes worked for me. . . . I am now in an amazing committed relationship with my life mate!"

—Renée Piane, author of *Get Real About Love:
The Secrets to Opening Your Heart and Finding True Love*

"You can't get what you want until you know what you want. Katherine Woodward Thomas helped me to define what I was looking for and helped me to create a path to call in the love of my life. Now, I'm proudly wearing a beautiful engagement ring on my finger, given to me by my wonderful life-partner. It works!"

—Debra Tennen, MD, ophthalmologist

"Working with Katherine Woodward Thomas opened my heart and mind to embracing and healing all aspects of 'The One' in me. Yes, I have called in the love of my life, my beautiful husband; a lover beyond my wildest dreams! Yet most important, I've called in—and live in—LOVE."

—Karen Russo, author of *The Money Keys:
Unlocking Peace, Freedom, and Real Financial Power*

"Katherine is brilliant at helping to create an inviting space for your divine-right partner to show up. When I first came across her teachings, I was in a relationship with a wonderful man who was just not the right person for me. Yet within a few months, that relationship was over and the man who would soon become my husband, Paul, showed up. We are now the parents of two wonderful children. I am so grateful for Katherine's wisdom, clarity, and inspiration."

—Wanice Mottola, mother and writer

"This course became my lifeline, best friend, and guardian. It gave me what I craved most: the compassionate understanding, loving support, and practical tools to guide me in releasing old blocks and patterns that were inhibiting love from entering my life. The work required some time and dedication, but as I'd made the commitment to do it diligently and honestly, I was amazed to find it comforting and pleasurable. Just a few weeks after finishing the course, I met my amazing husband, who is now the father of my beautiful children."

—Debra Kaufman, happy homemaker and mother

" 'The One' I had to call in first and foremost was myself, and this course gave me the tools to do that. Definitely a life-changing experience on many levels. A beautiful, healing journey into the heart, expanding it to let more love out, and welcome more love in. It helped me to stand in the vision of the great love I'd always wanted in my life, but never before truly believed I could have. I'm happy to say that I actually *DID* find 'The One' soon after completing the course! And our partnership is *so much better* than anything I had ever even imagined possible."

—Magda Molina, jewelry designer

Thought Leader Endorsements

"There are people in all our lives to whom we listen with our ears perked, and for me, Katherine Woodward Thomas is such a person. Katherine is a woman I look to for wisdom and counsel. How wonderful that her advice is available to all."

—Marianne Williamson, *New York Times* bestselling author of *A Return to Love*

"Katherine's grounded and fierce tenderness has been an inspiring force for me for years. . . . She is a visionary whose passion for both personal and global fulfillment is felt throughout her writing, presence, and teaching. I am so grateful for her."

—Alanis Morissette, multiple Grammy–winning singer/songwriter

"I have known Katherine Woodward Thomas for many years and can attest to the fact that she is a most brilliant teacher. Her articulation of the principles and subtleties of the adventure of relationship is impeccable. Regardless if one is seeking to bring their beloved into their life or release a relationship to assume another form, her teachings are stellar guideposts for this kind of sacred transformation. She's the real deal."

—Rev. Michael B. Beckwith, founder, Agape International Spiritual Center; author and creator of *Life Visioning*

"I love Katherine Woodward Thomas! She elegantly and articulately explains the cause of our relationship pain; and what's really required of us to heal our major wounds so we can become all of who we are, and move beyond previous limitations. She's incredibly clear and well-researched. Yet most important to me is her authenticity, her vulnerability, and her transparency. Her story is an inspiring message that weaves it all together and leaves us transformed."

—Jack Canfield, bestselling author, speaker, and entrepreneur

"Katherine Woodward Thomas is a master teacher and one of the great pioneers who is offering new perspectives, skills, and tools that will lead us into the depths of authentic loving, and to the true potency and power of relationship."

—Dr. Jean Houston, bestselling author of twenty-six books and co-founder of the Human Potential Movement

"Katherine Woodward Thomas is my relationship guru."

—Gabrielle Bernstein, *New York Times* bestselling author of *Miracles Now*

"Katherine Woodward Thomas touches and transforms people's lives with her quiet, graceful, exquisite elegance combined with an incredible power that moves through her and into us!"

—Debra Poneman, bestselling author and founder of YesToSuccess.com

calling in
"the one"

7 Weeks to Attract the Love of Your Life

Revised and Expanded

Katherine Woodward Thomas

Harmony Books

New York

Broadway Books, an imprint of Random House, a division of Penguin Random House LLC: Excerpts from
"This being human is a guest house" and "Lovers Think They're Looking for Each Other" from
The Illuminated Rumi by Jalal Al-Din Rumi, translated by Coleman Barks, copyright © 1997 by
Coleman Barks and Michael Green. Reprinted by permission of Broadway Books, an imprint of
Random House, a division of Penguin Random House LLC.

Harmony Books, an imprint of Random House, a division of Penguin Random House LLC: Excerpts from
"Looking for Your Face," "The Awakening," "The Agony & Ecstasy of Divine Discontent," "Do You
Love Me?" "I Am and I Am Not," "Looking for Love," and "Lost in the Wilderness" from *The Love Poems
of Rumi* by Deepak Chopra, copyright © 1998 by Deepak Chopra, M.D. Reprinted by permission of
Harmony Books, an imprint of Random House, a division of Penguin Random House LLC.

Daniel Ladinsky: "The Sun Never Says" and "Some Fill With Each Good Rain" from *The Gift: Poems
by Hafiz* renderings by Daniel Ladinsky (New York: Penguin Books, 1999), copyright © 1999 by
Daniel Ladinsky. Reprinted by permission of Daniel Ladinsky.

Parallax Press: Excerpt from *Present Moment Wonderful Moment: Mindfulness Verses for Daily Living*
by Thich Nhat Hanh, copyright © 2006 by Unified Buddhist Church. Reprinted by permission of
Parallax Press.

Library of Congress Cataloging-in-Publication Data
Thomas, Katherine Woodward.
Calling in "the one" : 7 weeks to attract the love of your life /
Katherine Woodward Thomas.— 1st ed.
Includes bibliographical references.
1. Single women—Religious life. 2. Mate selection—Religious aspects.
I. Title.
BL625.7 .T47 2004   646.7'7—dc22   2003017868

ISBN 978-0-593-13979-0
Ebook ISBN 978-0-593-13981-3

Printed in the United States of America

Book design by Jen Valero
Cover design by Kathleen Lynch/Black Kat Design
Cover art by Popova Anna/iStock/Getty Images Plus

8th Printing

Revised Edition

*To those of you
who've had your heart bruised
and dreams crushed
more times than you can count.
Yet who courageously, boldly,
steadfastly, and stubbornly continue to
believe in love. . . .
This book is for you.*

*And to Alexandria and Mark . . .
the sweet fruits of my labor.*

Special Thanks

If I have seen further it is by standing on the shoulders of giants.

—Isaac Newton

All accomplishments in life, both great and small, can be traced to the influences and efforts of many. This book is no exception. It has taken the love and support of many wise and caring people over the years to help me arrive at a place in my life where I have something valuable to say. The collective kindness and generosity that I have received in my life is a debt that I can never repay directly, and can only hope to pay forward for the rest of my life. I do, however, wish to thank certain people for helping me, not only to write this book, but also to become the person who was capable of writing this book.

To my original "vision keepers," Naomi Benghiat and Jennifer Holt, thank you for steadfastly holding the vision of what love could, and would, look like in my life, when I was too weary to care; and for the depth of your devotion to the fulfillment of my dreams. To Lora Cain, for providing hours of encouragement, editorial advice, and edification. To my agent, Angela Rinaldi, who, with great kindness and care, skillfully managed to shepherd this work into the world. To my first editor, Jennifer Kasius, for blessing this project with the magnitude of your talents and creative abilities. To Nancy Hardin, for your generosity, commitment, and common sense. To Carrie Thornton, for so graciously and adeptly stepping up to the plate as we came into the final stretch. And now to the wonderful Michele Eniclerico, whose talents as an editor were indispensable to this project.

To Douglas Evans, for being one of those rare and special people who actively seeks to bless and prosper those around you. And to Maureen O'Crean, for insisting I write all this down in the first place.

To every psychotherapist, spiritual teacher, and healer I've ever had, including

Dr. Anne Brooks and Rev. Chris Faulconer, for your amazing generosity, wisdom, and counsel as well as your willingness to travel into the depths to help me find my way home. To Marianne Williamson, whom I knew when, and who has consistently modeled for me what it is to be a woman on fire, burning brightly for the forces of love. To the Agape International Spiritual Center, Rev. Michael Beckwith, and Landmark Worldwide, for helping us all to expand our capacity to love and be loved.

I also want to thank the tens of thousands of clients and students I've had the honor of coaching and teaching over the past two decades. You've catapulted my own growth, both personally and professionally, and I've been blessed to work with each and every one of you. Appreciation as well to Claire Zammit, whom I had the honor of working with for well over a decade, and who did much to support the growth of the *Calling in "The One"* work in the world.

Great gratitude also goes to my Certified *Calling in "The One"* Coaches, particularly those of you who've been working with me for well over a decade to train other coaches, and to serve the many students who've come to us from around the world: Lina Shanklin, Jeanne Byrd Romero, Prem Glidden, Janet Webber, Jane Velten, Victoria Rose, and Lynne Michaelson. Thank you too to those *Calling in "The One"* Coaches who also support our community to flourish and thrive: Leila Reyes, Dr. Joan Bragar, Dale Sparage, Paige Ramsey-Palmer, Martina Meyer, Judy Waters, Cheryl G. Roberts, Susierra Willson, Eileen Jager, Melissa Monahan, Suz Bagstad, Jennifer Zundel, Isandra Muñoz Bonilla, as well as the thousands of *Calling in "The One"* Coaches I've trained and certified since the book was first published in 2004. Thank you too to my support team, with special mention to Kristi Capurso, Wendy Speigner, Kristin Rywalski, Jeffrey Kihn, and Gina Vucci and her fabulous team.

My gratitude would not be complete without appreciating all of my past loves and ill-fated romantic partners, from whom I've learned everything—thank you from the bottom of my heart and please forgive me my flaws.

Thank you too to my family. My kind-hearted former husband and awesome co-parent, Mark; our powerful and brave daughter, Alexandria; my brilliant bonus daughter, LeRoya, and her dad, Lee. My brothers, Todd Grupe and Scott Grupe; my mom, Sandra Pullman; and my dad, Bob Kersch. Thank you for supporting me through the many years it took to grow myself into the person I've become.

And finally, deep heartfelt gratitude to Michael. You are the star that lights the night sky.

Contents

Week Six | A LIFE WORTH LIVING 259

Week Seven | LIVING LOVE FULFILLED 305

Preface: My Story

Be realistic.
Plan for a miracle.

—Bhagwan Shree Rajneesh

This is what being single was like for me. I am an attractive, charismatic woman—petite, with a curvy figure, olive complexion, and unruly dark hair. I love people fervently and I have a profound need to be deeply connected to them. I loathed being alone in life. Yet, by the time I reached my fortieth birthday in 1997, I was a true-blue, card-carrying member of one of the fastest-growing groups in America, the "never-marrieds."

I had no problem meeting men. As a matter of fact, my favorite advice to my girlfriends was that old saying "Men are like buses. If you miss one, another will be along in ten minutes." In other words, don't spend too much time grieving when they disappoint you. And believe you me—I spoke from experience.

When I was nineteen, I had a boyfriend who, responding to my nurturing and caring nature, told me that it would be a tragedy if I never had children. His words haunted me as the *(tick, tick, tick)* years passed.

When in my late thirties, having just finished graduate school en route to becoming a psychotherapist, I sat reading Gail Sheehy's book *New Passages,* which at the time had just come out. In it, she devotes a whole section to women who, like me, had postponed childbearing. She quotes a gynecologist as calling this phenomenon "a mini-epidemic of . . . deluded, about-to-be desperately disappointed women in their mid-forties." My heart sank. I knew then that it just wasn't ever going to happen for me and that I'd just been fooling myself. Remember, this was before the promising option of freezing your eggs. So, the stakes felt incredibly high.

At least once a week, as though he or she had the right to humiliate me, someone

> All of our suffering in life is from saying we want one thing and doing another.
>
> —Debbie Ford

would say, "You've never been married? Why? What's wrong?" For years, I told them that it was because I hadn't met the right person. Eventually, though, I began to secretly wonder if it was because I'd never *been* the right person.

I kept trying to figure out what was *wrong* with me. Here I was, counseling others on how to have great and loving relationships, then coming home to an empty apartment night after night. Why wasn't anyone proposing to me? Why wasn't anyone asking me to be the mother of his children? God, it would have been better if I were at least divorced. Then I could say that *someone* had wanted me, only it didn't work out.

This was my pattern. I went for unavailable men: any type, shape, size, color, professional affiliations, or lack thereof. As long as it was an impossible love, I was in. I was a magnet for married men, engaged men, workaholic men, alcoholic men, commitment-phobic men, and gay men who wanted to explore. And because I worked with ex-cons as an art therapist for several years, I also seemed to possess an unfortunate allure for straight men who were on their way in or out of prison. All of these men found me fascinating and compelling and would go to remarkable lengths to bed me. I'd like to be able to tell you that available men found me uninteresting or unattractive or . . . something. But, truthfully, so few available men came into my life that I have no idea how they might have responded to me. Consequently, I was alone quite a bit.

Sometimes, I'd give in and become entangled in some drama that wasn't ever going to go anywhere and I'd feel terrible about myself. I'd berate myself for wasting my time on impossible relationships, yet it seemed the only alternative was to be alone. And, as I told you before, I loathed being alone. All too often, I found myself getting attached to a man whom I didn't respect, seduced by his desire for me. The occasional man I'd meet whom I did respect and who actually was available seemed to run like water through my fingers. He was always on his way elsewhere.

Finally, right around my forty-first birthday, I met a gracious and classy man named Daniel. He was a widower whose wife of twentysomething years had passed away a few months before we met. He was good-looking, kind, successful, spiritual, fun to be with, and very, very considerate of me. He told me over and over how beautiful and smart he thought I was and went out of his way to try to please me.

I thought I'd gotten it right this time, completely ignoring the signs that I was simply his transitional relationship in the aftermath of a long and happy marriage. Even though I had stopped dating anyone but him, the truth was, he had several girlfriends whom he was seeing. I was just waiting for him to come to his senses! Perhaps, in my heart of hearts, I didn't believe that I'd ever have what I really wanted. So, I just pretended that even though he wasn't committing to me, the crumbs were good enough. After all, it was a huge step up from some of the guys I'd dated. This included the one who thought being good to me was "letting" me feed his cats while he was away. Yet, when Daniel asked another woman out on New Year's Eve, I finally got the hint. Daniel was the last unavailable man I ever dated.

> *If you want the whole thing,*
> *the gods will give it to you.*
> *But you must be ready for it.*
>
> —Joseph Campbell

Meeting "The One"

Now I have to back up about six years, to 1992. I was dating William, whom I'd met through the personals. (That's back when people actually put ads in the newspaper to try to meet someone, pre–online dating!) William seemed to be the good guy I thought I was looking for—bright, creative, sweet, *law-abiding*, and *employed*. He actually paid for dinner at the nice restaurants he invited me to. I was in heaven. I did not yet know that William was a rageaholic. That part came later.

When I was invited by a friend to a gathering sponsored by a local spiritual group, I asked William to come along. Now, William had about as much interest in spiritual matters as I have in the mating patterns of armadillos. However, when a man is trying to get a woman into bed, he racks up lots of points by going with her to the kinds of events she's interested in, and this fact was not lost on William.

We made our way to the address I was given and rang the bell. A man who

> You don't have to go looking for love when it's where you come from.
>
> —Werner Erhard

introduced himself as Mark answered the door. Welcoming and polite, he invited William and me to join the group that had gathered in his living room. Although Mark gave no overt indication of being attracted to me, I've always had a fairly acute radar about these things. I could tell by the way his glance lingered just a moment too long that he was interested. I was flattered and somewhat intrigued. When he called two days later, I was not completely surprised.

On my first night out with Mark, we attended the backyard wedding of a friend of his. We were so absorbed in our conversation that we barely paid attention to the bride and groom. Afterward we went dancing. I assured Mark that my relationship with William was not exclusive. I convinced him that it would be perfectly fine for me to date both of them. I did this for two months, after which time I chose William over Mark. Upon reflection, I see that I let Mark go because he didn't fit the picture in my head of what "The One" would look like. I can also see that it was not the right time for Mark and me to be together. This was for a variety of reasons, not the least of which is that being with Mark would have required a certain level of maturity that I did not yet possess.

A year later, out of the blue, I received a call from Mark. I hadn't heard from him since our sad "I can't see you anymore" talk, due to my growing relationship with William. Yet by that time, I'd already broken up with William, and another "bus" had come along. Although my newest relationship had not yet progressed to exclusivity, we were knee deep in getting to know each other. In spite of this, I agreed to spend time with Mark, and we had a couple of magical dates together, one of which was going to see the just-released romantic comedy *Sleepless in Seattle*. As we began leaning in to connect on a deeper level, the man I'd been seeing caught wind of it and upped his game. After only two weeks, I had to admit that I wasn't able to pursue things with Mark, and I reluctantly let him know that, once again, I wasn't available.

For the next six years, I thought about Mark off and on. I would wonder how he was and if he was even single anymore. And I wondered if he ever thought about me. Each time I was between boyfriends, I'd toy with the idea of calling him. Somehow, I always decided against it.

Six Years Later

Back to December of 1998. In response to my little epiphany about my widower semi-boyfriend, Daniel (i.e., after six months of dating and no New Year's Eve date, get a clue, girlfriend!), I did what most of us do. I called one of my best friends to complain. Now, what I *wanted* her to do was to conspire with me in making Daniel and, for that matter, all men in general, wrong. Instead, she asked me what I was avoiding by choosing to be alone in life. The question startled me. I had so longed for a healthy, committed partnership with a man whom I could love and respect that I hadn't even considered that I might actually be invested in being alone. Yet, as much as the question irritated me, I had to confess that the idea resonated as true. The more I sat with it, the more I realized that I loved my freedom, in spite of my complaints to the contrary. I loved not being accountable to anyone. I loved keeping my options open. In fact, I had to admit that I was terrified of being emotionally dependent on anyone, and vulnerable to the possibility of being left.

Now, I became a psychotherapist from the inside out. Helping others to heal was a natural outgrowth of how I'd been healing myself for close to fifteen years by that time. Believe me, by then I knew my issues backward and forward, and thought I had most of the answers to my own perplexing questions and broken-hearted dilemmas. However, I was still acting in reaction to things that had happened to me as a child. Things like my parents' nasty divorce and losing contact with my father as a result. I still felt profoundly victimized by how these relational traumas of the past kept relentlessly showing up in the present, as persistent and dramatic setbacks in love. I wasn't yet looking to decipher the specific and habitual ways that I myself was unconsciously choosing to behave that were covertly re-creating these painful disappointments that I'd suffered as a child. It seemed to simply be my fate that these old hurts would show up again and again, and I was completely unaware of how I was actually surreptitiously perpetuating them. (More on this later!) Although I'd been focusing my

> The important thing is to be able at any moment to sacrifice what we are for what we could become.
>
> —Charles Dubois

efforts on endlessly mourning the countless ways my parents had failed me, the truth was, I was actually the one unconsciously propagating the lack of love in my life due to the many walls I'd built against it. In spite of my deep yearning for love, the truth was that I was actually somewhat conflicted about letting it into my life.

Becoming Available

You can work on yourself for years and then someone says one little thing and your whole universe shifts. My friend's simple question initiated a profound period of inquiry for me about how I might be the source of my own aloneness. I simply couldn't go on blaming others—my parents, men, the culture—for my circumstances. For years, I had made my desire to meet "The One" the central drama of my life. Yet I saw in that moment that in many ways, I'd been substituting drama for love. In an instant, I finally understood the difference between wanting love and being ready to receive it.

As luck would have it, it was around this time that I came across an inspired group of people who were committed to helping one another set intentions in order to manifest miracles in their lives. We'd hop on the phone once a week to share our intentions with one another, and created a somewhat informal accountability structure to help us stay on track to manifest those breakthroughs. What I didn't know then, but have since discovered through research, was that this was a really smart thing to do. In the past few decades, research has begun on the power of collective intention, led by such scientists as Roger Nelson and Dean Radin.

It began with the controversial PEAR studies done in the late 1980s at Princeton University, which demonstrated that an intention shared between a bonded group of people is actually six times more likely to manifest than an intention not shared with others. Most of the people in our group were focused on expanding their professional or financial success in the world, like doubling their income or buying their first property. Given my recent bruised heart (or perhaps it's more accurate to say, bruised ego), I decided to set an intention to find "The One." To make it official, I called a friend from the group. "Naomi," I said, "I'm going to be engaged by my forty-second birthday." Now, my birthday was a mere eight months away and I had absolutely no prospects for a husband, let alone a great one. Yet in response to my unreasonable assertion, she said something that changed my life.

"Katherine," she replied, "I will hold that intention with you and for you if you give me permission to hold you accountable for being the woman you would need to be by your forty-second birthday in order to be engaged."

Gulp.

And with that one little sentence my friend shifted me from running out like a crazy person to try to find love, to going within to discover all of the internal blocks and barriers I had unknowingly built against it.

> Don't tell me the
> story of your past.
> Tell me the story
> of your future.
>
> —Dr. Joe Dispenza

Now, before this, I'd been blaming my chronically single status on a host of things that were outside of my control. I thought maybe men didn't like powerful women, or that there weren't enough straight men to go around. I feared I was too old, that my thighs were too big, or that I was just too messed up from childhood. I was sure all the good ones were taken, and that I'd just never meet the right person. In trying to solve the mystery of why love had eluded me for so many years, I had all sorts of external reasons to justify my inability to find a committed union. Yet my friend's assertion invited me to go deeper and take a good hard look at the ways I'd covertly been working against myself, and unknowingly sabotaging my love life.

Declaring a future of love fulfilled is nothing like setting an intention to create something that one can actually control, like starting a nonprofit or getting a graduate degree. You can't write a business plan to find true love. Instead, you must rely upon your intuition to try to find your way to that future, and focus your efforts on becoming the person you would need to be in order for that future to happen. For this reason, I began each day in a visioning meditation. Which basically means I made a sincere attempt to sit in stillness for a few minutes before running off to the demands of my ridiculous schedule. I'd watch my mind rattle off its insistent to-do list, drop my awareness down into my body by paying attention to and then deepening my breath, and try to get hold of a deeper sense of center. Then I'd imagine that the miracle had already happened, and I was in a wonderful relationship with a kind and loving man. I'd lean in to try to listen to us laughing. To imagine I could smell the scents of the meal he was preparing for us. I'd pretend I could hear him singing in the shower or talking on the phone to a friend. I'd allow myself to feel his tender touch on the small of my back, or his fingers lovingly combing through my hair. I'd soften into what it might feel like to be in this relationship; safe, happy, grounded, loved, inspired . . . home. I felt at home with this person.

After a time of basking in the sweetness of this scenario, I'd ask the Universe three questions, inspired by a visioning practice I'd learned from my dear friend Rev. Michael Beckwith.

The first was "What will I need to give up to find my way to this future?"

The second was "What will I need to embrace and/or cultivate to prepare myself to receive this future?"

And the third, "What is my next step to co-create the fulfillment of this future?" (I added that one!)

Almost immediately, I found myself receiving a level of inspiration, clarity, and intuitive instructions that I hadn't ever experienced before in life. It wasn't like a burning bush, but more like a hunch, a gut feeling, an insight, or an idea that truthfully, I could easily have dismissed. Yet I didn't. Instead, I tentatively followed the guidance I was receiving, wondering all the while whether I was "just making it up" or if I really was being led to take certain actions and move in certain directions. Either way, the guidance I felt that I was receiving seemed sound enough, so I went with it. During this period, I spent Saturday nights at home alone going through my things, burning old love letters and deleting old emails that I'd saved for no reason other than to feel less lonely. I gave away jewelry given to me by former lovers. I put away love poems a past lover had written for and about me. I went through my apartment, removing any images that reflected loneliness, sorrow, or isolation, replacing them instead with pictures that represented love, union, and joy. I wrote page after page after page in my by-now-tattered journal, examining how I was the source of my own single status, reflecting upon all the ways that it actually worked for me to live a solitary life, and on all of the choices I made to ensure it, in spite of my protestations to the contrary. I started acting as if my assertion to manifest my perfect mate was real, and began organizing my life around the fulfillment of that future. I measured my choices and actions against a future where I was wildly happy in love. Within a month, my life turned completely upside down and inside out. Daniel and I had a genuine heart-to-heart, laying it all out on the table. We discussed what each of us wanted in our lives and decided to break up, transitioning our relationship into a friendship. I had some sincere conversations with a couple of men who'd been my flirting buddies. They brought clarity and, in one case, completion to our friendship. Like many of my relationships, it seemed founded upon the possibility of romance without any real availability on his part. And I finally released and mourned a relationship that had taken five years to run its course.

I also began showing up in new ways. Leaning in to discover who I'd need to be in order for this future to have even a chance at happening, I suddenly discovered a newfound clarity and courage to start setting boundaries I'd never been willing to set. To take risks I'd never been willing to take. To speak up where before I'd been silent. I stopped blaming and shaming anyone, myself included. Within a few weeks, I became unrecognizable to myself, and to others.

I'd like to say it was a joyful process but truthfully, it was incredibly uncomfortable to give up my old habits, safety strategies, and, frankly, my whole *identity* in this way. Most times, it left me with a tremendous void that danced in the pit of my stomach. However, I really believe that if you want to create a miracle in your life, if you truly want to make a big and life-altering change, then you've got to learn to tolerate the "in-between" time. That's the period in which we let go of who we know ourselves to be in order to allow for the possibility of who we might become.

Calling in "The One"

By now, it's February of 1999 and thoughts of Mark began popping into my head again. Yet, once more, I decided not to call him as I was absolutely convinced he must be married with two kids by then. One Sunday, I attended services at a church I'd gone to for ten years. In all that time, I'd never once seen Mark there. As far as I knew, he wasn't even aware of the place. Speaking with a friend in a crowd of several hundred people milling about the parking lot, I looked up. To my surprise, there was Mark walking across the asphalt! I immediately had a shy attack and turned away, hesitating just long enough to lose sight of him. By the time I gathered my courage to look for him, he'd disappeared. "Oh, well, I guess it wasn't meant to be," I told myself, to mask my disappointment.

Two weeks later, I was speaking with another friend on the phone. In spite of setting my intention and faithfully doing my inner work, I was complaining that I

> Hitch your
> wagon to a star.
>
> —Ralph Waldo
> Emerson

still wasn't even close to finding "The One." I was getting impatient. This was March and I was on a deadline! My friend suggested that I log on to an Internet dating site where she'd been meeting some interesting people. Now, this is back before Internet dating was a thing. In fact, at the time, no one even posted their photos. When I logged on to the one and only dating site my friend knew of, there were a quarter of a million faceless love seekers there waiting, identifiable only by their somewhat creative love handles like "Two Hearts Beating as One" or "Romeo Seeks His Juliet" as well as the brief profiles they'd written about themselves. Frankly, I found the whole thing a bit weird. Yet due to the urgency of my deadline, I was coachable. Following my friend's directives, I entered my age, religion ("Other"), location, and logistical preferences, and narrowed down this impossible number to a mere eighty men.

As I read through their profiles, one in particular captured my interest. The author said that he believed we were all interconnected and, therefore, ultimately a part of one another—a conviction I shared. He went on to describe himself as a well-rounded, happy, and successful man. I decided to respond. Feeling a little foolish and self-conscious, I quickly rattled off a brief and somewhat awkward paragraph about myself. I then continued scrolling through the other choices. Another man's profile made me laugh out loud with his dry and urbane sense of humor; but when I began crafting a response to him, my computer froze. Having little patience with technology, I turned off my computer and went to bed, losing the response I'd started.

The next evening, I turned on the computer to check my emails. As I heard the familiar "You've got mail," I noticed that the man I'd written to had written me back. His response had come straight into my email inbox, as was typical back then. Amazed, I stared at his name, which stood in parentheses next to his email address. The man was Mark. "Of course," I thought; "how perfect."

Since my identity was not obvious from my email address, Mark did not know who I was and he wrote to me as he would to a stranger. I responded warmly, as though to an old friend, and revealed my identity. Weeks later, Mark would tell me that he was so stunned to hear from me this way that he literally fell off his chair. Soon after, he collected himself and called to invite me out for coffee—a gesture, he later assured me, he would never have made if not for such an obviously meant-to-be encounter. Mark has a healthy amount of self-esteem and would not have asked me out again after my having turned him down twice before. As a matter of fact, he later confessed that he *had* seen me across the church parking lot that day and had deliberately left without speaking to me. So, you see, we needed a bit of a miracle to bring us together again.

Several days later, I found myself sipping a large cup of decaf across from this handsome, bright, kind, and gentle man. I knew within an hour that he was "The One" I'd been searching for. I was no longer ambivalent and afraid of love. I came home and excitedly emailed the friends who'd been supporting me, stating unequivocally that I'd just had a date with the man I was going to marry. And in fact, Mark proposed two months later, on the last day of May. Eight weeks *before* my forty-second birthday. We were married the next year and the following year, at age forty-three, I gave birth to our daughter.

We then happily rode off into the sunset, all three of us joyfully strapped onto the back of a beautiful white steed.

Living Happily Ever (and Even) After

Although most of us aspire to not need anyone to be happy and fulfilled, the truth is, we all need loving, supportive relationships in order to thrive. Yearning for love isn't pathological. It's *wise*. Inside of the nourishing environment of my happy home with Mark, my life blossomed in ways it never had before. We bought a beautiful home, I opened a healing arts center in a great part of Los Angeles, and I finally secured that coveted book deal that I'd dreamed of for years: the first edition of this book, which, much to my surprise, became a national bestseller within weeks of publication. Soon after, people from around the world began flocking to me, to teach them how to manifest a miracle in their love lives. Over the next few years, tens of thousands of people participated in my online and in-person transformative learning communities.

I was living the happily ever after story to the max. And like most of us, I anticipated that our love would last forever. Yet, brace yourself. Because ten years into our marriage, Mark and I chose to . . . well, get divorced. Now, for those of you committed to finding a lifelong partner, please don't let this news discourage you. Most people who find love by doing the *Calling in "The One"* program do stay together for a lifetime. In fact, those who offered testimonials in the opening pages of this book did so seventeen years ago, and I'm grateful to say they're all still happily partnered with "The One" they called in as a result of doing this work. That said, Mark and I did choose to separate. So, let's talk a moment about living happily *even* after, since many of you who are reading this book have also ended a marriage.

None of us, when walking down the aisle to pledge lifelong devotion to our one true love, assumes that we'll wind up on the wrong side of that tenacious divorce divide, and I was no exception. I had the added complexity of being a visible teacher of love in the world. To say I felt confused and humbled is an understatement. Yet what I discovered during this topsy-turvy time (due to a restless search on the Internet at 2 A.M.) was that the "Happily Ever After" myth we all assume to be the ultimate goal of love is actually only four hundred years old and that it was created when the life span of the average person was less than forty years of age.

Hmmmm. . . .

The truth is that in our day and age, in many parts of the world, serial monogamy is the new norm. Now, I'm not promoting this. I'm just reporting what's so. I'm actually a big fan of lifelong love, and wholeheartedly support anyone who's committed to manifesting a love that lasts forever, like those who gave their testimonials at the front of this book. Yet the truth is, in our very mobile and modern society, people change. To be specific, in this incident, I changed. Radically. And rather ironically, it was because of the loving-kindness and support of our connection that I was actually empowered to do so.

So, once past the disappointing realization that this was indeed happening, I turned my attention to ensuring that it happened with as much love and respect as was humanly possible. After all, I was and still am a lifelong student of love. I figured if I could crack the code on how to get unmarried without getting into a pissing match, and instead have it be decent, respectful, generous, and kind, that I'd be onto something. Mark and I were also motivated to have this go well for the sake of our daughter. We'd both experienced the loss of contact with one of our parents after their respective divorces, and understood firsthand how devastating this can be for a child.

I also knew how horrible breakups could be from the many bad splits I had in the past. I was familiar with the kind of sleepless soul-shattering separations that happen in response to the all-too-common raging, blaming, and shaming that can go on when people take on untangling their lives from one another. Given my toxic history with relational trauma, I knew how badly this could go.

Yet, one saving grace of our separation was the thoughtful, generous, and honoring way we chose to go about it. Having aligned upon a shared intention that our daughter have a happy childhood, we mindfully completed our relationship as spouses and re-created it as mutually supportive, cooperative co-parents, giving birth to what Mark and I now affectionately call our "happily *even* after" family. After finding a conscious, loving way to transform our relationship to its new form of family without doing damage to ourselves, each other, and our daughter, I was also able to create the five steps of *Conscious Uncoupling*. I feel proud to say that my hard-won new teaching made it into the lexicon when actress Gwyneth Paltrow and her "wasband," musician Chris Martin, used my term to announce their divorce in 2014, and created a new possibility in the world for how we might break up in a kinder, more humane and decent way.

I'm happy to say that our daughter is now in college and close to us both. Mark and I have created what we call our "expanded family," which includes his other former wife and their daughter, his lovely new partner, and my wonderful new partner, Michael.

For those of you who want to use my divorce from Mark as evidence that *Calling in "The One"* doesn't work, I ask you to consider suspending your judgment. A few years after our divorce, when I decided in my early sixties that I was ready again to manifest a new love, I used this same course that I present to you in this book to miraculously "call in" gorgeous, extraordinary "Big Love," with a kindhearted king of a man who delights me and fills my days with sweetness, inspiration, and joy. The work works.

This Course

There is a huge chasm between wanting to find a great love and being truly available to create a loving union when that person appears. This course is about bridging that chasm. It shows you how to set a strong intention to love and be loved, then outlines in clear, specific steps what you can do to make your intention your lived reality.

By providing forty-nine lessons that can be done in just seven weeks, I've structured an approach that is practical, accessible, psychologically sound, and incredibly transformative and effective. In fact, some twenty years down the line, I'm grateful to say that it's helped hundreds of thousands of people who've followed in my footsteps to create life-altering miracles of happiness and fulfillment in their lives as well. And although I can't promise that you'll actually have "The One" in your life in just seven weeks, I can promise that after doing this course, you will be open and available to receive love into your life, magnetic to its impending arrival.

The road to finding love can be a long and arduous one. It can be fraught with wrong turns, dangerous potholes, and circuitous routes that sometimes feel as if they're leading us nowhere. But the very fact that you've been drawn to this book indicates that you are seriously searching for a change in your life. You are now being presented with an extraordinary opportunity. You are standing at the fork in the road. One path leads to more of the same. It's a safer journey, in many respects, but usually leads only to an all-too-familiar disappointment. The other path takes you to freedom from the past and the very real possibility of deeply satisfying love in your future. I encourage you to say yes to the latter. This course will guide you along that road, and lead you step-by-step to create the miracle of love in your life. I promise to give you daily support and direction, taking good care of you once you decide you're ready for the journey.

No matter how disappointed you've been, or how weary and resigned you've become, your past does not define what's possible for you in love. You do! Take heart and be not discouraged. Love belongs to all of us.*

---

* I think it valuable to make transparent that though many examples in the book are of straight women looking for a male partner, I'm very aware of those who choose someone of the same gender as their intimate partners. This book is for those in the LGBTQ community just as much as it is for those who are cis and/or straight. Please know that I've held those of you who are gay, bi, lesbian, trans, poly, asexual, queer, questioning, and all other unique and creative ways of being sexual in my heart as I wrote this book. Love is indeed for us all.

Introduction

We are all born for love. It is the principle
of existence, and its only end.

—Benjamin Disraeli

Most of us want someone to tell us the concrete, practical rules of this crazy love hunt. "When she does this, you should do that." "When he texts this, you should wait three hours and then text that." When to speak up, when to shut up, when to put up, and when to put out. Hey, the more information the better! There's nothing wrong with looking at dating and mating this way, and there are a lot of great teachers out there writing about love from this perspective. But that's not what this course is about. In this course, you will not find the surefire secrets to getting someone to fall madly in love with you and propose marriage within the year. What you *will* find, however, are tools to radically and permanently transform your love life from the inside out.

Before we begin, however, there are three basic premises I must ask you to consider. These premises are imperative to the success of our work together, as they are the very foundation of the course.

Premise #1

Life is an ever-emerging creative process.
Our thoughts, beliefs, assumptions, choices, actions, and words
are the tools we use to invent our experiences and our circumstances.

> Every moment of your life is infinitely creative and the universe is endlessly bountiful. Just put forth a clear enough request, and everything your heart desires must come to you.
>
> —Shakti Gawain

Most of us live as though there were a future "out there" somewhere that we will one day just bump into at some designated and preordained time. This is a fantasy, and a rather harmful one at that.

What's closer to the truth is that our lives are a creative work in progress. Yet in order to access the power to change deep-seated patterns and create that which we've never managed to create before, we must give up the idea that we are victims. Victims of our circumstances. Victims of our culture. Victims of the unconscious behavior of other people. And even the victims of our own wounded psychology, which would limit the possibilities we hold for happiness and fulfillment in love. This may not be easy for some of us. We may have difficulty giving up the heavy burden of victimization for several reasons. We may have built an entire identity around it, knowing ourselves only through the lens of our wounded story. We may feel that being a victim brings us much desired love and compassion from others. Perhaps we are attached to punishing our perpetrators by making them witness our suffering year after year. Or we may not feel that anyone has truly heard and understood our pain as of yet, so we couldn't possibly just let it go. These are all understandable reasons to continue on under the weight of victimization. Yet the price tag is incredibly high. Simply put, remaining a victim will cost you your ability to manifest a miracle in your love life.

> There is little sense in attempting to change external conditions, you must first change inner beliefs, then outer conditions will change accordingly.
>
> —Brian Adams

Premise #2

We have the ability to create circumstances and opportunities in our lives by setting clear intentions, and by committing to and living in alignment with these intentions.

Most of us live our lives not by setting intentions, but by having expectations. These expectations go largely unfulfilled and often lead to feelings of disappointment and resignation. This is because we do not see ourselves as needing to be an active agent in the fulfillment of our own dreams and desires.

> Life consists of what a person is thinking about all day.
>
> —Ralph Waldo Emerson

By setting clear intentions and then striving to make choices and take actions that are in integrity with the future we're standing for, we access unprecedented power to evolve beyond painful patterns, and realize our higher potentials in life and in love.

Premise #3

When we alter our relationships with ourselves,
the externals of our lives will organically alter accordingly.

———————————————

The issues we struggle with in our relationships are usually mirroring back our own internal issues with ourselves. If you are having difficulty sustaining loving, nurturing, and committed relationships, the place to look first is at your relationship with yourself. Ask yourself: "In what ways am I failing to love, nurture, and commit to myself?"

> Every issue, belief, attitude, or assumption is precisely the issue that stands between you and your relationship to another human being; and between you and yourself.
>
> —Gita Bellin

Without changing how we relate to ourselves internally, the external changes we manage to create with others are destined to not last. Yet when we transform our relationship with ourselves, we effortlessly adjust our behaviors with others to manifest a new and improved experience. It happens outside of conscious awareness. For example, if you start speaking to yourself in kind and respectful ways, you'll soon find others relating to you with greater thoughtfulness and respect as well.

Because you have dealt with the source of the

> The future is not there waiting for us. We create it by the power of imagination.
>
> —Pir Vilayat Khan

problem, once you transform your inner experience, your outer world will forever be altered. And not just for as long as you remember to follow a set of rules and regulations that may feel forced and unnatural to you.

These three premises are very much the operative principles of this course. The definition of a premise is "something that is to be taken without the need for proof." You may or may not agree with these three premises or you may not be sure, in this moment, of their relevance to you. However, for the purpose of our work together, I ask that you try them on for size. Just give them a chance to work in your life. You can always discard them later if you find they're not helpful to you. Truth be told, once you master these premises in service to bringing your beloved to you, you'll be able to use them to create the fulfillment of your deepest desires in all areas of your life.

How to Do This Course

I define a "spiritual" person not as one who believes in a particular doctrine or religion, but rather as one who is actively pursuing the qualities of character that constitute a life of goodness and love. I have met the most devoted religious people who think little of examining their own hearts authentically to ferret out selfishness and deceit. I have also met those who profess to be atheist or agnostic and who go to great lengths to cultivate the qualities of loving-kindness, compassion, and goodness in their lives. Because of this, I have come to disregard those labels and credentials that normally make up the definition of a "spiritual" person and grown to appreciate profoundly the complexities and uniqueness of each person's particular path.

COURSE SUPPLY LIST

Journal (physical or virtual version)

Modeling clay (optional)

Lighter or matches

Online vision board app

or

Drawing paper

Cardboard and/or other backing for collage

Drawing markers and/or crayons

Scissors

Glue

Magazines and/or other resources for pictures and images

Highlighter

As you go through this course, you may find yourself challenged by some basic spiritual principles that I employ. If these moments occur for you, I ask you to remain open-minded and willing to experiment with ideas and practices that may be somewhat new and unusual for you. I ask that you not become too distracted by specific religious tenets but rather that you focus more on the essence of the practice and the effect it is having upon you.

As long as you're willing to stay open to the magic of life, then those of you who are steadfastly atheist or agnostic should have no more difficulty in successfully navigating this course than anyone else. I promise you, I have no interest in converting anyone. My experience of God is very personal and, frankly, ever-evolving. I am much more interested in continuing to discover my relationship with the Divine than in proselytizing who or what I believe that Being to be. I assume that you have your own understanding of spiritual matters and are growing yourself according to longings of your own heart. There are simply some things for which there are no words.

If all you can do is crawl, start crawling.

—Rumi

When the word *God* is used . . .
you may substitute the thought
good orderly direction or *flow*. It
is not [my] intent . . . to engage in
explaining, debating, or defining
that flow. You do not need to
understand electricity to use it.

—Julia Cameron

This course integrates many spiritual traditions, psychologically sound teachings, transformative technologies, and ancient healing methods, moving between meditations, physical activities, writing assignments, art projects, and suggested actions to take in your life. These practices, as they are called, are meant to engage you in a holistic process of healing, awakening, growth, and transformation. As such, you cannot do this course effectively on the level of intellect. While it's fine to read through the course before going back to actually do the practices, I can only promise you authentic movement in your life to the extent that you are willing to *do* the course and not just *read* the course.

To those of you who would tell me that you've "already done this" (and I'm sure you have), I would suggest that doing this course is more in the realm of taking on a spiritual practice than it is experiencing a onetime event. Few of us would forgo prayer because we've prayed once before. Nor would we avoid going to the gym because we've worked out in the past. And whereas one can read volumes on the subject of meditation, there is simply no substitute for sitting down and spending twenty minutes or so giving it your best shot. This course is an on-the-court experience. It is designed to help you transform your life, which means that you must be willing to put your money where your mouth is by taking concrete actions and doing the work.

I suggest you get a special notebook that you dedicate specifically to doing the course. You may also wish to have a particular pen that you love writing with. Find a safe and private space to keep these items. Your writings need to be kept confidential so that you feel safe enough to really tell the truth, no matter what. You don't need to worry about the possibility of someone looking over your shoulder. Your work is for you and you alone. Unless, of course, you choose to share it with someone. Many people have created a ritual such as lighting a scented candle or listening to meditative music each time they sat down to do the course. This is your time. Give it to yourself. And if you notice you're having a hard time doing so because of all of the demands on your schedule, then ask yourself if you're in the habit of putting yourself last. If the answer is yes, then consider that your happiness in love might actually matter more than your to-do list, and the never-ending demands of others.

> If grass can grow through cement, love can find you at every time in your life.
>
> —Cher

If you do the course as written, it will take you seven weeks to complete. I have a preference for doing it this way, straight through with one lesson a day for forty-nine days. If you do it like this, you should plan on setting aside twenty to forty-five minutes a day, preferably in the morning. While I understand that this might seem like a lot of time to some of you, consider the amount of time an intimate relationship is going to require of you and assume that commitment starts now.

I have discovered that some people prefer to work in a less linear way, perhaps reading a chapter at a time, which represents a whole week's worth of lessons. They then divvy up the practices so that they are doing a practice a day, or two one day and none the next, working in the context of the entire week. As each week focuses on one overall theme, this has proven to be quite effective. Another group of people will read through the book in its entirety before returning to Lesson One to actually *do* the practices. And then some will just amble along at their own pace, taking two or three days per lesson (or three to five months to complete the course).

It's important to keep in mind that there is no right or wrong way to do this course. This course is not an invitation to beat yourself up for not doing things perfectly. In fact, it's not possible to do the course perfectly and, if you try to, you should consider loosening up a little more in life. This isn't about perfection. This is about growing and stretching yourself. It's about discarding things that no longer work in your life and embracing things that do. Here's the truth. I wrote this book to include more than you could comfortably do in just seven weeks. I did that deliberately for those of you who might want to return and do it again, and maybe go deeper next time, getting all the juice out of it you can. The course is rich and succulent, and, frankly, you could feast on it several times through. So savor. Enjoy.

Having said all that, if you find that you are taking longer than six months to complete the course, you might want to ask yourself if you actually want a relationship at this time. Too much delay could suggest a strong ambivalence about opening yourself up to the experience of intimate, romantic love. If you find that

> How much longer will you go on letting your energy sleep? How much longer are you going to stay oblivious of the immensity of yourself?
>
> —Bhagwan Shree Rajneesh

you are taking a long break between lessons, procrastinating doing the practices, and/or getting stuck on various lessons, I recommend that you ask yourself how it's working for you to be on your own and unpartnered in life. I assure you, you'll find some part of you that thinks this is the safest way to go. However, engaging your own ambivalence directly will give you the opportunity to rethink some of the assumptions you may be holding on to. You may assume that you'll get swallowed up if you let someone into your life, instead of committing yourself to learning healthy boundaries in order to prepare for love. Or maybe you fall back on the belief that everyone always leaves you and that no one will ever really show up for you, as opposed to committing yourself to learning healthy communication skills in order to keep love safe. Let me reassure you that doing this course doesn't mean that you *have* to "call in" an actual relationship at the end of our seven weeks together. You can simply set an intention to be free of the baggage that has you so frightened by the possibility of letting someone into your life. This way, you can choose freely and from a centered, healthy place within you to either have a relationship, or not to have a relationship.

If you're really stuck, you may want to talk about your feelings with someone you trust, such as a *Calling in "The One"* Coach, a therapist, or a spiritual adviser. They might be able to help you see more clearly what could be keeping you from completing the course. You can find a *Calling in "The One"* Coach directory on my website, CallingInTheOne.com. All of our coaches work virtually and can coach you from anywhere in the world.

If you find that, in general, you are moving forward in the course but occasionally get "stuck" on a particular lesson because of its profound impact on you, there is nothing wrong with simply marking that lesson to return to once you've completed the entire forty-nine days. You can also mark those practices that make your heart happy and your spirit light, and begin to integrate them into your regular routine. The course is comprehensive. It travels through a plethora of subjects. Some of these will be more relevant for you than others. The "hot" issues, the ones you discover you need to work on some more, should be noted and returned to later. Not everything is going to be transformed in a day. You are engaged in a process. Please trust it. Much of the value of the course has to do with its ability to bring clarity regarding your particular blocks to love. Make note also of those practices that you find especially helpful, so that you can incorporate them into your life after you've completed the course.

A word of caution. The course can be intense at times. I will warn you as best I can when these times are coming up. However, if you've been the victim of severe abuse, which includes neglect and emotional mistreatment, as well as verbal, physical, and sexual abuse, you may find that you need extra support to move through the feelings of anxiety and fear that may arise as you expand your availability to love. Pay attention to yourself and be willing to get professional support if you need to.

If you don't have a coach or a therapist and feel it might be helpful to speak with someone, don't be afraid to interview two to four people before choosing someone to work with. Choosing a coach or a therapist is a little like dating, in that it takes some time to find the right "match." Look for someone you respect, who shares your values and your philosophy of life, as well as someone you feel safe and comfortable with. For those of you who have financial considerations, know that local clinics often provide low-cost counseling in exchange for the training of graduate students who are studying to become therapists. Often, these students have a lot of talent and some excellent supervisors guiding them. What they lack in experience is often made up for in commitment and enthusiasm. You might want to reach out to our community as well, as we often have *Calling in "The One"* Coaches-in-Training who are looking to provide low-cost or free coaching as part of their training to become certified relationship coaches.

DOING THE COURSE WITH OTHERS

Most of us have been working on ourselves for a while by now, diving deep to try to figure out why we're having the relationship challenges we're having. What happened when, where, with whom, and why. And it's helped, for sure. Yet, if we're really honest,

We are meant to midwife dreams for one another . . . Success occurs in clusters.

—Julia Cameron

> Intending as a group create[s] an ecstasy of unity—a palpable sense of oneness.
>
> —Lynne McTaggart

we might admit to being a bit discouraged by how slowly the changes have come and how tenacious the patterns have been. And at how often we've slid back into the old self-defeating habits we thought we'd long ago outgrown. Yet what I've seen countless times over the years is that it's nearly impossible to create radical lasting change by ourselves, in isolation. We need a relational field in which to grow our capacity to love and be loved. Love doesn't flourish by writing about it in our journals, and healing doesn't happen just by reading a book. It happens in the space between us.

For this reason, if at all possible, I encourage you to consider doing this course with others. As you are doing it in the hope of creating a deeper and more profound experience of love, I can think of no better way to prepare yourself than by allowing others to support your journey. Sharing with people who care about you and truly grasp the significance of the changes you're making will demonstrate your willingness to let more love into your life, as well as give you the opportunity to extend your love and support to others.

Allowing others to hold your intention with and for you could significantly increase the likelihood of your success at manifesting a miracle in your love life. Because of this, you'll want to make sure that each person in your group has adequate time to share his or her vision of what love will look like in their lives. You might even encourage one another to create vision boards and share them with each other, so that everyone in the group really knows what you're committed to creating. It's wise to allow others to hold your vision with you and for you, particularly when you experience a disappointment, setback, obstacles, or delay. It's in these moments we can too easily give up, dim down our expectations, and settle for less. Yet, a strong circle of friends who can hold a sense of possibility for you, when you're unable to do so for yourself, can help you stay in a positive, generative place of anticipation and faith.

Lastly, those in your support circle will be able to serve as witness to what it is that you're letting go of in life: a toxic relationship, a self-destructive habit, or a long-held hope that a past lover will return. This witnessing provides much-needed compassion for the pain that you have been through, which, in turn, will help you give it up. Many times, we have a difficult time releasing the past simply because we haven't felt that the suffering we've endured has fully been recognized and held with love by others.

If I've convinced you that doing this course with others is the way to go, here are a few guidelines that I would suggest for your group.

> The only currency in this bankrupt world is what you share with someone else when you're uncool.
>
> —Philip Seymour Hoffman
> in *Almost Famous*

1. MEMBERSHIP. I suggest you make this a closed group. This means no more newcomers after the first or second meeting. I also suggest you choose members who can attend most, if not all, of your meetings. If someone knows that they'll miss more than one or two meetings, it's best they wait to join another group. You're also encouraged to stay in contact between meetings. Members may want to choose buddies they go through the entire course with, or perhaps the group may prefer rotating buddies each week.

2. MEETINGS. I suggest you meet for at least nine weeks, which will allow for a "Getting to Know You" introductory meeting and a "Closure" meeting, as well as the seven weeks of the course. The location, dates, and times of your meetings should be decided upon in advance, so that everyone understands what they are signing up for. Make sure the location you choose is private enough for people to share deeply from their heart.

3. HOSTING. You may want to share the role of host, choosing the host for next week's gathering at the end of each meeting. The host will be the one who brings drinks and snacks should you be meeting in person, and who would also contact everyone should there be a change in the time or location of your meeting. The host can also serve as timekeeper by dividing the available time between members, and keeping everyone on track for all members to have equal time to share.

4. HONOR CONFIDENTIALITY. The most important way to create safety and group cohesion is to protect the confidentiality of each member. That means to not reveal the identity of members to anyone outside of the group. Do not repeat what is said in a meeting to others, including those not in attendance.

Do not post photos online of members without their express permission. Do not record your meetings without permission from all members. Do not gossip about one another or in any way violate the trust and integrity of your group. Relate only in ways that build respect, trust, and appreciation. Without establishing this level of safety, the group's effectiveness will be undermined and may actually be sabotaged entirely.

5. OFFER ADVICE ONLY WHEN ASKED. Rather than offer your advice or opinions about the shares of others, simply share what touched, moved, and inspired you. Though it's sometimes difficult to refrain from "fixing" others, it's important to remember that the simple act of lovingly listening can be extremely helpful and healing. Bottom line: Make sure that the word *I* is being used far more often than the word *you*. For example, *"I noticed how much I wanted to make it better for you when you were sharing,"* instead of *"You really shouldn't feel that way."*

6. ABSTAIN FROM ALCOHOL AND/OR NONPRESCRIBED DRUGS BEFORE AND DURING MEETINGS. As you're coming together each week to do deep inner work inside of a shared commitment to transform your love lives from the inside out, it's probably best to save the martinis for *after* your meeting, and not before or during.

For a handout on these guidelines, please go to CallingInTheOne.com/Doing TheCourseWithOthers.

Yet if after all of this, you still want to do the course alone, at least let your close friends know what you're up to. It will be helpful to have at least one or two trustworthy friends who are holding your vision with and for you. I'd also encourage you to give your friends permission to hold you accountable to live in alignment with your intention to call in a great love. Invite them to lovingly give you a nudge if they think you may be going back into an old pattern, such as dating someone unavailable, or getting into an abusive situation.

> Friendship is a sheltering tree.
>
> —Samuel Taylor Coleridge

You're now ready to begin. As we move through our next seven weeks together, please feel free to be your imperfect, messy, unenlightened self, as well as your magnificent, powerful, and brilliant self. I had a woman register for one of my workshops who almost canceled the day before because she hadn't yet "gotten rid" of her commitment-phobic, neglectful boyfriend. She thought she had to have it all together before she came to the workshop. I reminded her that that was *why* she was coming in the first place!

You don't have to be perfect before, during, or after doing this course. Just be authentic and risk telling the truth—first to yourself and then to others. Because that's where the transformation and healing can happen.

Blessings to you as you embark on this magical, mystical journey to the fulfillment of love in your life.

Preparing for Love

Someday, after we have mastered the winds, the waves,
the tides and gravity, we shall harness for God the
energies of love. Then for the second time in the history
of the world, man will have discovered fire.

—Pierre Teilhard de Chardin

Too often, we believe our private agonies are ours alone to bear, forgetting that we are part of a vast collective where the majority of our concerns are shared with others.

This week, we will:

- Explore the impact that the culture around us is having on our collective ability to create loving and meaningful relationships
- Commit to growing your capacity to love and be loved as the foundation from which to create healthy, happy love
- Prepare yourself for love by exploring and expanding your capacity for healthy interdependence
- Cultivate a vision of great happiness in love, and begin organizing your life around a future of love fulfilled
- Begin taking specific actions that are generative of that future fulfilled

Expanding Your Capacity to Love and Be Loved

If you want to learn to love, then you must start the process of finding out what it is, what qualities make up a loving person and how these are developed. Each person has the potential for love. But potential is never realized without work.

—Leo Buscaglia

One reason so many of us do not have the love we are longing for is that we've not yet become the people we will need to be in order to attract and sustain that kind of love. Most of us have dramatically elevated our standards of what we expect from a romantic partner far beyond what our parents or grandparents ever expected from their relationships. Yet we may not have evolved our level of wellness and maturity to the point where we can manifest and maintain the love that we are hoping to create.

Romantic relationships today are a tentative and uncertain thing. In our postmodern world, where serial monogamy is the new norm and more people over fifty are divorced than widowed, no longer is getting married the safe and secure way to go. Whereas once upon a time people tended to stay together for the long haul no matter what, and perhaps even married out of economic and social necessity, we now seek to form long-term unions in an attempt to create authentically soulful and deeply meaningful lives. Yet, much of the time, falling in love means that we end up standing by helplessly as we watch it all slip through our fingers. Why can't we seem to hold on to the glorious transcendence of love? Why can't we seem to harness passion, root it down, and make a home of it?

Some would say that romantic love is an illusion. A trick of nature meant to entice us into procreation. In the aftermath of a devastating breakup, we find ourselves asking, Was he or was he not my soul mate? Was it or was it not real love? The most beautiful moments of our lives become reduced to their lowest common denominator: hormones, lust, and those most dreaded of words—"It was just infatuation."

Yet many understand, if only intuitively, that romantic love holds a promise that we have yet to fulfill. Instinctively, we know it holds a key to our expansion. Because romantic love has such a profound capacity to bring out the best—and the worst—in us, many of us have identified it as our newest frontier for spiritual growth and development. Rather than calling us into seclusion, the spiritual path now beckons us deeper into the quality of our connections. This premise is the very crux of the relatively new term "spiritual partnership," which describes the relationship that most of us aspire to. What exactly is this new kind of union, and how does it differ from the old paradigm of marriage that our parents and grandparents were looking for? A study was done back in the sixties, where young women attending college were asked, "If you met a man who met all of your criteria for a husband yet you did not love him, would you marry him?" More than 70 percent said yes, they would. In other words, as long as the guy came from a good family, had a job, smelled good, and didn't drink too much, then he must be "The One!" Apparently, the main objectives of the old paradigm were economic stability and morally sanctified sex. Yet what most of us care about today is finding someone who can help us become who we came here to be, and realize the fulfillment of our potential in all areas. Spiritual partnership implies the goal of inspiring and supporting the unfolding of each other's souls in this journey through life.

An intimate relationship today means allowing ourselves to become immersed in knowing and being known fully by another human being, with all of our brilliance, beauty, failures, and flaws. It means learning the terrain and the language of love through a shared commitment to mutual growth and awakening. It means opening our hearts fully and learning how to love in ways that are vulnerable, authentic, and undefended, while at the same time remaining independent

Love can only be found through the act of loving.

—Paulo Coelho

and autonomous in ways that would allow us to live 100 percent true to ourselves. It means going beyond the pervasive ideas of our parents' generation that romantic union was about martyrdom and sacrifice, and moving into an experience of romantic love as an invitation to creatively expand by generating inclusive win-win solutions that take everyone's needs, feelings, and desires into account. It means discovering how to be completely responsible for your own feelings and needs by understanding the lens through which you are interpreting, then responding to whatever's happening between yourself and others. It means honoring your own needs and perspectives while being open to hearing those that are completely the opposite of your own, without needing to make one of you right and one of you wrong. It means holding people accountable for treating you with respect, in ways that are respectful of them. In other words, those who still believe that romantic love and spiritual love are two different things understand little about the direction that either has taken.

This is not a book for those who wish to hide out. This is a book for those who aren't afraid of a challenge. It is designed to help you get from who you are today to who you will need to be in order to call in the best possible partner for you in this lifetime, and create deep happiness and health in your relationship with that person. That means that the journey must begin with an interest in how one might become a more loving person.

Years ago, long before he became a friend of mine, I heard Jack Canfield, co-editor of the *Chicken Soup for the Soul* books, tell a moving story of a woman who'd had a near-death experience. She'd had an accident and was pronounced dead soon after. While dead, she saw the tunnel of light we so often hear about. She followed the light and soon came upon an Angelic Being who was radiating an enormous amount of love. The Being told her that it was not yet her time to die. However, before she was sent back into her body, she was asked two questions. The first was: "What wisdom have you gained in this lifetime?" and the second was: "How have you expanded your capacity to love?"

If you want to be ready to bring "The One" into your life, then you must be willing to grow yourself beyond the person you know yourself to be. Because the person you are today is the same person who's

> We waste time looking for the perfect lover, instead of creating the perfect love.
>
> —Tom Robbins

created the experiences you've already had. As they say in the twelve-step programs, "Our best thinking got us here." As such, your task is to grow yourself healthier and more mature in order to create a space for a remarkable love to take root in your life. As long as we are acting out the wounds of our childhood and in reaction to the disappointments of our past, we will most likely remain frustrated and unfulfilled in our attempts to find true love. However, once we've done the work to heal and transform, it then becomes possible for us to bring the best of who we are to others. In return, we will draw in those who are willing and able to bring the best of who they are to us. At the very least, we will be able to distinguish early on those who can't or won't do this, knowing that, although this person might have "great potential," he or she is no one to open our hearts to.

> In the orchard and rose garden
> I long to see your face.
> In the taste of Sweetness
> I long to kiss your lips.
> In the shadows of passion
> I long for your love.
>
> —Rumi

In order to attract an extraordinary love, and sustain relationships that are characterized by authenticity, kindness, and respect, then we must outgrow our tendencies to unconsciously duplicate the relational traumas of our past, and replay over and over again our deepest disappointments in love. Instead, we must consciously evolve our capacity to experience authentic, adult love with a heart that is strong enough to love, even when confronted with all that is not love. Until we do, we will likely either have difficulty creating loving relationships, or sustaining the love that life sends our way.

I invite you therefore to give yourself fully to the pathway of happy, healthy relatedness. Build your life upon the wise decision to grow your ability to love and be loved. To expand your capacity to have love, to grow in love, to live in the essence of love. For in order to have a great love, one must begin by becoming a greater lover.

I was there in the beginning and I was the spirit of love.

—Rumi

It's important to realize that you do not need to be with a partner to open your heart and begin expanding your ability to give and receive love. You simply need the willingness to start by opening yourself to the opportunities to love and be loved that surround you today.

PRACTICE: OPENING TO LOVE YOGA EXERCISE

The following is a simple yoga practice to help open your heart.

If you are able to, sit cross-legged on either the floor or a pillow to do this exercise. If you are unable to cross your legs in this way, simply sit up with a straight back, legs stretched out, and feet together on the floor in front of you, or try placing a pillow under you while sitting up on your knees.

Begin by stretching your arms out in front of you, palms together, elbows straight, with your arms parallel to the floor. As you inhale through your nose, open your arms widely to the sides, expansively bringing your shoulder blades as close together as possible. As you stretch, place your awareness on your heart. Imagine your heart opening and expanding as you fill your lungs with air by continuing to breathe in deeply. Stretch your arms out as far as they can go as though they were giant wings, while keeping them parallel to the ground.

With each expansion, silently say to yourself:

"I open myself fully to give and receive love."

After each inhale, exhale strongly through your nose, bringing your arms slowly back to their original position. Again, press your palms together, keeping your arms parallel to the ground.

If you are able to, repeat this movement thirteen times. If you are very strong, try challenging yourself to reach twenty-six times, all the while keeping your eyes closed and slightly rolled up and focused just above and between the eyebrows (your "third eye" point).

Do this exercise at a moderate pace. Allow yourself to relax between expansions, if necessary, by bringing your arms down to rest upon your knees.

Bonus: Practice in Action

Throughout the day, whenever you think of it, breathe deeply into your heart, repeating silently to yourself:

"I open myself fully to give and receive love."

Looking Through Laura's Eyes

A human being is a part of the whole . . . He experiences himself, his thoughts and feelings, as something separated from the rest, a kind of optical delusion of . . . consciousness. This delusion is a kind of prison for us, restricting us to our personal desires and to affection for a few persons nearest to us.

—Albert Einstein

A friend of mine who was born and raised in India used to confide in me how desperately lonely he felt in the United States. "There is so much isolation here," he'd say. "How do you Americans stand it?" As a licensed marriage and family therapist, I'm more privy than most to the inner worlds of those I come into contact with. And, after thinking about his question for quite some time now, I'd have to answer him by saying, "Not very well, my friend. Not very well at all."

Too many of us feel isolated and alone. My friend and bestselling author Dr. Lissa Rankin tells us that loneliness is now the number one health problem in America; as dangerous to the body as smoking fifteen cigarettes a day and predisposing us to a multitude of illnesses. In our materially abundant and technologically sophisticated society, we tend to organize our lives around goals meant to grow our net worth, rather than cultivate the true wealth of relatedness. The importance of developing a nourishing circle of caring connections is somehow off our radar, or plays a secondary role to our goals and aspirations. The result unfortunately is that the majority of our interactions are transactional in nature. Rather than being "in and for each other," as my dear friend and bestselling author of the wonderful book *Evolutionary Relationships*, Patricia Albere, calls it, we're basically in it for ourselves and relating to others as though they were objects in our world, either helping or hindering our ability to get what we want. Which leaves us with the pervasive, somewhat subtle, and haunting experience of feeling unseen, unknown, and unloved. Many of us know this experience all too well from our efforts to connect through the impersonal multibillion-dollar online dating industry, which occurs for many of us as a kind of transactional meat market, and often leaves us feeling more lonely and uncared for than ever.

Several years ago, I lost my dear friend Laura to breast cancer. Two days before she died, I went to see her in the hospital. I anticipated that she'd be morose and sad, given that she was dying before she'd reached her fiftieth birthday. Yet when I walked into the room, I found her lit up with an unexpected joy as she warm-heartedly welcomed me to her bedside.

Sometimes, when someone is dying, they become almost radiant right before they leave their bodies. This was the case with Laura. In the excited voice of a child, she told me of the love she saw when her nurses walked into the room to care for her, and even when the janitor came by with his broom to sweep the hallway. In her heightened state of awareness, she could see love in each and every interaction as a beautiful, fluid, and very tangible energy that was freely moving between herself and others.

I sometimes wonder what life would be like if we were all able to see even partially what Laura could see on that day. How would life be different if our natural collective currency was our ability to care for one another?

> In the modern world we also tend to see everything as if it were a machine, including our most precious relationships.
>
> —Thomas Moore

For though it seems that we Westerners place a high value on love, in reality, I'm not so sure. In spite of our plethora of love songs, romantic comedies, and romance novels, we're too often a "what's in it for me" society. I would even suggest that our preoccupation with romantic love may actually be a symptom of a certain inner poverty that we've come to call normal—a pervasive and distressing shortage of connection and care that most of us assume is a personal pathology.

In *Gila: The Life and Death of an American River*, author Gregory McNamee writes about an anthropologist who once asked a man from the Hopi tribe why so many of his people's songs were about rain. The Hopi replied, "Because water is so scarce. Is that why so many of your songs are about love?"

Our fascination with romantic love tends to focus on the finding of love and not the substance of what truly makes up a loving relationship. Rarely do our movies or our songs deal with the day in, day out minutiae of what true love actually requires of us. But the experience of loving for the long haul, of generously extending oneself day after day after day, while receiving the kind of constancy and kindness that weaves one's broken heart back together again, is about as high drama as we'll ever hope to find in this lifetime. It always amazes me that we tend to skip that part in the movies. For truly, it is the absolute best part of love and yet most of us have no idea what it even looks like. Being consumed with falling in love as opposed to the sustaining of love is a little like stopping at foreplay.

George Bernard Shaw once said that our ". . . worst sin toward our fellow creatures is not to hate them, but to be indifferent to them." Most of us don't walk around harboring strong negative emotions such as hatred or rage. Yet, the challenge for many of us is to overcome the apathy and indifference we have toward one another: to be available and attentive to those we pass in the aisles at the market, the co-workers we pass daily in the halls, and those acquaintances we regularly notice in our social or spiritual circles.

The qualities that make up a loving relationship are the same whether we love our neighbor, our friend, our student, or our husband. Attentiveness, compassion, generosity, tolerance, and kindness are the foods we all most hunger for. Yet the spiritual self-study program *A Course in Miracles*, published by the Foundation for Inner Peace, tells us that the only love missing is the love that we ourselves are not giving. To overcome our tendencies toward isolation, or counteract your impulse to hoard your love for that one special person you're hoping to finally meet one day soon, I invite you to consciously generate a feeling of connection and care with all those you come into contact with today.

> The biggest disease today is not leprosy or tuberculosis, but rather the feeling of being unwanted, uncared for and deserted by everybody.
>
> —Mother Teresa

> Loneliness is proof that your innate search for connection is intact.
>
> —Martha Beck

Our sense of community is fostered readily during or in the aftermath of a tragedy. Yet, a sense of belonging must be cultivated and valued in and of itself for us to feel truly fulfilled in our lives. As Einstein suggests, in order for us to transcend the "delusion of separateness," we must learn to "free ourselves from this prison by widening our circle of compassion to embrace all living creatures and to the whole of nature in all its beauty."

PRACTICE: AWAKENING TO CONNECTION MEDITATION

Today we're going to cultivate an awareness of the interconnectedness that binds us all together always. I invite you to begin the day with a simple meditation designed to open you to an awareness of the inherent love and connection between yourself and others. I suggest that you read through the meditation once or twice and then do it by memory. Do the best you can in recalling the meditation but don't worry if you don't do it exactly as written.

I recommend that you don't try to meditate lying down, as it's too easy to fall asleep, particularly first thing in the morning. If you can, sit up straight and cross your legs in front of you. Rest your hands gently on your thighs and close your eyes.

NOTE: For some of you, sitting still like this presents a challenge. If this is you, I'd rather you try a walking meditation than skip the meditations included in this book entirely. Instead, try taking a mindful walk around the block, while doing the assigned meditations to the best of your ability.

1. **Become Still.** Close your eyes and take a nice deep breath, as though you could breathe all the way down into your hips. Move into a place of deep listening and receptivity. Become aware of

all of the feelings and sensations in your body, noticing where you may be holding any tension. As you find it, simply let it go. With each breath, allow yourself to soften even more into a place of stillness and surrender, recognizing that you are safe to let go.

2. **Expand Your Heart.** Imagine that you could breathe straight into your heart. In your mind's eye, imagine that with each breath, your heart is growing lighter, stronger, and more vibrant.

3. **Extend Your Heart to Others.** Now, think of your neighbors whether or not you know them. Notice that there is vibrant energy that connects your heart to their hearts and back again from them to you. Silently say to yourself:

"I am connected to everyone and everything."

Now think of your co-workers or others you come in contact with on a regular basis. One person at a time, notice beautiful force fields of energy connecting you with everyone you see. Whether you know the person by name or not, repeat the phrase to yourself with each person you think of.

Now imagine that you are walking down a street. Again, in your mind's eye, see the energy of care connecting you with each person that you pass, and continue to repeat the phrase.

Next, think of those whom you are currently estranged from. Maybe it's because there is unresolved anger between you. Perhaps it's because time has passed and you've lost touch. Whoever comes to mind

> You have a feeling of being lonely—this will pass through you quickly unless you make up a story about how you're lonely because you're unlovable and worthless and nobody will ever love you and you're going to be alone forever.
>
> —Dr. Lissa Rankin

is fine. As you repeat the phrase with each person who comes to mind, imagine a beautiful energy passing between your heart and theirs, connecting you in love and compassion.

Spend at least three minutes doing this exercise. If you are able to sit for a longer period, I encourage you to do so, but you need not do it for longer than three minutes.

Bonus: Practice in Action

Today, I invite you to spend the day looking through Laura's eyes. Frequently throughout your day, connect with your own heart and repeat silently to yourself:

"I am connected to everyone and everything."

A strange passion is moving in my head.
My heart has become a bird
Which searches in the sky.
Every part of me goes in different directions.
Is it really so
That the one I love is everywhere?

—Rumi

Consciously relate to those around you, looking to discover the connections between yourself and others. Make eye contact, speak to someone you would not ordinarily speak to, smile at someone you might normally look away from, ask someone how they are and pause long enough to listen to their response.

NOTE: If any of this makes you uncomfortable, just breathe through your discomfort. Do not allow your discomfort to stop you from doing the exercise throughout the day.

At the end of the day, take out your journal and write down the moments when you experienced a sense of connection, relatedness, and belonging that passed between you and another person, whether or not you knew them. It could be that a stranger looked at you and smiled. Perhaps you opened the door for an elder or someone called you for business purposes and you made an effort to relate to them as a real person. Remember, we are looking through Laura's eyes, so look to generate a sense of belonging and connection everywhere.

Accessing the Power to Manifest a Miracle

[A person's] chief delusion is [their] conviction that there
are causes other than [their] own state of consciousness.

—Neville Goddard

Getting into a place of possibility—where you can actually imagine yourself in a happy, healthy, loving relationship—can be heavy lifting for those of us who've had our hearts put through a shredder time and time again. After so much evidence to the contrary, what makes us think we can now just set our minds to manifesting this miracle, then pull *that* rabbit out of a hat?

Most of us feel stuck in a pattern that seems hell-bent on happening, no matter how much time we put in sitting on the meditation cushion or the therapist's couch. It happens again and again: a cycle of getting involved with unavailable people, or winding up in long-distance love affairs, or being abandoned or abused. Never being the one chosen, always finding yourself the third wheel in a triangle, or waking up one more time to realize you're with yet another narcissist and it's all about *them.* Even always being alone is a pattern, because the absence of a pattern is actually the pattern!

In order to access the power to manifest a miracle in your love life, you're going to have to step back and see this pattern clearly, and begin to see how the pattern is actually happening *through* you, and not just *to* you. Through the unconscious and habitual choices you're making, the automatic actions you're taking, and the chronic ways you show up (or don't show up) in your relationships with others.

Right now, it feels like you're just a victim of the pattern. Like the pattern is bigger than you and it's just happening over and over again against your will. Somehow, it's just your fate to never have love, or to always wind up alone. Maybe you feel as though the Universe has it rigged that somehow other people get to have love, but not you. Perhaps it's in your astrological chart that you'll always struggle in love. Or maybe it's in your lineage that the women in your family—your mother, grandmother, and great-grandmother before her—were always cheated on or somehow left deeply disappointed by the men they loved. You may feel that the effect of things that happened to you in childhood has somehow doomed you to forever suffer in love. That somehow you are now victimized by your own consciousness and the beliefs you formed in response to the immature, selfish, or just plain bad behavior of your caregivers.

> This is your life. You are responsible for it. You will not live forever. Don't wait.
>
> —Natalie Goldberg

When I suggest you seek to discover how you might be the source of your own patterns, I'm not suggesting you're "to blame" for what's happened to you. Surely, there are factors that are outside of your control. And certainly, if you're struggling with the residue of having been abused in childhood, you were never responsible in any way for the unconscious, disturbed, or even evil behavior of others. Yet I am suggesting that by becoming curious about how you're showing up with others now as an adult that is allowing, and even encouraging, the pattern to continue, you just might access the power you need to finally outgrow it.

Aida always seemed to get involved with self-absorbed men whom she called "takers." Men who lacked the ability to give her the love and commitment she craved, yet who felt entitled to, and even demanding of, her loyalty, care, and devotion. At first, these men seemed like desirable partners. They'd impress her with an intoxicating sense of confidence, seduce her with an almost uncanny ability to know just what she was thinking, and shower her with flowery words of adoration and praise. Yet after she was all in, they'd start giving less and expecting more. Suddenly, they would let their eyes and attentions wander to other women, while expecting fidelity of her. They would do things like walk two steps ahead of her, forget to call her on her birthday, or fail to introduce her when they ran into others whom they seemed to know quite well. The pattern happened differently with various men, yet the dynamic was always the same. The relationship was about *him*. What *he* felt, what *he* needed, and what *he* wanted, with little room for her feelings or needs. When she tried to talk about this, she always somehow left the conversation feeling ashamed of herself for wanting and needing too much.

Inside of this pattern, all Aida could do to reclaim her right to take care of herself was to end the relationship and go back to being alone. "Either I get to be a whole person who can take care of my own feelings and needs, or I am in a relationship which requires me to abandon my own feelings and needs to serve the other person." The way Aida rationalized this pattern was to tell herself that men were fundamentally narcissistic and entitled. That they got their esteem from controlling women, and asserting dominance over them. This was certainly what she saw growing up in a home where her mother seemed to almost be in servitude to the man she loved, no matter what he did or did not do.

When I first asked Aida how she was the source of this pattern, she was actually a little offended. Was I blaming her for the toxic way men treated women? Yet when we took the blame and shame out of it, and simply looked to discover the actual choices she was making that may have fed into, and even encouraged, the self-centeredness of the men she dated, she suddenly started seeing all sorts of covert ways she was showing up that contributed to, and sometimes even caused, the pattern to happen.

Looking at it from this perspective, she saw that when she was in a relationship with someone she wanted to make a commitment to her, she put all of her attentions on pleasing him, usually at the expense of herself. She would start dismissing, and even disappearing, her own feelings, needs, and desires by negating them entirely. On the rare occasion that she *was* aware of her feelings and needs, she stayed silent, not wanting to appear needy or difficult, for fear he wouldn't choose her. Or worse yet, leave. When a man would try to coax her into sharing her true feelings and needs, she would deflect his attentions elsewhere, minimizing her own internal experience and thereby teaching him to do the same. She was shocked to see this so clearly. For years, she'd blamed men. Yet suddenly she started seeing how *she*

> Change the way you look at things and the things you look at change.
>
> —Dr. Wayne Dyer

was actually the source of the pattern. In always making the relationship about them and disappearing herself, she was actually encouraging them to do the same.

In letting go of being a victim and being willing to understand how the pattern was happening *through* her and not just *to* her, what opened up was the power to make different choices. No longer acting out her mother's unhealthy modeling, or in reaction to what she thought others wanted or expected from her, she could start making choices that would allow her to create the kinds of relationships that she would actually want to be in. Immediately, she pledged to start showing up differently. To stay aware of her feelings, needs, and desires when she was with others, and start expressing herself more authentically to others. To take the risk and responsibility of making her deeper feelings and needs known to others. In this way, she was finally able to more accurately assess someone's character, as well as their capacity to love her, *before* jumping in fully. She also was able to give others a chance to express to her how much they cared. Before, inside of her self-imposed invisibility, she just assumed that no one cared about her feelings and needs. Yet once she started making them transparent to others, she was surprised to discover that some people actually adjusted themselves accordingly, as a way of showing her how much they did care about her.

Aida didn't wait until she was in a new relationship to begin making these changes, but she began showing up this way with her friends, family, co-workers, and neighbors. I'd love to report that they were thrilled. Yet we all know it doesn't always work that way. Some people were happy and some weren't. Aida lost a few "friends" who liked her better as a doormat. Yet some were able to make the change with her, applauding her courage to start being more visible, and grateful for the chance to know her more deeply.

Aida is now married to a loving, kind man who looks out for her and listens deeply when she shares her feelings and needs. The first step of this heartwarming transformation was not trying to figure out how she could change others, or better protect herself from predatory, narcissistic men, but in looking to understand how she was actually causing the old pattern outside of conscious awareness, and awakening to her power to make choices that could create a different experience.

> Happiness and true freedom come only when we assume full responsibility for who and what we are.
>
> —Leo Buscaglia

PRACTICE: SEEING YOURSELF AS THE SOURCE

Most of us have been searching for ways to explain to ourselves and others why we've been having such a hard time finding the right mate. *"All the good ones are taken." "Men don't like powerful women." "There aren't any queer folks where I live."* And the one *we've all said to ourselves at one time or another . . . "I just haven't met the right person."* (All the while secretly wondering if it's because I've never *been* the right person.) While these external explanations are interesting and worthy of discussion, they all have one thing in common. None of them is anything we can control. Yet in looking to identify yourself as the source of your painful relational patterns, you're seeking to discover the *internal* reasons why you're chronically unsatisfied in love, in order to transform your love life from the inside out.

Take out your journal.

1. **Let's begin by identifying your pattern in love.**

    Journal on your experiences of love to date to try to identify the painful and disappointing experience you tend to have time and time again. *For example, I get involved with unavailable people. I'm never the one chosen. Men don't commit to me, then marry the next person they date. Women are judgmental and critical of me. I'm always in a long-distance relationship. I'm always lied to and betrayed. No one ever shows up for me when I need them.* Although the external conditions might be different, the same pattern emerges each time.

    Do your best to describe what actually happens versus your emotional interpretation of what happens. *For example, "Men reject me"* is what actually happens. *"Men don't like me and think other women are better than me"* might be the emotional interpretation of what happens. Right now, we are looking to identify the theme of your love life. What story do you find yourself stuck in no matter how hard you try to have it go another way?

> You and I are essentially infinite choice-makers. In every moment of our existence, we are in that field of all possibilities where we have access to an infinity of choices.
>
> —Deepak Chopra

2. **Notice where you feel the pain of the pattern in your body.**

Close your eyes and take a deep breath as though you could breathe all the way down into your hips.

Notice where you feel the emotional pain of the pattern in your body.

Extend a sense of love and support to the part of you that is holding the hurt of the pattern.

See if you can identify what you are making the pattern mean about you. In other words, your emotional interpretation of the pattern. *"I'll always be alone." "No one cares about me." "I'm not good enough." "There is something wrong with me."*

When you see this clearly, open your eyes and write it down in your journal.

This is how you've been explaining to yourself why the pattern keeps happening. Let's assume, however, that whatever that internal dialogue is, that it's just a story you made up a long time ago in response to a wounding, and not necessarily the truth about you.

3. **Notice who or what you've been blaming the pattern on.**

Journal on the following question:

What have I been blaming for this pattern?

For example:

- *I've been blaming my mother for being so negligent.*
- *I've been blaming myself for being too fat, too skinny, too short, too tall, etc.*
- *I've been blaming women for being so manipulative.*

4. Identify a way you've been the source of the pattern.

Inside of your emotional interpretation, you have most likely shown up in ways that have unconsciously generated the pattern. It feels like it's happening *to* you, but it's actually happening *through* you. *For example, inside of Aida's emotional interpretation of the pattern, "Men don't care about my feelings and needs," and her assumption that this was because men were selfish, it didn't even occur to her to share what she was feeling and needing. Yet in not sharing what she felt and needed, she never gave others a chance to demonstrate that they might actually care about her feelings and needs, if only she had the courage to share what they were.*

Journal on the following question:

Inside of my emotional interpretation, how do I show up in ways that generate the pattern?

For example:

- *Inside of the assumption I'm all alone in life, when I feel hurt by someone, rather than pick up the phone to try to work it out, I withdraw and put up a wall to protect myself.*
- *Inside of the assumption I'm not good enough, I overgive to try to prove my value, and in the process covertly communicate I'm not very valuable.*
- *Inside of the assumption I'm not safe, I'm combative and defensive and I put others on defense, causing a lack of safety in our relationship.*

Identify at least one way that you are the source of your painful pattern in a way that opens up the choice to do things differently moving forward.

Bonus: Practice in Action

Make one new choice today to show up differently. Based on what you discovered about yourself as the source of your painful pattern(s) in love, try showing up in a new way that has the potential to generate a new experience. *For example, share your true feelings with someone you'd normally stay silent with, say no rather than automatically give someone what they want, negotiate for your own needs and desires, or take the risk to set a boundary with someone you want to like you.*

Starting with the End in Mind

The secret of change is to focus all of your energy,
not on fighting the old, but on building the new.

—Dan Millman

You may have felt frustrated and limited by the relational traumas you suffered as a child. "My dad left when I was four." "My mom made me take care of her for most of my childhood." "My big brother emotionally abused me for years." We all have our stories to tell.

What's most maddening about these stories, however, is not what happened thirty years ago, but what just happened thirty minutes ago, when we repeated that same wounding once again with someone new. When once more, someone left whom we'd hoped would stay. Or one more time, we gave and gave and gave to someone who had little to give in return. Or yet again, we found ourselves tolerating abuse from someone we want to love us. We're burdened by the tenacity of these wounds, and imprisoned by the residue they've left in their wake. It's understandable, then, that we'd assume our emancipation would come from getting to the bottom of whatever happened way back when.

For years, we've been rummaging through the past, believing that by doing so, we'll somehow access the power we need to finally transform the present, and unlock the possibilities of the future. By now, however, many of us understand the metaphysical principle that whatever we focus on grows stronger. Though we've had great faith in leaving no stone from our childhoods unturned, digging through the dirty ditches of all the damage done and assuming this to be the Holy Grail of our healing, we must admit, it's been only somewhat helpful. Truth be told, most of us live with only minor variations of the same disappointing themes year after year, in spite of spending hundreds, if not thousands, of hours and dollars diligently "working on ourselves." Years of analyzing who did what to us when and how we feel about that has actually served to solidify the "self" we formed in response to what we endured. Which may be the absolute worst thing we could possibly do to try to get beyond it. Because wherever we are centered at the level of identity is where we will generate our lives from.

Bestselling author Dr. Joe Dispenza tells us that "[i]t's impossible to create any new future when you are rooted in your past." Understanding your past can help you heal. It can support you to unpack the lies of your childhood, and assist you in creating a cohesive narrative that makes meaning out of all you had to endure. It can bring you much-needed acceptance and closure. But it cannot cause a miracle in your love life.

Luckily, however, *you* can. You are a maker of miracles. You possess the power to declare a future that is very different from your past, and begin leaning in to discover who you will need to become in order to manifest, then sustain, that experience. You have the power to set a bold intention to create something that likely won't happen unless you stand for it, then begin taking actions and making choices that are aligned with, and generative of, the fulfillment of that future. To begin inquiring into who you'd need to be in order for that future to manifest, you'll need to step into that which Drs. Hazel Markus from Stanford University and Paula Nurius from Northwestern University call the "Possible Self"—the "you" that you are inside of that future fulfilled. In this case, happy, loved, confident, and contented. In trying on and beginning to identify with the self of your future, you're essentially inviting that possibility to begin pulling you toward its own fulfillment.

Rather than running away from the you of your past, you are running toward becoming the you of your future.

Most of us, however, have been engaging our quest for love emotionally anchored in the wounded,

> The only person you are destined to become is the person you decide to be.
>
> —Ralph Waldo Emerson

traumatized selves of our childhoods. The ones we keep trying to heal with all of our prodding around in the past. We project the alone self, the unwanted self, or the inferior self into the future, creating a sort of desperation to find someone to finally rescue us from this sad story. Rather than spend your time dreaming of all the many possibilities your life holds for deep happiness in love, you may be motivated to find "The One" by the "lonely you" who imagines yourself to have nowhere to go next Christmas, or by the "humiliated you" who has no date to bring to your sister's wedding. Or by what Drs. Markus and Nurius call the "selves we are afraid of becoming." Which are basically projections into the future of who we've already known ourselves to be.

In order to awaken your power to manifest the miracle of love, I invite you to look to your future and not your past, and begin defining who you are as it relates to that future fulfilled. Ask yourself what it might actually feel like to be loved by "The One" you love, and imagine being in that experience now. Ask yourself what it looks like, sounds like, smells like, and tastes like to be this in love. Swim in and savor these sweet images and emotions. Let them begin to influence and inform how you show up in your life now.

When you have the courage to stand for a joyous, healthy, loving, committed union that is a complete departure from anything you've experienced before, you're stepping into the recognition that life is an endless act of invention and reinvention. You'll see that you are a force of nature who has been given the gift of imagination to unleash the creative process! Your past is not necessarily your fate, but rather fuel for the future you're standing to create. So often, I hear people go on about how uncreative they are, unaware that we are all creating our very lives in every moment of every day. Most of us are living as though we were reading a novel, assuming that one day we'll get to the end to see how it all turned out. We're not present to the fact that we are constantly generating our lives, as though they were great works of art. And the tools we've been given to do this are the thoughts, beliefs, assumptions, actions, choices, and words we use, which are organic to the self that we are identified with and generating our lives from, in any given moment.

Consciousness precedes all matter.

—Albert Einstein

PRACTICE: SETTING YOUR INTENTION

Having identified your painful pattern(s) yesterday, we now know what you don't want to create in your life any longer. No more unavailable people, no more betrayals, no more abuse, no more lonely stretches of months or years on end between lovers. Today, however, we are going to give you permission to dream of what you do actually want. A beautiful, wise, kindhearted lover whom you can count on and who lights you up like a Christmas tree every time she walks in the room. A wildly happy and healthy committed partnership with a powerful king of a man who claims you as his queen.

To engage the following exercise, please read it through a couple of times, then do it from memory as best you can:

1. **Close Your Eyes and Relax Your Body.** To begin, close your eyes and take a deep breath as though you could breathe all the way down into your hips. Become aware of all of the feelings and sensations in your body, noticing any tension. As you find it, just let it go.

2. **Feel the Future as Though It Were Now.** As if God were in a good mood, and deciding it was His pleasure to give you anything and everything your heart desires, allow yourself to imagine having the kind of love you long for. Imagine that the miracle has already happened, and you are now happily in love with a wonderful partner who is happily in love with you.

    Ask yourself:
    - What does it taste like to have this love in my life? See if you can taste the wine on your lover's lips kissing them.
    - What does it sound like? Imagine hearing your beloved singing in the shower.

- What does it smell like? See if you can smell the scent of the fresh flowers they bought you today.
- What does it look like? Imagine seeing a beautiful engagement or wedding ring on your finger.
- What does it feel like? Imagine your beloved spooning you from behind in bed, lovingly kissing your back.

3. **Identify Who You Are in This Future Fulfilled.** Sense who you are in this future, and allow yourself to "try on" the Possible Self of your future. Let yourself linger in the emotions of being this version of yourself.

Now imagine yourself at work as this version of yourself. Having lunch with a friend. Visiting with a family member. Notice how you show up differently from this place of being loved, supported, honored, valued, nourished, cared for, and seen. Make the decision to begin showing up this way everywhere and with everyone starting now.

4. **Set an Intention to Manifest This Future.** Create an intention to manifest this future. State it in the affirmative. So rather than say what you won't have any longer, declare to the Universe what shall be so. For example, "I will be happily partnered with an amazing man whom I respect, love, and admire by Christmas of this year," or "I will be in a committed relationship with a loving, sensual woman."

You need not know how this future will happen, who it will happen with, or when it will happen. You need only have the courage to put your stake in the ground and let the Universe know what it is that you are committed to creating at this point in your life.

Your past is not your potential. In any hour you can choose to liberate the future.

—Marilyn Ferguson

Finish this sentence:

My intention is to manifest _____

_____ (feel

free to include descriptive adjectives here . . . *bighearted,
loving, happy, sweet, sensual,* etc.).

NOTE: By including a date by which your intention will manifest, you're lighting a fire under yourself to get busy transforming now. If you hesitate doing so for fear of being disappointed, just remind yourself you already have your PhD in surviving disappointment. Just gather your courage and go for the gold! The game isn't so much to have a relationship by the date you set, as it is holding yourself accountable for being who you will need to be in order for it to happen.

Bonus: Practice in Action

Take a bold action that's generative of the future you are standing for. For example, join a dating site, sign up for a class where you can meet new people, throw a dinner party and invite everyone to bring one single friend.

Honoring Your Need for Others

We are each of us angels with only one wing.
And we can only fly embracing each other.

—Luciano De Crescenzo

A friend, Stuart, and I had lunch a while back. We met at a small restaurant overlooking the bay in Marina del Rey on a beautiful, clear afternoon. As I bit into an overstuffed turkey burger, Stuart leaned in and asked me a question. "Do you know the difference between heaven and hell?" he inquired.

"I'm not sure," I replied. "Why don't you explain it to me."

"Well," he said, leaning back in his chair, "hell is like this. You enter a beautiful dining hall, decorated with the finest linens and china. Over in the corner, an orchestra plays exquisite music. You look around and see that everyone is dressed in elegant clothes and draped in splendid jewels. They are all sitting around tables abundant with fine food and drink. You think you've arrived.

"But slowly you start to see that something's wrong. The people don't look happy. In fact, they look sad and confused. In spite of the magnificent array of food laid out before them, they can't eat any of it because their utensils are too large. Though they can manage to get the food onto their forks, they can't actually get it into their mouths. The handles on their silverware are simply too long. You notice they are starving to death." He sat quietly.

"And heaven?" I asked, taking the bait. "Oh, heaven," he replied, with a mischievous smile. "You walk into the same dining hall. Same fine linen and china, same exquisite music, same magnificent food, even the same utensils. Only this time the people are flourishing, laughing, talking, and having a wonderful time. And the only difference is that, whereas the people still can't feed themselves, they've learned to feed one another."

> Man is but a network of relationships and these alone matter to him.
>
> —Antoine de Saint-Exupéry

This story touches us because we know, intuitively, that most of us are living a little too close to hell. We're unclear about how much we should be feeding others, and expect to be fed in return. Aren't all expectations bad? Isn't total autonomy good and the goal to which we should be aspiring? In our therapeutically savvy culture, we've collapsed our unhealthy tendencies toward codependence with a fear of healthy interdependence, uncertain about the difference between the two. Inside of our uncertainty, some of us have learned to deny and turn away from needing others, assuming our needs to be infantile, unattractive, and decidedly negative. Our misguided goal has become total independence and self-sufficiency lest, God forbid, we be thought of as "too needy."

We have to connect the dots between this attitude and escalating reports of an epidemic of loneliness. Particularly in the Western world where, according to a recent article written by the brilliant David Brooks, nearly half of adults in America are now single and unpartnered. As the nuclear family has been our primary source of relatedness for the past seventy years, many are now rethinking how we might grow a healthy sense of belonging to one another.

My friend Aviva was diagnosed with stage 4 lung cancer while only in her mid-thirties. She had two beautiful children, a boy who was five and a girl who was three, a loving husband, and a wonderful career ahead of her to live for. When she first heard the news, she called together a healing circle, inviting her community to gather with her and her family. About sixty of us showed up bearing gifts, poems, prayers, and offers of help. One woman brought a gold ring her mother had given her on her wedding day. She laid it at Aviva's feet, telling her she was giving it to her to give to *her* daughter on her wedding day. No one was without tears that day.

Aviva's illness allowed us all to band together in a way that is uncommon in our culture. Her best friend, Rachael, put all of us on a schedule. Some people did the grocery shopping. Some cleaned the house. Others cared for her children one day a week, and some took her to her medical appointments. You would think that this community would be morose and heavy with sorrow, but nothing could be further from the truth. People were so happy to be needed in this way. They wanted to contribute to Aviva and her family in a way that made a difference for them. There was always laughter and joy coming from that house. Ultimately, Aviva surrendered to death. But even on her deathbed, people were helping out, praying, and reassuring her that all was well. That her children would be well loved and cared for, making it safe for her to leave. One of the saddest things in Aviva's passing is that we all soon returned to our own isolated lives. She used to confide in me how embarrassed she was that so many people "had to go out of their way" to help her. I tried to tell her many times what a gift she was giving to others. Most likely, she understands now.

The simple truth is that we humans need one another to be well and happy in life. While we may no longer require one another for economic and physical survival, we do need one another for emotional, psychological, and spiritual well-being. We all need to feel connected, valued, cared for, and respected. These experiences don't exist in a vacuum. They exist in relationship to one another.

Some of us have become so afraid of appearing needy when dating, that we've given up a healthy sense of entitlement. I frequently counsel those who are afraid to insist that they be treated well, tolerating all sorts of dismissive, disrespectful, and confusing behavior from others simply because they don't want to scare someone off by appearing "too demanding" or "too needy." Because of this, many of us have given up entirely on expressing our needs to others. Yet in doing this, we've severely handicapped our ability to make good choices about which relationships to invest our hearts, bodies, and souls into, and which to steer clear of. How can we assess whether someone's mature enough to love us, if we've taken such pains to hide our need for love? How can we assess whether someone's willing to extend themselves beyond their own needs to at least try tending to ours, if we've gone to such lengths to pretend we don't have any?

Li Jing stood up at a recent *Calling in "The One"* workshop to share the sad story of her recent breakup. She thought she'd found the perfect man: handsome, smart, successful, and looking for the mother of his children. And so, Li Jing set out to be

the perfect woman. She dressed impeccably, she educated herself on his interests, and worked hard to win
the approval of his family and friends. When upset,
she kept it to herself, as she did not wish to appear like
a "high-maintenance woman." (Her words, not mine.)

Six months into the relationship, however, her family went through a financial crisis. Li Jing flew home to help her parents through their fear and despair. It
nearly broke her heart. She was so upset, in fact, that she failed to keep it to herself. She reached out to her boyfriend for emotional support, fully anticipating he
would be there for her. Imagine her confusion and hurt when she discovered that
he had little to no interest in offering her a shoulder to cry on. It turns out that in
going to such lengths to protect him from "burdening him" with her feelings and
needs, she'd failed to notice that her boyfriend was incapable of empathy. Nor did
he have any interest in cultivating any. He was on to the next woman before she
even returned home.

Often, when my clients report that they're too needy, I discover that the people
whom they're spending time with are unwilling or unable to provide them with
what they'd need to feel safe, cared for, and loved. I assure them that it may not
necessarily be that they are too needy. Rather, they may be choosing people who, for
whatever reason, aren't taking their needs into consideration. Of course, this then
leads us to explore how willing they are to take their own needs seriously.

I become so disheartened sometimes listening to people telling me why they
don't need anyone to be happy in life. As though needing others was somehow a
crutch. The truth is, we human beings are a pretty needy bunch. We need a whole
lot of things from one another in order to feel happy and well in life. We need to
know that we belong. That we're valued, respected, wanted, and loved. That our
feelings, our needs, and our desires matter to those around us. That we can count
on a select group of intimate kin, whether biological or chosen or both, to have our
backs. To be rooting for us to accomplish and create all that we feel called to. That
we can trust what others are telling us. That they'll be there when we fall with a
kind word, an outstretched hand, a compassionate ear, and sometimes even a Band-
Aid in the form of rent money or a ride to the doctor's office. This is of course a
two-way street, as others also need these things from us. To the extent that we find
people to love and be loved by and grow our capacities to relate in these healthy

> The bird a nest, the spider a web, man friendship.
>
> —William Blake

interdependent ways, is the extent that we will be fundamentally well and happy in life.

Now, I understand that many of us are carrying around unhealed wounds from the past that occur in the present as neediness. Yet it's important to distinguish our healthy needs from our unhealthy ones. If we're coming from the perspective of the unwanted two-year-old, we can never get enough validation. In fact, our attempt to get the validation we crave will actually covertly create more evidence that we're not wanted. It's a vicious cycle. And so, inside of not knowing how to deal with these unhealthy needs of ours, we'll start hiding our needs, afraid that they'll engulf anyone who gets too close. In an effort to not appear inappropriately needy, some of us will shut down our needs entirely. The appropriate ones get thrown together with the inappropriate ones and we'll swallow them whole. Yet this, in turn, creates only more hunger because it's simply not normal for us to not have needs in our relationships. When we try to pretend our needs don't exist, or treat them as though they were pathological, we only feed the hunger in our hearts that much more intensely.

The following is a partial list of some of our most basic necessities in a relationship. These needs are not only valid and appropriate, but also actually healthy to have:

Acceptance	Empathy	Respect
Affection	Encouragement	Responsibility
Appreciation	Forgiveness	Responsiveness
Autonomy	Honesty	Safety
Belonging	Inspiration	Security
Boundaries	Integrity	Support
Communication	Intimacy	Touch
Companionship	Kindness	Trust
Compassion	Mutuality	Understanding
Consideration	Nurturing	Validation
Consistency	Presence	Values Compatibility

To prepare for love, it's important that you take some time to identify and own what you actually need to be well and happy in a relationship, without judging and making yourself feel wrong for it. Until you can take full responsibility for what you want and need in a relationship, you may waste a lot of your time with people who either don't have what you want or, for whatever reason, simply aren't interested in giving it to you.

PRACTICE: IDENTIFYING AND TENDING TO YOUR NEEDS
Identify What You Need in Your Relationship

Take out your journal. Read through the list of healthy needs and choose five to ten things you need to be well, happy, and safe in your relationships. Feel free to add something that is not on the partial list.

Write each one out as a full sentence. As you write, own your needs as valid and worthy of consideration.

Be specific, such as:

- "I need to know that others are being honest and telling me the absolute truth."
- "I need others to listen to my feelings and needs and respond by doing their best to accommodate them."
- "I need others to respect my boundaries, particularly around important self-care practices like giving me the space to meditate."

NOTE: In this moment, don't worry about how to get those in your life to give you these things. You may have been training people for years that your feelings and needs don't matter, so turning things around may take some time. For now, simply acknowledging your needs as valid, appropriate, and healthy is the right direction.

Make a Promise to Give Yourself What You Need

Because our relationships with others can never be any better than our relationship with ourselves, I invite you to begin raising your healthy expectations that others acknowledge and care for your needs by making the choice to start acknowledging and caring for your own needs.

Now, close your eyes, put your hand over your heart, and take a deep breath. Go through your list and, one by one, promise yourself you will do all you can to start giving to yourself that which you need. Do this either by speaking your promise out loud, or simply by saying it silently to yourself.

For example:

- *"I need to know that others are being honest and telling me the absolute truth"* becomes *"I promise to start being completely honest with myself and telling myself the absolute truth."*
- *"I need others to listen to my feelings and needs and respond by doing their best to accommodate them"* becomes *"I promise to turn toward and listen to my own feelings and needs, and respond by doing all I can to accommodate and tend to them."*
- *"I need others to respect my boundaries, particularly around important self-care practices like giving me the space to meditate"* becomes *"I promise to respect my own boundaries, particularly around my self-care practices like meditating each morning."*

Write the promises you are making to yourself ten times each in your journal. As you write, feel it to be so in your heart.

Bonus: Practice in Action

Carve out some quiet time today to craft a private letter to yourself, written to you from your Beloved-to-Be.

Begin with *Dear _____ (Your Name),*

Then imagine this person lovingly, tenderly pledging themselves to caring for your deepest needs and desires, softly whispering words of great tenderness and love into your ear. As you write this down, allow your heart to open to receive this person's devotion.

For example:

Dear _____,

My Beloved, I will always have the courage to be honest with you. To guard your heart and protect the integrity of our love by telling you the truth. I am also willing to hear your truth, and invite you to be completely honest with me as the foundation of our love.

Beloved, I welcome your true feelings and needs and I promise to do my best to accommodate them whenever possible. Rest assured that your feelings and needs matter to me, and I am grateful to be the guardian of your heart.

Beloved, I'm happy when you take care of yourself first and foremost! I honor your boundaries and support you to do everything you know to do to take excellent care of your heart, soul, body, and mind.

> What makes a happy marriage? It is a question which all men and women ask one another . . . The answer is to be found, I think, in the mutual discovery, by two who marry, of the deepest need of the other's personality, and the satisfaction of that need.
>
> —Pearl Buck

As you write your letter, imagine yourself receiving the experience of having your needs acknowledged and tended to by your Beloved-to-Be, who loves, respects, cherishes, and honors you. When you've finished writing your letter, read and reread it as often as you like, each time allowing yourself to experience the love and care your Beloved-to-Be is extending toward you, as though it were happening now.

Cultivating a Vision of Love Fulfilled

Like a great athlete, we must have a very clear vision of what we want to accomplish before we make a move. Vision, in preparation for an action, is as important as the action itself.

—Marianne Williamson

I 've met many people who can't imagine having the kind of relationship they would actually want. Where their fundamental needs for love, intimacy, and support are met, and the relationship is a foundation for the full flourishing of their lives. It's for this reason that some of us who want love the most, are the ones most likely to push it away. It's called being "love avoidant." That's when we unconsciously assume that an intimate partnership will actually take from us more than it will give us. We may desperately want intimacy, belonging, and closeness, yet we're terrified to allow it into our lives.

A beautiful and talented young woman named Kimberly attended a live *Calling in "The One"* workshop with me more than a decade ago. She's a first-rate singer who traveled around the world performing her original music. On her way to our workshop, she got lost, which caused her to be a half hour late. She apologized to everyone, saying how happy she was to be there, as finding her life partner was her number one priority. However, as the day wore on, it became clear that Kimberly was afraid of making a commitment. She was devoted to her music career and feared a relationship would prevent her from achieving her professional goals. She believed she had to choose between finding a husband and becoming a known and celebrated singer-songwriter. Kimberly ended up leaving the workshop early because she got a singing gig, promising to enroll in the next workshop. To date, she has never returned. The last I heard, her career had plateaued, and she was very much still single.

Many of us see our desires as mutually exclusive. Either I get to have a successful career, or I get to have love. Either I get to pursue my passions in life, or I get to start a family. Those of us who have a calling to be of service to humanity in some meaningful way are particularly vulnerable to this either/or way of thinking, and our lives can easily end up taking on a certain holy, nunlike quality. As in empty "holes" and "none" to describe our intimate love lives.

When we speak of creating a vision of love fulfilled, we'll want to stretch ourselves to consider having all that we desire—love, purpose, creativity, self-expression, career success, belonging, health, abundance, intimacy, and autonomy. Success that is made possible not just in spite of love, but because of the stability, encouragement, and well-being that your relationship provides. Passions that are fulfilled not just in spite of your relationship, but because of the support and inspiration you receive from your partner that make it all possible. You must make sure you don't default to your automatic assumptions about what love might have looked like for your parents and grandparents. Most of us aren't looking for an antiquated role-based relationship, but a soul-based connection. A love that expands what's possible for you, rather than contracts or limits it, and is inclusive of all you desire to experience and express in life.

When envisioning what a loving relationship might look like for you, be careful not to narrow down your sights to a list of attributes (attractive, successful, fit, college-educated, funny, spiritual, and on and on). While I agree we should be clear about what we want, most of us forget to include the way we'll actually feel when in this relationship: inspired, safe, heard, seen, supported, trusting, happy, and well loved. Instead, we tend to focus on the external attributes we think we want in a partner. Some of the lists I've seen have been so detailed that they specify what the person does for a living ("I want to fall in love with a writer"), where the person lives ("I want someone who lives in Beverly Hills"), or what kind of car they drive ("I need

> Soulful marriages are often odd on the surface.
>
> —Thomas Moore

someone fun who drives a sports car"). Dating coach Logan Ury calls this "relationshopping," where we're reducing potential partners to a mere commodity. But bringing in a mate isn't like ordering a meal—I'll have the dressing on the side, extra tomatoes, and hold the cheese, please. The external attributes we think

> I am enough of an artist to draw freely upon my imagination. Imagination is more important than knowledge. Knowledge is limited. Imagination encircles the world.
>
> —Albert Einstein

are so important actually have little to do with the heart of a person or the emotional tone of a connection. In other words, the aspects that reflect what we call soul.

A recent study done at Rutgers University polled a group of singles between the ages of twenty and twenty-nine, asking whether they agreed or disagreed with the statement "When you marry, you want your spouse to be your soul mate first and foremost." Ninety-four percent agreed. Obviously, most of us aren't looking for just someone. We're looking for "The One" with whom we can build a soulful and meaningful life.

In his book *Soul Mates,* author Thomas Moore defines a soul mate as ". . . someone to whom we feel profoundly connected, as though the communicating and communing that take place between us were not the product of intentional efforts, but rather a divine grace." A soul mate relationship is characterized by such things as shared values, a sense of comfort and ease, and a genuine liking of each other. A secure relationship is distinguished by qualities such as friendship, trust, and a feeling of togetherness that has space for individual differences and healthy autonomy. So the qualities you want to weave into your vision of love fulfilled are experiential in nature. Rather than say you want someone with a graduate degree, try on what it might feel like to enjoy how your partner thinks. Rather than say you want someone with a buff body, try on what it will feel like to be inspired to realize your own goals for physical health and vitality.

Wear your expectations of what that person should look like lightly. Because soul mates have a way of arriving in unusual packages. In her book *Soulmates,* Dr. Carolyn Miller tells us,

> *"Our soul . . . directs us to individuals who share our purpose in life, complement our strengths, and supplement our weaknesses. But there is no guarantee*

> Hope is . . . an orientation of the heart; it transcends the world that is immediately experienced, and is anchored somewhere beyond its horizons.
>
> —Václav Havel

that these ideal mates are going to look the way we expect, or be of our own background. That's only one of the reasons why they are so easy to miss if we are not listening for guidance."

Until you are able to *see* yourself living the life that you truly want to be living, it will be difficult for you to create and sustain it. We will be doing a lot of work in our next few weeks together to grow your ability to imagine your life abundantly fulfilled in love, and inclusive of the fulfillment of all your deepest desires.

PRACTICE: BEGIN A VISION BOARD OF LOVE FULFILLED

I invite you to begin a vision board today that you can work on at your own pace throughout the course. You can create your collage virtually on your computer, or as a concrete art project. If you choose to do it as an art project, you will need some supplies, such as a piece of cardboard or a canvas, a stack of magazines, scissors, and some glue.

Begin by anchoring into your vision for love by taking out your journal and writing a list of your deepest desires and all you yearn to accomplish in this lifetime. You'd love to create a soulful marriage, along with moving to the country and growing a lush vegetable garden. You're dreaming of starting a successful business and raising a family. Along with a big golden retriever! You yearn to be fit and healthy and contribute to your community in beautiful and meaningful ways. Let yourself dare to dream of your very best life in all areas!

Now look for images and/or words that represent the fulfillment of what love looks like for you. Make sure that you include images of *all* of the various parts of yourself where romantic love coexists with other things that you love and need in your life in order to feel fulfilled. Begin looking for photos and images that touch your heart. Look at paintings created by masters or unknown artists that inspire you. You may even wish to draw or paint your own images into the collage. Consider including words and phrases that light you up, either ones you create or cutouts from magazines.

Allow yourself to be creative and unconventional.

If you wish to spend the day working on this project, that's great. However, if the most you can do today is simply locate one or two pictures or phrases to include, that's fine.

As you collect your images, you may want to keep them in a special, sacred place, gathering them all together before you begin designing your virtual vision board, or gluing them onto a piece of cardboard, canvas, or wood. Or you may prefer creating your masterpiece as you go.

Place your images where you can see them often. Whenever you look at the images, allow your awareness to drop down into your body, take a deep breath and feel what it will be like to receive this into your life. Silently say to yourself, *"Yes. This is for me. Thank you, Universe [God, Spirit, Life]."*

Bonus: Practice in Action

Many of us have been looking for a partner with a checklist of qualifications in mind, judging and assessing people according to our preconceived ideas of what we think we want. It's what philosopher Martin Buber called an "I-It" connection, where we're relating to others as though they were simply objects in our world.

Today, I invite you to begin doing this differently by consciously connecting with others from a more heart-centered and curious place. Let go of your mind's agenda and practice opening your heart to others to discover who they are. It's what Buber referred to as an "I-Thou" connection, and it is the foundation of all true intimate connection.

Throughout the day, instead of assessing people with your

> This or
> something better
> now manifests
> for me in totally
> satisfying and
> harmonious
> ways, for the
> highest good of
> all concerned.
>
> —Shakti Gawain

preconceived notions of what you're looking for, try dropping down into your heart to notice how they actually *feel* to you. Are they warm and inviting? Is there kindness in their eyes? Do you feel seen? Are you intimidated? Are they off-putting and arrogant? Do you feel liked? Wanted? Cared for? Objectified? Is this person someone you could be friends with? Laugh with? Trust with a secret? Are they someone you feel safe with? Judged by? Rather than be captivated by their external attributes, do your best to notice the tone of the connection between you.

Remember, you're calling in your soul mate, not your perfect ego mate. That means you want to be looking primarily with your heart, and not just your head. Tonight, before bed, take out your journal and write down your thoughts and impressions on your connections with others. Explore your interactions with others not from obvious things about them like gender, political affiliation, financial status, or professional position, but from the way you actually *felt* when relating with them.

Making the Space for Love

The space in which we live should be for the person we are
becoming . . . not for the person we were in the past.

—Marie Kondo

One gray night, I was traveling with a group of about fifty on a large, chartered bus. We were inspired and relaxed after an exciting conference that had ended several hours earlier. People were sharing snacks and songs, telling silly jokes and simply enjoying one another's company. I found myself sitting across the aisle from a man I'd never met before, and I began a conversation with him.

Jeffrey was in his late thirties and he had just gotten engaged. He was beaming with contentment. I asked him how he'd met his wife-to-be. With a great smile of satisfaction on his face, he told me that she was nothing like he'd pictured his wife would be. For years, he had a list of qualifications that he was looking for that he now described as his "rigid criteria." He said that "The One" hadn't shown up in his life until he'd given up the attachment of what he thought she should look like. The real work, he confided, was that he needed to open himself to love and be loved. When I asked him how he did this, he smiled sheepishly and leaned in to tell me his secret. "I cleaned out my closets," he confessed. "I literally created a space in my bedroom closet and cleared out a drawer so that when she showed up, she'd have a place to put her things."

If you want to call in a great love, you must create an open, warm space for that person to come into, so they feel welcomed when they arrive. Even if your home is too small for two people and you are certain that you will move when you

Our lives will mirror our surroundings. Choose thoughtfully.

—Karen Ann Tompkins

find them, it is important to make room for this person where you are right now, if even symbolically. There's a lot of wisdom in the age-old advice: If you want a relationship, go out and buy a double bed.

The best room to begin with is, of course, the bedroom. The purpose of the bedroom is twofold: rest and intimacy. If you have your office set up in your bedroom or if any other activities go on there, you may wish to move these to another part of your home or at least screen off that area so it is separate from your sleeping quarters. Your bedroom is your personal space and it is important to dedicate this one room to the exchange of love, warmth, affection, rest, and rejuvenation.

If your bedroom is filled with stuffed animals left over from childhood, pictures of your parents, relics from former love affairs, or framed copies of your advanced graduate degrees, I invite you to reconsider how you are using this room. One woman I worked with complained to me of depression and exhaustion. She was having difficulty separating herself emotionally from her ex-husband and often found herself sleepless, irritable, and upset. During the course of our conversation, I discovered that, in her attempt to avoid looking at the mounds of paperwork that were being generated from her difficult and ongoing divorce proceedings, she was storing all of the legal documents underneath her bed. I was stunned. No wonder she was unable to get a good night's sleep. Needless to say, I advised her to get them out of there at once and to store them appropriately in another part of the house. She immediately started to sleep better at night.

When I began designing my environment to support calling in "The One," one of the first things I noticed was my bed. Although it was queen-size, it was pushed up against the wall so that it could only be gotten into from one side. It was not a big adjustment to turn the bed cater-cornered so that it could be accessed from both sides.

So many of us, when single, tolerate living in environments that have little meaning for us. Too often, we procrastinate creating a loving and nurturing space until we have the right partner, only to find that our dissatisfaction with our lives is aggravated by a home that feels temporary, empty, and undernourishing. Worse yet, many people are living in homes that hold reminders of a former relationship, thereby keeping it alive in their space. If any of these describe you, I suggest you begin creating an environment that reflects and supports the future you are calling in.

Feng shui is an ancient Chinese art and science first developed some six thousand years ago. Very simply, feng shui is about the energy flow in a given space, concerning itself with how the placement of objects affects how people feel when they are in that environment. In feng shui, using pairs of items accentuates the possibility of romantic union. Pairs of pillows, pairs of pictures, pairs of candlesticks all bring forth the feeling of a harmonious relationship and evoke a feeling of intimacy. I once heard actress and minister Della Reese share a sweet story about being single in her sixties and wanting to call in a mate. The first thing she did was go out and buy herself two place settings. She began setting her dinner table every night for the two of them. When she'd walk in after a long day's work, she'd open the door and say, "Hi, honey! I'm home. What's for dinner?" It wasn't long before there "he" was, dining with her at that very table each night.

When calling in romantic partnership, feng shui also encourages us to reflect both masculine and feminine energies in our environment. If you have lots of puffy, lacy, flowery things throughout your home, you may wish to balance this with more masculine motifs, colors, and lines, and vice versa.

While driving to a recent *Calling in "The One"* workshop, Cynthia, a charismatic woman in her early forties, shared that she found herself becoming irritated at the very thought of sharing her bedroom with anyone. She described her bedroom to us, noting that she had a different nightstand on each side of the bed. One nightstand had shelves for her books and a nice-size lamp so she could read at night. The other had no shelves and was too small to hold a lamp. When she met her man, she assumed that she would feel compelled to give him the nicer of the two nightstands, thereby leaving her with one that would be inadequate for her needs. Already she was a martyr, resenting a man she hadn't even met. At least she could laugh at herself. The group encouraged her to purchase another nightstand to match the one that she liked, and to get rid of the smaller one entirely. A suggestion that she took. Imagine how delighted she was when she discovered that the man she called into her life loved to read before bed as much as she did.

Sometimes we have to work from the outside in. My good friend, feng shui

> Above all, love your home. . . . You cannot expect love to come and stay in a place that is unloved. A place that is loved for being home will invite more love in.
>
> —Rosemary Ellen Guiley

expert Marie Diamond, tells us that our environments serve as a vision board of sorts, instructing our unconscious, as well as the Universe, what we are (and are not) open and available for. It is for this reason that I'm admonishing you to let go of clutter and to clear your space of anything that anchors you into the past that could present an obstacle to love. Give up using the other side of the bed as your library. Give away or return your former boyfriend's jacket that's still hanging in your closet. Take down any artwork that reflects loneliness and solitude. One woman I worked with had a collection of lonely portraits throughout her home. When I suggested that these images should be replaced with pictures of happy friends, family, and lovers, she balked. She'd been collecting art reflecting isolation and solitude all her life because, she explained, it was how she felt inside. "Yes," I replied, "that's the problem. And you've now built a shrine to reinforce these feelings! Yet if you hope to shed your habit of being so chronically alone in life, you'll do well to begin by welcoming images of union, togetherness, and love into your home."

Creating space for the love of your life isn't just about your physical environment. Make sure that you have breathing room in your schedule so you have the time to explore relationships and let new people into your life. You may feel particularly driven to fill your life with constant activity in an effort to create a sense of meaning and purpose. Many people I know make themselves excessively busy in an effort to avoid the pain of coming home to an empty apartment at the end of the day.

Tolerating the void is not for the faint of heart. Yet we all must master the ability to release who we are for the possibility of who we might become. As the saying goes, "In order to fly, you have to give up the ground you are standing on."

PRACTICE: PREPARING YOUR HOME FOR LOVE

Today, take a few minutes to walk through each room of your home. Notice whether or not each room is welcoming and inviting. Is this a place you'd feel comfortable inviting someone into? Is there space here for another person? Is your home clutter free? Clean? Does it smell good? Do you have pairs of things throughout your home? Do you have spaces where the two of you can enjoy each other?

When doing this awareness exercise, my friend Dr. Joan Bragar, who wrote the lovely book *Never Too Late for Love*, noticed she had only one armchair in her bedroom where she would sit each morning to meditate and read. She decided to go out and buy the matching chair as preparation for finding her husband, who she hoped would be a man who also had a spiritual practice. For seven happy years now, the two of them start their day together by sitting in those chairs to do their morning practices side by side.

Take out your notebook. Make a list of at least five things you could alter in your home to create a more welcoming environment for the intimate partner you are calling into your life. For example, buy a pair of matching pillows for your bed, buy that person a bathrobe that matches yours and hang it in your closet, take down any artwork that reflects loneliness or loss, or clean out a drawer so they'll have a place to put their things.

Add to your list one or two things you could do to alter your schedule so that there is some breathing room in your life to explore new relationships.

Bonus: Practice in Action

Make one or more changes in your home today to reflect a more welcoming environment for the partner you're inviting into your life. Also make one or more plans that create possibilities for you to meet new people (e.g., make a date to go out dancing with a friend, ask a co-worker to set you up on a blind date, schedule some downtime in your day to go outside for a walk, read the newspaper at a coffee shop, or just window-shop at the local mall).

Suggested Study Guide for Group Discussion

1. How connected to and/or disconnected from others do you feel, and what do you do to discourage or lessen a sense of connection? How might you begin to generate a greater sense of belonging and a connection with others?

2. What is/are your pattern(s) in an intimate relationship up until now and how have you been the source of that pattern? What habitual actions have you taken, or choices have you made, that have perpetuated this disappointing pattern time and time again? In seeing this clearly, what new choices and actions might you now begin to take?

3. What do you need in your most intimate relationships, and how are you beginning to fulfill your own needs in preparation to receiving this from your Beloved-to-Be?

4. Share your vision of love fulfilled in your life and how it feels to be in a happy, healthy, loving relationship.

5. What specific changes did you make this week in your home and schedule to create space for love in your life?

Completing Your Past

Your task is not to seek for love, but merely to seek and find all of the barriers within yourself that you have built against it.

—A Course in Miracles

Now is the time to roll up our shirtsleeves and get down to the nitty-gritty work of actualizing love in our lives, as we begin a two-week process of identifying and releasing all that is in its way.

This week, we will:

- Challenge ourselves to undergo the necessary losses of those things that are diminishing our chances for success in love
- Explore the process of true release and forgiveness to complete the past
- Examine the toxic relational ties that are preventing healthier relationships from taking root in our lives
- Identify and let go of old agreements that no longer serve us and re-create new ones that do
- Redefine our relationships to the wounds we've endured to create a deeper opening for love

Allowing Loss

To give oneself over to love and marriage is to say yes to death.

—Thomas Moore

Most of us want something for nothing. We want to be thin without exerting ourselves, successful without taking a risk, and loved without losing anything. This "all blessings, no burdens" idea of how life should be is very American, since America is the only culture in the world that seems to expect life to be comfortable and relatively pain free. However, in most spiritual traditions, we find countless examples of the inevitable relationship between joy and despair, fullness and emptiness, life and death. Philosopher Alan Watts said, "Good without evil is like up without down, and . . . to make an ideal of pursuing the good is like trying to get rid of the left by turning constantly to the right."

The first time I considered the possibility that finding "The One" might necessitate some losses was the day I asked my happily married hairdresser, Carrie, about her courtship with her husband. She recognized him as the man she wanted to partner with almost immediately: She felt both a great respect and an intense attraction the moment they met. Yet even though she was overjoyed they'd committed their lives to each other, their engagement was actually a difficult time for her. As the date of their wedding grew closer, the reality of joining her life with this man compelled her to examine certain habits and patterns she'd had for years. She recognized that her image of herself as a strong and fiercely independent person was counterproductive to creating an enduring bond with him. She had to allow herself to give up the emotional armor she'd grown so used to, becoming more vulnerable and undefended than ever before. She also had to give up a fantasy she'd had since

> Like the moth longing for the flame, insane for the light that will extinguish its very life, the lover longs for the beloved partner.
>
> —Connie Zweig

childhood that she would please her father by marrying a man just like him. Her fiancé was nothing like her father, and the two men, although polite and respectful, were actually a bit uncomfortable with each other. Little by little, Carrie was compelled to give up that which was incongruent with the life she was committing herself to creating. Thus, their courtship was a major adjustment period that included many losses and much maturing on her part.

We are so captivated by our collective myth of the happy ending that we rarely acknowledge the amount of loss and letting go that can be involved in getting there. The truth is, each gain in life represents the loss of something else. We simply never move forward in life without losing something. No wonder most of us are resistant to change, even when those changes promise to be positive. As much as we want our lives to be different, the truth is, surrendering to change means letting go of being in control. And we don't like it much when our illusion of being in control is challenged because the feeling that we're in charge gives us leverage against feeling the void of a loss. Yet, these efforts to circumvent emptiness are the cause of much anxiety and angst. At the heart of worry is always a fierce holding on, even when that which we're clinging to is no longer appropriate or beneficial to us.

Early on in my teaching career, I noticed something odd. When asked what brought them to a *Calling in "The One"* workshop, people would share their deep yearnings for a loving relationship. When asked to expand upon their vision of what that relationship might look like, they'd share in great detail their elaborate lists of what they were looking for in a mate. Yet when asked what they'd need to give up to make room to receive this great love in their life, such as the habit of closing their heart and putting up a wall when someone disappoints them, their righteous resentment toward a former partner, or their preconceived ideas about what "The One" is supposed to look like, there'd be dead silence in the room. The truth is, many of us would secretly rather stay the same and not be challenged to give up anything, even if that means we continue to suffer. But life isn't really set up to allow us to stagnate where we are. When we refuse to sacrifice something up in order to move forward, it becomes clear within a relatively short period of time that, in fact, we've begun to move backward. Refusing to risk taking the next step to let go of who we've known ourselves to be for the possibility of who we might become, we discover a loss of vitality. We become uninspired, depressed, stuck, and resigned. Not the best states of mind to attract love, although it might make the longing for love even more acute, since life is so devoid of its spark.

One of the most important skills we can acquire in life is the ability to let go when letting go is appropriate. And to recognize that the very human experience of setbacks, losses, breakdowns, and disappointments is what grows our wisdom, deepens our compassion, and initiates us to a more mature version of ourselves.

The first step in doing so is to give up the assumption that, when we suffer a loss, something is "wrong." Nothing is wrong. Loss is an integral part of life. Sometimes there is a sadness, a silence, a despair, or a loneliness that just needs to be listened to and learned from. The ancient Sufi poet Rumi says it best:

> *This being human is a guest house.*
> *Every morning a new arrival.*
> *A joy, a depression, a meanness,*
> *Some momentary awareness comes*
> *As an unexpected visitor.*
> *Welcome and attend them all!*
> *Even if they're a crowd of sorrows,*
> *Who violently sweep your house*
> *Empty of its furniture.*
> *Still, treat each guest honorably.*
> *He may be clearing you out for some new delight.*

Our lives are always in motion. As such, we will continually be asked to give up the life we have for the life we are creating. Particularly so in the aftermath of setting a powerful intention to create that which we've never had before. Contrary to our often overly optimistic expectations, the first stage of a breakthrough is usually a breakdown; the bottoming out on a bad habit, or the crash and burn of a false friend. One by one, out the door go distractions, defenses, and illusions. Anything incongruent with the future we're standing for must now make way for the new life you're calling in. For those of us who've

> He who loses his
> life shall find it.
>
> —Jesus

suffered traumatic losses, particularly ones that occurred in early childhood, the feelings that we associate with loss, fear, anger, and frustration can be unsettling and frightening. However, it's important to learn how to feel these feelings without needing to run back to the safety of the lives we've known, and to the people we've known ourselves to be.

Let me give it to you straight. When you decide to improve your life, your first experience will likely be loss. The first act of creation is always destruction.

Soon after declaring my intention to call in "The One," I was confronted by the need to initiate the death of three relationships. The first was with a former boyfriend, whom I was still hanging on to, both through the desperate hope that he'd change and a fierce resentment that he hadn't. The second was with the man I'd been dating, Daniel, who was very clear with me from the start that he had no interest in creating a family. Although Daniel remained my friend, my hope of us moving into an exclusive, committed partnership had to be surrendered so we could each be true to ourselves. And lastly, I let go of a friendship with a man who'd been flirting with me for more than two years, dangling the carrot of "maybe someday" he'd leave his live-in girlfriend and we would build a life together. These relationships had to be released before I could receive Mark into my life. More accurate, the me that had created these relationships in the first place had to die and be replaced with the me who had higher and healthier expectations about what was possible for me. The old me used to believe that I was "inferior to other women," that I was "too old to find someone" and "too difficult" for anyone to want to deal with me. No wonder I compromised myself by hanging on to unavailable men. On some level I thought that my choice was either that or be alone.

In order to live rich and meaningful lives, we must be willing to endure the necessary losses of life without distracting ourselves with drama, or needing to be rescued from the unknown. We must be brave enough to allow the organic ebb and flow of life, and learn to value those things that can be found only in the letting go—a deepening of our commitment to ourselves, a resolve to stop settling for less, and a learning to love our own company. Or the epiphany that sometimes you have to give up saving face, in order to save your own ass. A willingness to finally stop controlling everyone and everything in order to discover that no one actually dies when you do. These are all

> Every day a little death.
>
> —Stephen Sondheim

experiences that liberate us from that which is no longer working for us, and which have the capacity to expand our ability to love and be loved.

There is a Chinese proverb that I find very beautiful.

My barn having burned to the ground,
I can now see the moon.

Loss is like that. Our job is to simply surrender those things that block the experience of love, trusting the promise of the Psalmist that "weeping may endure for a night but joy cometh in the morning."

If there is one thing to bear in mind until the truth of its words eases the heart troubled by apparent failure and loss, it is this: *The new life is always greater than the old.*

—Ralph Blum

PRACTICE: WELCOMING LOSS TO CREATE ROOM FOR LOVE

Take out your journal. Make a list of three or more losses you've suffered and thought you wouldn't survive and your subsequent gain.

For example:

LOSS #1

Benjamin broke up with me right before what was to be our dream vacation. I cried for three days before I decided to go anyway.

SUBSEQUENT GAIN

Discovered that I could make friends anywhere. It opened up a whole new world for me to know that I could travel alone and have a great time. Now I vacation alone at least once a year.

Ask yourself and journal on the following:
What would I need to release from my life to make more room for love?
Hint: Look to discover the necessary losses that you've been trying

> One may not reach the dawn save by the path of the night.
>
> —Kahlil Gibran

to avoid to inform what you will need to let go of to create more room for love. For example: "I've been trying to avoid giving up my ex-boyfriend even though I know the relationship is bad for me. What I need to release is trying to make this re- lationship work when it's clearly not working," or "I've been trying to avoid getting rejected so I've not been putting my- self out there to meet new people. I need to release organizing my life around my fear of rejection," or "I've been trying to protect myself from getting hurt again by keeping my guard up and not opening up my heart. What I need to release is the wall I've built around me."

Bonus: Practice in Action

Take one or more actions today to release something from your life to make room for love. For example, ending a friendship that clearly isn't working for you anymore, burning an old love letter from an ex that you've been holding on to through prolonged grief, or going through your closets and getting rid of everything that you haven't worn for a year or more and making room for your Beloved-to-Be to put their things.

Asking a More Beautiful Question

Always the beautiful answer who asks a more beautiful question.

—e. e. cummings

Most of us have been trying to complete the past for a while now—sitting quietly on our meditation cushions, or scribbling furiously in our tattered journals. Or faithfully perched on a couch for fifty minutes, pouring our hearts out to someone who we hope is wiser than we are. Rummaging through our histories, trying diligently to reflect on how we became who we know ourselves to be, and hoping with all our hearts to figure out how to become who we sense we could be, and perhaps even should be.

The connections we make in these reflective moments are usually good ones. Yet if our attention stays captivated on the grief, sorrow, anger, or insult of how we were once mistreated or wronged, we could begin to make a home of victimization. Thereby solidifying the sense of ourselves that we created in response to the painful experiences we once endured. The classic therapeutic question, "How do you feel about that?" is only one part of trauma recovery. The next question needs to be along the lines of, "And what did you make that mean about you, or about the possibilities you hold for love in this lifetime?" Followed by, "And from that perspective, how have you been showing up in life in ways that have then validated and even perpetuated that story, often outside of conscious awareness?"

When we talk about discovering ourselves as the source of our painful patterns in love, we are talking about you accessing the power to create a future that is different from your past. You can't change anything if others are always to blame, because you have little to no control over others. You can change your life only when you decide to take 100 percent responsibility for yourself and your patterns. Does this mean you are to blame? No. Because usually, you are not the sole reason why a pattern keeps happening. Patterns almost have a life of their own. They are like a river that predictably flows in one direction solely by habit, day after day, month after month, and year after year. In fact, your part in perpetuating a chronic and painful pattern might actually be quite small and subtle. You have a habit of turning away from and dismissing your own deeper knowing. Maybe you habitually ignore your own feelings and needs, caring instead for the perceived feelings and needs of others. Perhaps you lack the courage to speak up for yourself in key moments, for fear that others might become angry with you.

Many of the ways we're the source of our own chronic unwanted experiences are covert in nature. Yet those of us who have the spiritual integrity to try to understand ourselves as the source of our own patterns will often do it in ways that set us up for failure. We ask ourselves questions that are decidedly shame-based and therefore designed to not change a thing. One simply cannot change if they are stuck in shame.

Patricia, a high-level high school administrator, had not been asked out on a date in more than twenty years. Though she yearned for love, she was at a loss as to where to even begin. When she came to a live three-day *True Love Awakening* workshop I offered in Los Angeles, she had the courage to stand up in front of the group to confess her deep confusion as to why love had eluded her for all of these years. It seemed to her that she was just invisible to men. She felt embarrassed and even ashamed that a woman of her education and professional success in life would be so clueless about something that seemed to come so easily to others. When we explored how she was internally processing the feedback of no one asking her out, we discovered she was basically asking herself the same question over and over again. Which was basically the shame-based inquiry of "What the #*&% is wrong with me?" Inside of this unsophis-

There is one art of which people should be masters—the art of reflection.

—Samuel Taylor Coleridge

ticated inquiry, she became more and more shut down and
isolated, unable to even ask her girlfriends for advice, and
paralyzed to the point of complete powerlessness.

Because of her courage to stand up in front of the group
and share so authentically, we were able to help Patricia
come up with some new, and more empowering, questions
to start asking herself. How might she be showing up in
ways that broadcast "stay away"? What part of her didn't want a man to approach
her? How might she be presenting herself in a way that suggests she's not available for an intimate connection? These were much more nuanced and sophisticated
questions than the one she'd been asking herself, and they opened up the possibility
for her to begin showing up in new ways with others. The changes she made were
subtle yet significant. She took a bit more care with how she presented herself, paying more attention to her appearance than was typical for her. She then learned
a few fun flirting techniques and started practicing them on a couple of men she
found attractive at work. She had new photos done by a professional photographer,
and posted a profile on an online dating site. Within three months of that workshop,
she met a good-looking, successful widower. The owner of a construction company
who had a lot of time and money to lavish on a woman he loved. He fell for Patricia
immediately, and they've been lovers ever since.

The questions that inspire us to grow beyond the painful patterns of our past
are ones that are thought-provoking, sophisticated, and nuanced. They inspire us to
think more deeply about ourselves as the source of our patterns, and in ways that
promise to bring about true transformation.

> You cannot have
> a meaningful life
> without having
> self-reflection.
>
> —Oprah Winfrey

PRACTICE: EMPOWERED SELF-REFLECTION

Today's practice is about becoming aware of the automatic questions you tend to ask yourself when looking to understand yourself as
the source of your experiences, and to identify the more empowering
ones you could ask instead.

Take out your journal and write on the following:

1. **Identify Your Painful Pattern in Love.** *For example, "No one ever asks me out," or "I get involved with unavailable people," or "I always wind up with narcissistic people."*

2. **Notice Where in Your Body You Feel the Pain of the Pattern.** Focus on the lowest place in your body where you can feel the energy of the emotion you feel when the pattern happens. For example: in the center of your solar plexus, or heaviness on your heart.

3. **Make the Automatic Question You're Asking Conscious.** Breathe deeply into this part of your body, and notice the automatic inner conversation you find yourself engaging around this situation over and over again. *For example, "What's wrong with me?" "Why can't I ever get what I want?" "How can I be so stupid?"*

   Notice the lack of room for true evolution and growth in these disempowering questions.

4. **Create a More Empowering Question That Could Lead to Growth.** Stepping back from this inner conversation, come up with a question that could support you to grow in the area of love and relationships. *For example, "What am I avoiding being responsible for in this situation?" "How does it serve me to be without a partner in life?" "What is the deeper truth about me, and how can I align my actions and my choices regarding this situation with what is really true?"*

Bonus: Practice in Action

Choose the most powerful question you came up with this morning, and live this question throughout the day. For example, if your question was "How could I let men know that I'm interested in being asked out?" then take the risk to play with ways you might do just that.

Be more invested in taking actions that are aligned with your commitment to call in your partner-to-be than you are in getting what you want. If you take a risk, then you win big-time and you should celebrate your courage and commitment! If you end up actually getting what you want from someone, then that's just the icing on the cake.

Letting Go of Your Past

Pause at the word: "for-give." "For-to-give." Forgiveness is such
a gift that "give" lives in the word. Christian tradition has tried to
make it a meek and passive word; turn the other cheek. But the
word contains the active word "give," which reveals its truth.

—Michael Ventura

For several years, I did my best to attend a three-day silent-meditation retreat on New Year's with spiritual leader Rev. Michael Beckwith. Through the years, the retreat grew in size. Yet back then, there were usually about fifty or sixty of us convening around 9 A.M. and sitting together in silence until about 9 or 10 P.M. under Rev. Michael's guidance, with very little eye contact so as not to distract our attention outward.

One retreat in particular was difficult for me. I'd made the assertion I would be engaged by my forty-second birthday a few weeks earlier and I was in the early stage of my process. I was dealing with intense feelings of anger and a desire for revenge toward an ex-boyfriend, who was already in love with another woman. I struggled the entire weekend to let go of the hostile feelings I was having, to no avail. I was completely consumed by the agony of unresolved resentment.

I had every right to be mad. From my perspective, my former boyfriend had wronged me deeply. I had brought an idea to him several years before to run transformational workshops with professional songwriters and people who had, at one time, been homeless. I wanted to help these men, women, and adolescents tell their stories of hope, healing, and renewal through music, thereby solidifying and celebrating the gains they had made while also highlighting solutions to homelessness.

My former boyfriend, a music publisher, loved the idea and, together, for five years we ran these very special workshops on Skid Row in Los Angeles between those in recovery from homelessness and some of the best songwriters in the world. I was completely in love with

What! Must I hold a candle to my shames?

—William Shakespeare

the difference we were making in people's lives and the music we were helping to create. The workshops were sheer magic and the first time I felt that I was having a real impact on the world around me. Yet the relationship between my former partner and myself was troubled and unfulfilling for both of us. I couldn't figure out how to leave the relationship but keep the project since, at that point, it really belonged to both of us. It was as though we had birthed a child together. When I finally did leave the relationship, my worst fears occurred. The project stayed with him and I ended up losing them both.

I was furious. I simply could not talk myself out of the victim position on *this* one: *I* was the one who'd had the original vision! I was the one who'd invited him to participate and now I was the one who had to give it up. It just wasn't fair. To make matters worse, I didn't believe the project would survive losing me, and it seemed I was right. After we broke up, the project was dying from inactivity. Not one workshop had been produced, not one song written or recorded. So, not only did he "steal" the project by refusing to relinquish control of the organization, but he also neglected (and thereby destroyed) it.

For two days I wrestled in the silence with the idea of forgiveness, unable to release the resentment I felt. I knew that, in order to not bring that baggage with me and be a clear space for someone new to enter my life, I would have to let go of this bitterness.

At the end of the second day, after meditating for hours, I had what might be called an epiphany or a spiritually transcendent experience. It was late at night and I was standing outside on a bluff, looking up at a large, bright, and perfectly round moon as it shone through the bare branches of an old gnarly tree. Suddenly, the moon became illuminated and I was transported into another realm of awareness. I sensed the presence of a multitude of ethereal beings who spoke to me, not as an external voice but as an internal knowing, saying, "We understand your suffering and know well of your loss. You are right that you are owed a great debt. However, we have now incurred that debt and are the ones holding it. We will make sure that

> In this life-creative
> adventure the criterion
> of achievement will
> be . . . the courage to
> let go of the past, with
> its truths, its goals, its
> dogmas of "meaning,"
> and its gifts: to die to
> the world and come to
> birth from within.
>
> —Joseph Campbell

all that is due you will be paid above and beyond that which you can even imagine. But in order for us to do this, you must first release him, for your attachment to getting restitution from him is preventing us from being able to give you your due." In that moment, I let go of my resentment toward him completely, never again to be plagued by feelings of bitterness or rage toward him. In place of hostility, I suddenly found compassion, acceptance, and understanding.

Not surprisingly, the next day, I began to understand my part in our relationship much more clearly. It seems that when I was finally able to quiet the internal tirade against my former partner, I was available to see how I myself had created this difficult situation. I saw that I had actually given away my power five years before our breakup when we set up the original structure of the organization. Instead of delegating parts of my vision to him and offering him a 49 percent or less portion of ownership, I had made him a 50 percent full-fledged owner and partner right off the bat. What made me do that? I barely knew him at the time. I had to confess to myself that the only reason was because I didn't believe in the value of my vision, or in my ability to make it happen. As I thought more about it, I remembered feeling uneasy about the partnership right from the start. My intuition was trying to speak to me but I had been too insecure to listen.

I suddenly saw that throughout my entire life, I'd consistently devalued and doubted my ideas. And I saw how I'd suffered because of it. Yet, the project we created was extraordinary. Hundreds of people throughout the Los Angeles music community had happily participated in the songwriting workshops we set up. The songs written were inspiring, uplifting, and just plain great music. We'd held a nationally televised concert and made a CD with star artists that was selling in record stores throughout the country. I had the time of my life doing that project—the project that I had been afraid to believe in—an idea that I feared was foolish and insignificant and consequently gave away.

What I learned is this: that I had paid too high a price for the self-doubts I had carried since childhood; that I was through with giving away my brilliance and creativity because I thought my ideas were worthless. In that moment, I gave up being willing to allow self-judgment and self-criticism to stop me in life.

Even more important, I learned something about love. Not because I loved my former boyfriend so well but because of how much I withheld love from him. We were engaged in a severe power struggle that went on for years, and withholding love was my number one weapon of choice. Whatever potential our relationship held for true love was pretty much starved to death. Because of that relationship, I came to understand that there are certain lines you don't cross when you are building a trusting, loving connection with another person. Now, that may seem simple enough but I honestly didn't know that before. I experienced, firsthand, that being right often costs us being loved. I learned that dumping all of your negativity and judgments onto someone under the guise of "communication" was destructive. I learned that power struggles were the currency of war, not love. I hoped I wouldn't have to repeat those lessons, as I never wanted to experience the cost of that unhealthy behavior ever again.

A lot of us think that we have to wait until feelings of hurt and anger are resolved before we can forgive someone. This is not always so. Forgiveness is actually an intentional and deliberate decision we make to align our will with the life-affirming perspective of using the mistakes made—both ours and theirs—to grow our wisdom, learn our lessons, and pay forward the amends in how we live. It's a decision that restores vitality, possibility, and integrity to your life. As such, magnanimous feelings of appreciation and benevolence are often the last things to fall into place, if they ever do at all. Realize that you are only resentful to the extent you've given your power away. If you're in full possession of your personal power, you can afford to be generous when someone else is behaving poorly. It's only when you're not owning your power fully that it shows up as resentment.

Ultimately, to forgive someone means to cancel the debt you believe they owe you, with faith in the overall goodness of Life. It's a surrender of the need for restitution from the one who hurt you and the willingness to value the lessons learned and to make good on that wisdom moving forward. That doesn't mean that you agree with what the person did, condone their behavior, or ever invite them back into your life again—often, it is unwise to do so.

> The weak can never forgive. Forgiveness is the attribute of the strong.
>
> —Mahatma Gandhi

Sometimes we hang on to resentment because anger is all that we have left. We're afraid to tolerate the void of letting go. However, when that's the case, we usually end up creating even more emptiness and loneliness, because we so thoroughly block any new possibilities of love from coming to us.

Many of us need to give up having the person who hurt us understand the agony they've caused us. We'll spend weeks, months, and sometimes years suffering, hoping they finally see the consequences of their bad behavior. As though that really means much anyway. Look, it's great to get an apology, but it's not really necessary. The real value in these situations is to see your own part clearly and to recognize how you need to change moving forward.

Soon after that night when I'd had the transcendent experience looking up at the moon, blessing upon blessing began coming into my life—meeting my first husband, effortlessly getting pregnant with my daughter at the age of forty-two, coming into an unexpected large sum of money, moving into a home that I had wanted to live in for years. The list goes on and on. When I forgave my former partner and took responsibility for my actions, I opened up a space for love and abundance to come toward me, and come it did.

The antidote to resentment is acceptance. The truth is, I had to accept the loss of my beloved organization. I had to accept a situation that, at first glance, did not seem at all just. I had to accept that the years I spent buried in the intensely hard work of creating that organization had turned to dust in my hands because I hadn't bothered to protect what I had built properly. Most important, I had to accept full responsibility for how I, and I alone, had caused the pain that I was in.

It was also important to assess the gains I'd made during that time of my life. When I was able to let go of being a victim, I could finally acknowledge my former boyfriend for having brought my seeds of a vision into a bona fide reality. Because I hadn't believed in myself, I can't imagine that I would have done what was necessary to bring the project anywhere near the level of success that it achieved. That was his tenacity—the same tenacity that I called stubbornness, which drove me bananas and that I constantly complained about. This was the same man who'd made my dream come true and ultimately demonstrated to me that my ideas were valuable and worthwhile.

Forgiveness is . . . the means for correcting our misperceptions.

—Gerald Jampolsky

You'll know that you have really completed your relationship with someone when you don't have a lot of energy in it anymore—when you can acknowledge the relationship from the perspective of being 100 percent responsible for having created it, if even by just being able to locate exactly when, where, and how you gave your power away. When you are able to recognize the lessons you've learned and appreciate the gifts that you've received from that experience. While that may, at first, appear to be a tall order, nothing short of complete neutrality toward those we've resented will do. When it comes to creating more love in our lives, we stand ready, like samurai warriors, to release all that is not love from our hearts.

PRACTICE: RELEASING YOUR RESENTMENTS

Take out your journal and make a list of people you resent, particularly those you've been connected to romantically.

Whom do I resent?

Go through your list and choose the person who feels the "hottest" to you.

Journal on each of the following questions for that person. When you have the time, return to this list and complete the following questions with everyone on your resentment list.

- What do I resent this person for?
- What can I be responsible for in this situation? *(For example, Where or how did I give my power away to this person?)*
- What lesson(s) did I learn? (For example, *How is this experience helping me to mature and grow?*)
- What amends can I make to myself moving forward? (For example, *What will I never do again or always do moving forward in life?*)
- What can I now let go of and accept so that the situation is complete?

Bonus: Practice in Action

Write a letter to someone you are ready to forgive. In the letter, write about the resentment you felt from the perspective of what *you* can be responsible for. How did you yourself create the situation? How did the situation help you to grow and mature? What lessons did you learn that will influence your choices and actions moving forward? Did anything good come from this situation that you can share with this person? Declare the situation complete by stating your willingness to forgive this person and release them from the debt you've believed they've owed you.

You can send the letter, or you can burn it or rip it up in a ceremonial release. If you're uncertain whether or not to send the letter, you can keep it to consider sending in the future. You may, however, wish to keep it as a reminder of the stand you've taken to let go and release the debt you have felt this person owed you.

Evolving Toxic Ties

If you have been operating in the dark, there is now enough light to
see that the patient on the operating table is yourself.

—Ralph Blum

All relationships are an energy exchange. Each connection either feeds us power or sucks it away; i.e., "draining" our energy. If we saw all of our relationships from this perspective, we would see that "toxic ties" are those attachments that cause us to lose personal power.

The associations we form have the capacity to nurture and inspire our growth, catapulting us into being the best that we can possibly be. However, the flip side is also true. Sometimes, we form attachments that can, and do, block the experience and expression of love in our lives. The most obvious example of this is, of course, a romantic attachment to a person who, for whatever reason, is unwilling or unable to love us.

Paul came to see me because he was in deep emotional pain over his relationship with his business partner of four years, Susan. Paul and Susan, both songwriters and music producers, were lovers for a few weeks shortly before they formed their business, a small recording studio. He had been trying to get back together with her for the duration of their business relationship. He sheepishly admitted that this was one of the reasons he had wanted to go into business with her in the first place.

Paul and Susan call each other often, speaking up to ten times a day. They spend countless hours together working on producing her songs and trying to get her a record deal. Susan has some unhealed childhood wounds that cause her to be an excessively insecure and frightened person. Paul spends many hours of his day

> When love grows diseased, the best thing we can do is put it to a violent death; I cannot endure the torture of a lingering and consumptive passion.
>
> —George Etherege

talking to her about her problems and encouraging her to believe in herself. His own recording projects have fallen by the wayside. Paul reports that Susan says she "loves him as a friend," yet she is uninterested in him as a sexual partner. She is now seeing another man and he is outraged and obsessed with "getting her back."

Although Paul is only thirty-five, he confides that a recent doctor's visit determined he's an imminent candidate for a heart attack and he was immediately put on medication. He is about thirty pounds overweight because, he explains, he is overeating out of anger and sexual frustration. And, he admits, he is broke, as he and Susan are entangled in a huge debt that they jointly incurred while launching her career. He also mentions offhandedly that all of their joint debt is actually in *his* name, since she has problems with her credit.

Much of my work with Paul has been to help him accept Susan's lack of romantic interest, to give up blaming her for failing to love him, and to be responsible for the many attempts he has made to manipulate her through his excessive "helpfulness." I encourage Paul to examine what his relationship with Susan reflects in his relationship with himself. He is able to acknowledge that her lack of sexual attraction to him mirrors his own disgust with his body, as he is furious with himself for being "too fat." His resistance to taking care of himself, even with the threat of a heart attack, makes it clear that he is trying to get Susan to love him while he is adamantly refusing to love himself. In fact, Paul can see that he has actually succeeded in getting Susan to reject him in exactly the same way that he rejects himself.

Even the most sagacious of us may be tempted to behave destructively in an effort to avoid facing the disappointment of unrequited love. However, try as we might, the truth is, we have absolutely no power to sway another person when they have decided to close their heart to us. It is one of life's great paradoxes that, though we are the authors of our own experience, we have no ability to superimpose our will onto another person. An unwillingness to accept this will be the source of great suffering. For even if we are successful at maneuvering ourselves into a "significant-other" position, the relationship itself will most likely be characterized by resentment, excessive dependency, disappointment, and power struggles, thereby making it a toxic tie.

Perhaps you're on the other end of the spectrum, having succumbed to the efforts of another to entice you into loving them for all the wrong reasons. Many of us have made choices out of the most needy, dependent parts of ourselves and then suffered the consequences of feeling the dreadful, dull ache of being stuck in a relationship that has absolutely no chance of a future.

> The best advice for people who can't seem to end an unsatisfying relationship might be to stop waiting for something from the other person. Probably what it is will never come.
>
> —Thomas Moore

I once had a client who was quite beautiful but, unfortunately, quite insecure and secretly self-loathing. Like Narcissus, she spent vast amounts of time looking in the mirror, fussing with her clothes, her hair, and her makeup. She dressed in sexy, seductive clothing that brought her lots of attention from men, and she spent an inordinate amount of time and money in an effort to enhance her beauty. It was not surprising to me, then, when she confided in me that she was deeply entangled in a relationship with a man whom she actually didn't even like, let alone love. When we explored how this had happened, we discovered that she was so captured by his constant admiration of her beauty, that she just allowed herself to become entangled with him. Now she felt trapped and frightened by his ever-increasing possessive behavior toward her. She hadn't seen the warning signs at the beginning, because his obsessive preoccupation with her beauty had simply mirrored her own. Her excessive neediness had attracted a man who intuitively knew her weakness and had used it to his advantage.

Susan Forward, author of the wonderful book *Emotional Blackmail,* talks about the "blinding FOG"—Fear, Obligation, and Guilt that characterizes most "toxic tie" relationships. Unbridled fears that we are unworthy, that we will never truly be loved, or that we will be abandoned by someone we desperately need, top the list of anxieties that can entice us into giving away more and more of our personal power. Often, due to an undeveloped ability to set healthy emotional boundaries, we will feel overly responsible for another's feelings, and allow an inappropriate sense of obligation to dominate how we make choices about the relationship. Or we'll feel consumed by feelings of guilt and shame, as though we owe another our very life force for the ways we have allegedly hurt them in the past.

When someone capitalizes on these vulnerabilities of yours, they are simply

> There are always risks in freedom. The only risk in bondage is that of breaking free.
>
> —Gita Bellin

exerting a manipulative effort to get what they want at your expense. Real love will never use fear, obligation, or guilt to influence you. Until you clear your life of these "*un*true" loves, you will block "true" love from being able to come to you, and you will always know, in your heart of hearts, that you are settling.

These types of relationships—often with people who are not easily gotten rid of like a sibling, parent, or boss—suck the life force right out of us, draining much of our creativity and power, and reducing us to the least of who we are. When in these unhealthy relationships, some of us will justify all sorts of bad behavior, and hope the other person will change. Yet, people aren't projects. They generally don't respond well when we try to "improve" them. And, the truth is, we are always training people how they need to treat us by how we respond to their behavior. What you tolerate *will* happen again . . . and again . . . and again. This is why it's more important to evolve a toxic tie than simply try to get rid of the person whose behavior is troubling you. Certainly, if someone is committing a crime, or abusing you in a tangible or dangerous way, then get out immediately. Yet if you are dealing with a habitually harmful dynamic, where you feel continually drained, diminished, or devalued, then it's better to graduate than to just get out. Instead of chronically tap-dancing around your truth or failing to set necessary boundaries, foster the courage to show up differently and outgrow your part of that dance.

If you find yourself engaged in a toxic tie, it's not just the other person's fault. If you are allowing someone to use you, manipulate you, and treat you poorly, then you must ask yourself what the relationship is reflecting in your relationship with yourself. How is it that it's somehow okay with you to throw yourself under the bus, simply because someone expects you to? How is it that it's somehow all right with you to borrow against your own well-being, to accommodate someone else's overly entitled demands? Until you make the decision to stop dishonoring yourself, others will happily continue doing so.

As unhealthy as the other person may be, toxic ties are usually the result of two unhealthy habits on your part. Number one, failing to speak your truth. And number two, failing to set appropriate boundaries. When we fall into these lethal practices, it's usually because we find ourselves in a bind. Someone is emotionally unwell and so we fear they'll fall apart if we speak our truth. Or someone is seriously narcissistic and we fear they'll punish or attack us if we set a boundary. Here's the thing about that: It may be true. But how long will you sacrifice yourself to their sickness when they themselves are unwilling to do anything about it? We have to remind ourselves that organizing around the weakest parts of others is not ultimately to anyone's benefit, theirs included.

> Relationships are not sporting events. Stop wrestling for control. No one ever wins this kind of match except divorce lawyers.
>
> —Leo Buscaglia

Toxic ties undermine and weaken our vision of what is possible in our lives. We perpetuate them because we think it's better to hold on to a little bit of love rather than risk not being loved at all. Or we're captured by the dramatic pull of the person who seems to desperately need us, as though needing someone were the same as loving them.

If you are operating under the illusion that you can continue to engage in toxic dynamics that you know are not good for you, and still create an extraordinary life filled with love and fulfillment, then you are fooling yourself. Toxic relational dynamics cost us, and they cost us big-time. If you are feeling stuck in your life, look to see who or what it is that you are stuck to. Then have the courage to put your commitment to call a happy, healthy love into your life above the pull to stay loyal to the unhealthy demands of a relationship that's been draining you of your power.

PRACTICE: WAKING UP FROM THE FOG (FEAR, OBLIGATION, AND GUILT)

Take out your journal and answer the following questions.

NOTE: Don't limit your answers to those you've had romantic encounters with. Include anyone who comes to mind, be it friends, family, co-workers, etc.

- What relationship(s), if any, do I suspect may qualify as a "toxic tie"? (For example, What relationship[s] is/are characterized by fear, obligation, or guilt?)

Choose one of these relationships to work on today by completing the following questions. When you can, return to this list and complete the following questions with everyone you've listed.

- What fear(s) is/are dominating me in this relationship?
- What obligations do I feel compelled to fulfill?
- In what ways am I allowing myself to be manipulated through feelings of guilt and shame?
- What does this relationship reflect in my relationship to myself?
- What truth could I tell that would increase health and wellness in this relationship?
- What boundaries could I set that would increase health and wellness in this relationship?
- What can I give up in order to restore my own sense of personal power? *(For example, avoiding having that person be angry with me, doing for that person what he won't do for himself, etc.)*

Bonus: Practice in Action

Promise yourself to give up participating in all toxic-tie dynamics by righting your relationship to yourself first and foremost. Take at least one action today to right your relationship with yourself (e.g., if you've discovered the abuse you've been tolerating from another is a reflection of how you've been abusing yourself, take an action that represents your willingness to treat yourself with greater respect). In addition, take at least one action today to either speak your truth and/or set a healthy boundary with someone you've been engaged in a toxic-tie relationship with. Both will require courage and a commitment to live in integrity with the healthy, mutually respectful relationship you are calling into your life.

Renegotiating Old Agreements

*We must be willing to get rid of the life we've planned,
so as to have the life that is waiting for us.*

—Joseph Campbell

The first time I was in love, I was fifteen. Frank was kind and thoughtful, frequently going out of his way to make me happy. When with him, I felt protected and loved. When I was seventeen he asked me to marry him. My mother was beside herself. She insisted that I go to college and get a life before committing to someone I met when just a sophomore in high school. It became a war between us. The harder she tried to separate us, the harder I fought to keep him. At one point, she even threatened to call the police if he so much as stepped foot in our driveway.

You can imagine the heightened sense of drama that surrounded the relationship amid such an onslaught of protest. However, my mother's concerns proved all too true when, in our last year together, we began fighting about the choices I was facing as I turned eighteen. I wanted to go to college. Frank, however, had decided against college in favor of going into his family's business. He was dead set against me pursuing an education when he hadn't. No discussion, end of story, and, sadly enough, end of relationship.

Our breakup wrenched my heart and sent me reeling into an anguished grief. One of the ways I dealt with my overwhelming sorrow was to make a promise. Since

> The old skin has to be shed before the new one can come.
>
> —Joseph Campbell

I couldn't bear the thought that I would never see him again, I tried to make a deal with Frank. With my eighteen-year-old logic, I suggested we go our separate ways now, but pledge to find each other again when in our sixties when we would have lived our lives and made all our choices. By then, my thinking went, we would be free to reconcile, as we'd finally be available to love each other completely. Obviously, Frank ignored my desperate plea because a year later he married his next girlfriend and was soon the father of three.

Twenty-plus years later, I'd all but forgotten this promise. Yet one night, about a month into my quest for "The One," I remembered this agreement and realized it was somehow always in the background of my life, living like an unfulfilled longing. Those crazy, desperate young-love words of passion, spoken in a moment of complete despair and unbearable sorrow, were still hanging out there somewhere, waiting to be fulfilled.

I hadn't spoken to Frank in all that time and was reticent to contact him, lest I risk harming his marriage. And so I settled for speaking to him in a "Soul to Soul" conversation, calling him, figuratively, into my meditation practice. I sat quietly and focused on my breath for a few minutes before silently saying his name several times and imagining him sitting in front of me. When I could see his face in my mind's eye, I told him how sorry I was for the ways I might have hurt him all those years ago. I let him know how much I'd missed him in my life and that I appreciated all the love he'd given me at a time when I needed it so much. Then I told him that I couldn't keep the promise I'd made to him and why. It was holding me up from finding someone else that I could be happy with, and preventing me from creating a life where I might not be free when I was in my sixties. I asked him to let me go if he'd been holding on to that promise and to please forgive me for not being able to keep it. And then I let him go, freeing myself from the contract I'd made so many years before.

All relationships have their agreements. Actually, it could be said that the very definition of "relationship" is to enter into a covenant with another. As such, relationships are determined by a series of pacts and promises that are sometimes spoken out loud, but most times are simply assumed or implied. Those agreements that are made without words—often matters of loyalty and expectations—will usually remain covert in nature while exercising a strong pull over decisions made and paths taken. Covert agreements can even influence us to violate our own values and beliefs, gaining leverage through our innate need to be a part of a tribal community.

I once had a young student, Deja, who desperately wanted to get a college education. However, no one in her family had ever gone to college and they felt threatened by her aspirations. They ridiculed her desire and succeeded in their efforts to prevent her from even applying to school, through a thinly veiled threat to withdraw their love and support from her should she try to "make herself better than them."

> Life is full and overflowing with the new. But it is necessary to empty out the old to make room for the new to enter.
>
> —Eileen Caddy

Although Deja's case sounds extreme, in truth, many of us make covert agreements with those in our family of origin to not be more fulfilled and successful than they are. Therefore, forming a loving, happy partnership, when no one in your family has been able to do so, can feel nothing short of disloyal. It's not uncommon for us to sacrifice ourselves out of a fear that our success will cause pain for our parents or siblings, or at least aggravate the parts of them that are unhappy and unfulfilled.

Consider Shanice, a beautiful and bright woman who attended a *Calling in "The One"* workshop several years ago. Like many of the women I work with, it appeared as though she should have no problem finding the right partner. Yet there she was, complaining about being close to forty and husbandless, with no prospects in sight. She seemed somewhat confused about her single status.

During the workshop it became clear that Shanice adored her father, describing their relationship as "very close." In fact, her father played a very active and dominant role in her life; he lived close by and they spoke almost daily. She confessed that she felt safe, particularly as a single woman, due to his "overprotectiveness" of her. However, what began to disturb the group, but unfortunately not her, was the way that her father weeded out the men who got too close to her. She saw this as part of his protectiveness and, therefore, an expression of his love for her. The more she shared with us, however, the more obvious it became that Shanice would actually choose men who were a little dangerous so that her father could rescue her from them, thereby proving his love for her and reinforcing their bond.

When pressed, Shanice admitted that underneath their dynamic was an unspoken agreement she'd made with her dad years before. When she was a little girl, she witnessed the deterioration of her parents' troubled marriage. Her mother seemed to handle this well, but her father became more and more depressed and despondent as the years went on. She recalls feeling a tremendous and persistent sorrow for him. So she made a decision. Although her mother did not seem to love him, she would make sure that her father always knew that *she* did. He would always be the most important person in the world to her. And, in fact, she did become "the light of Daddy's life."

Though she could admit to the agreement, Shanice resisted seeing its potential impact on her relationships with men. As she left the workshop, she was still justifying and rationalizing that this wasn't that big of a deal. Actually, she wasn't ready to give it up yet and so she didn't. Yet truthfully, I doubt that she will be available to love another man until she renegotiates this unspoken agreement with her father either in person or simply within herself.

Our need to be a part of something larger than ourselves is one of our most basic instincts, and we will often go to great lengths to protect our sense of tribal belonging. Margo was the third generation in a lineage of strong, smart, and powerful firstborn females. Her primary sense of identity is with her matriarchal ancestry—her mother and her mother's mother before her. The three of them all look alike and are ambitious, educated, and accomplished. They've also all had their share of difficulties with the men in their lives. It's no wonder then that, as a way to survive their romantic disappointments, they've developed a "humorous" little banter that "just slightly" diminishes the men in their lives. It's a covert thing—a roll of the eyes, a sideways snicker and glance, a subtle shake of the head. They have formed their own little matriarchal club and the membership dues are to scorn any man who gets too close. Inside of her commitment to "call in 'The One,'" Margo saw the absurdity of trying to find a man to love and be loved by, while, at the same time, keeping her covert agreement with her mother and grandmother to disrespect and diminish all men.

While writing this book, I heard about a woman whose stepfather incestuously pursued her when she was a preteen. The girl was so distraught by his advances that she made him a desperate promise. If you leave me alone now, she assured him, when I turn twenty-five, if you still want me, then I will marry you. It worked and he stopped his unwanted advances. Somewhere along the way, he divorced her mother but stayed in contact with her. She repressed her unpleasant memories of his advances and completely forgot about her promise to him. When she was twenty-four, she received a proposal from a decent man whom she did not love. She promptly accepted and married him right before her twenty-fifth birthday. Years later, when getting a divorce, she couldn't understand why she had married a man she did not love. After many hours of self-examination, she finally remembered the horrible pledge she'd made in her youth, and she understood. She married her ex-husband as a way to avoid keeping the dreaded promise to her stepfather.

There's another type of agreement that's important to mention: the agreements we make with ourselves in an attempt to deal with an emotional injury that we've suffered. Nancy is a fiftysomething-year-old friend of mine. When Nancy was a child, not more than two, she had to have a lifesaving operation on her throat. When Nancy was young, many doctors believed that small children did not know the difference between their mothers and other caregivers. The hospital Nancy was admitted to did not allow the parents to visit their children when they were in the intensive care unit. It was believed that the nurses could do a better job if their care was uninterrupted and unchallenged by the parents.

So, there was little Nancy, subjected to a terrifying operation at the hands of strangers. And, although these strangers were most likely competent and kind, they were not people whom Nancy felt close to or bonded with. They were, therefore, unable to comfort her the way her parents could have. Nancy spent the entire week at the hospital without seeing a single member of her family.

> We learn wisdom from failure much more than from success: we often discover what will do by finding out what will not do: and probably he who never made a mistake never made a discovery.
>
> —Samuel Smiles

> To everything
> there is a season,
> and a time to
> every purpose
> under the heaven.
>
> —Ecclesiastes 3:1

Though Nancy was just a young child when this happened, to this day, she remembers being furious at her mother for leaving her at a time when she most needed her. The thing she remembers most profoundly is that she made a decision at that time to never trust anyone again. Her mother validated Nancy's recollection by admitting, many years later, that their relationship was never the same after that week. She reports that Nancy became distant and detached from her and others in their family from that time on, unwilling to bond with and depend upon them to the same extent that she did before the operation. As you can imagine, this decision was causing her much difficulty in her adult relationships. It was a resolve that desperately needed to be renegotiated.

The agreements we make, both conscious and unconscious, have a profound impact upon our lives, for they literally serve as intentions that we set. These intentions have weight and authority in the universe to affect that which comes our way—and that which doesn't. Never underestimate the power of your agreements to influence your life.

PRACTICE: RE-CREATING YOUR AGREEMENTS

Today, we will examine the agreements, both spoken and unspoken, that you've made with others and yourself in order to re-create them to be consistent with the future of love fulfilled.

Take out your journal and complete the following sentences, answering as many times as you wish for each sentence stem. Don't censor yourself. Write whatever comes to mind even if it initially does not seem to make sense.

- The agreements, both spoken and unspoken, I made with my mother were:
- The way(s) these agreements are influencing my relationships today are:

- A new healthier agreement might be:
- The agreements, both spoken and unspoken, I made with my father were:
- The way(s) these agreements are influencing my relationships today are:
- A new healthier agreement might be:
- The agreements, both spoken and unspoken, I made with _____ (any other significant person in your life, such as a stepmother, stepfather, ex-boyfriend, sibling, etc.) were:
- The way(s) these agreements are influencing my relationships today are:
- A new healthier agreement might be:
- The agreements I made with myself regarding closeness and love are:
- The way(s) these agreements are influencing my relationships today are:
- A new healthier agreement might be:
- By staying single and unpartnered in life, I am keeping my agreements to:
- A new healthier agreement might be:
- In order to renegotiate these agreements, I would have to let go of:
- The new agreements I am now committing myself to are:

Bonus: Practice in Action

Complete and/or renegotiate at least one agreement that no longer serves you. You can do this by contacting the person directly to have a conversation, or by engaging an imaginary "Soul to Soul" communication in your meditation. Tell them what agreement you wish to renegotiate and why. Let them know the new agreement(s) you are making in order to manifest and sustain a loving, happy relationship.

If you prefer, you can do it the old-fashioned way, by writing an actual letter. You can either keep it as a reminder, or you can send it. You can also pretend to send it by putting the letter in an envelope with a stamp and writing only the first name of the person on the envelope with a silly address like Main Street, Anytown, USA 00000, placing it in the mailbox. Or you may just want to burn it, rip it up, and/or throw it away.

Appreciating
Your Sacred Wounds

What do sad people have in common? It seems they have all
built a shrine to the past and often go there and do a strange wail
and worship. What is the beginning of happiness? It is to stop
being so religious like that.

—Hafiz, translated by Daniel Ladinsky

I f we are overly identified with the wounds of our past, it will be as though we
are locked inside invisible prisons—captured by the iron bars of our sad stories,
and hopelessly confined inside the cold, impenetrable concrete walls of a fate we
are powerless to change. Sometimes it seems, no matter how hard we try to escape,
that we will forever be prisoners of our own painful past, doomed to repeat the
same frustrating patterns over and over and over again, in spite of our wishes to
the contrary.

Inessa sat hunched over, rocking back and forth, staring at the floor in front of
her. The other women, gathered together for a *Calling in "The One"* workshop, sat
quietly in the circle as though holding vigil, patiently waiting for her to speak. "I
can't get past the feeling that I'm dirty!" she spoke in a strained, frustrated voice.
"I'm damaged goods and I can't seem to forget it, even for a moment. And every
single relationship I've ever had ends up just as broken and damaged as I am. When
do I get rid of this ugliness inside of me? When do I get to be free? When do I get

to have love in my life?" By now tears were streaming down her face as she recalled being sexually molested by her father when she was a mere four years old.

"Inessa, do you really believe that you are dirty, as if that is the core truth about you? As though God made the mountains, God made the sun, and God made you dirty and damaged?" I asked softly. "Yes!" she replied without needing to think about it. "It always comes down to this truth: I am a dirty, dirty person."

I invited Inessa to take a deep breath and to tell me some of the best things about herself as an an adult woman of forty-one. She began to share some of her core strengths and competencies—how she was a good friend, a loyal employee, and had grown herself spiritually strong over the past several years as a devoted practitioner of meditation. As she spoke, she relaxed and began to be centered in her forty-one-year-old adult self. At which point, I invited her to imagine that she was sitting before a four-year-old girl. I asked her to send love to that sweet girl before inviting her to picture a grown man, her father—a man who, we would hope, would protect and love her—instead now molesting her. "What do you think of this little girl?" I asked. "Would you look at her and say to yourself, 'What a dirty, dirty little girl. No wonder her father is sexually abusing her'?"

Inessa burst into tears as, for the first time, she could actually feel her innocence. The foolishness of the belief that she was dirty was finally evident to her. At last she felt a deep compassion for herself, claiming her blamelessness as the truth of who she was.

"I am so sick of walking around wounded, desperate for someone to come and fix this in me." She sighed. "Why do I have to carry the burden of this betrayal into every relationship? When can I get rid of it?" she asked me with complete trust and simplicity. "Well," I replied carefully, "I don't know that we ever 'get rid' of our woundedness, but we can change our relationship with it. Rather than relate to our hurts and the meaning we made in response, such as 'I'm dirty' as the truth, we can hold our suffering as an initiation into wisdom, compassion, and depth. We must, however, give up defining ourselves by what happened way back when, and stop overly identifying ourselves with the pain we have suffered at the hands of those who were either too weak, too selfish, or too sick to do it any differently. This is not a denial of what we've been through but, rather, an awareness that the essence of who we are is far beyond it."

As Inessa pondered my words, I continued. "In addition to being a terrible burden to bear, the wounds we've suffered—particularly those that have threatened to crush and bury us beneath a mountain of guilt, shame, and despair, can also be the gateway to our greatness. If we can cast aside the meaning we made in response to what happened, and step outside of our identity of 'victim,' we can also see that the process of healing from our wounds can inspire us to heroic heights of nobility and kindness. We can create beauty and great goodness for the world. Art, poetry, music, philosophy, and philanthropy are all born from the terrible grace of hardship and hurt.

"Our wounds can become a part of who we now grow ourselves to be, in the best of ways. I know for myself that I've learned more about loving relationships from the absence of love than I have from its presence. And that understanding has led to a lifetime of devotion and, in many ways, is now the best of who I am. This is why your past traumas are your 'Sacred Wounds.' Because wherever you have suffered the most is where you now have the opportunity to contribute the most."

My comments startled Inessa, who had always seen the goal of her healing work as getting rid of the abuse—forgetting it and distancing herself forever from the impact it had had upon her life. Remnants of a smile appeared on her face as she comprehended, for the first time, that this wound had had a tremendous bearing upon the kind of woman she had become—a fighter, who was devoted to personal and spiritual growth both for herself and for others. In fact, Inessa's life was largely defined by her desire to give generously of herself to others. Her rigorous candor and authentic sharing that weekend served to move the entire group to a much deeper level than they would have gone had she not been there.

As much as we profess to hate our brokenness, we'll often set up camp, root down, and build our entire identities around our tales of woe. In her book *Why People Don't Heal and How They Can*, Caroline Myss writes, "The sharing of wounds [has] become the new language of intimacy, a shortcut to developing trust and understanding." Consider the friendships we form based upon what Dr. Myss calls our "woundology," where we bond with another through complaining about our victimization and the sad state of our lives. What happens

> People want you
> to be happy. Don't
> keep serving them
> your pain!
>
> —Rumi

then, when one person, out of a commitment to heal, suddenly decides to give up being in the victim position? Oftentimes, such a friendship will not survive a "betrayal" of this sort, since the silent agreement is to reinforce the oppression of each other.

Many of us even choose our significant others based upon their ability to understand our wounds and their willingness to dance around them and not expect too much from us. This usually works for a time. But what happens if and when the "wounded" party decides to get better? Relationships whose currency is "woundology" don't have room for people to thrive and become their best selves, because the covert agreement is: If one person is "broken," then the other gets to prop up their self-esteem either by (1) caretaking them and/or (2) being superior to them.

Many people have a difficult time bringing in a loving relationship, because they are still too invested in being damaged to allow their tragedies to transform into something beautiful. These people will usually continue to attract romantic partners who are also very attached to being damaged and are, therefore, not healthy enough to be suitable life partners.

We have to ask ourselves how attached we are to our pain. What is driving us to cling so fiercely to our sorrow? Sometimes, women will hold on to a sense of victimization because they're acting out a collective myth of "damsel in distress." This of course will attract those who source their value from rescuing, and who unconsciously need their lover to stay a bit desperate and dependent in order to feel good about themselves. This traps the "damsel in distress" in her habitual drama and covertly sabotages her from escaping it totally. As long as we cling to the pain of the past, it continues to live—and it continues to hurt us. When we do this, we are behaving as though the past were more powerful and significant than the present. The truth is, it's never what happens to us that matters as much as what we *do* with what happens to us. Those who hurt you in the past—who failed to love you the ways you needed to be loved, the ones who left you, neglected you, diminished you, and abused you—have no authority to determine whether or not you will now live a life of love and fulfillment, unless you yourself give it

> From suffering I have learned this: that whoever is sore wounded by love will never be made whole unless she embrace the very same love that wounded her.
>
> —Mechtild of Magdeburg

to them. For *you, and you alone,* are the only one holding the power to determine what's possible for you in love.

We can't "get rid" of our wounds, but we can find a way to make them meaningful. In his book *Man's Search for Meaning,* Viktor Frankl, a prominent Jewish psychiatrist who survived the camps of Auschwitz and Dachau, writes of an elderly man who came to him two years after the death of his beloved wife. The man was severely depressed, as he was unable to overcome his loss. In the face of such suffering, Dr. Frankl was wise enough to sit quietly, listening intently as the man poured out his grief and his sorrow. When the man was finished, Dr. Frankl asked him the following question: "What would have happened if you had died first, and your wife would have had to survive you?" "Oh," the man answered, "for her this would have been terrible; how she would have suffered!" To this, Dr. Frankl replied, "You see, such a suffering has been spared her, and it was you who have spared her this suffering—to be sure, at the price that now you have to survive and mourn her." The man was so moved by Dr. Frankl's words, that he simply stood up, shook his hand, and left, never to return again. Dr. Frankl concludes this story by writing, "In some way, suffering ceases to be suffering at the moment it finds a meaning."

In his book *The Power of Now,* spiritual teacher Eckhart Tolle writes, "If you are trapped in a nightmare you will probably be more strongly motivated to awaken than someone who is just caught in the ups and downs of an ordinary dream." For those of us who have had to endure incredible losses and sorrows, life demands an awakening of a much more profound nature than those who have not. We must find lessons and weave meaning out of the sorrows we've had to bear. For many of us have been challenged to live out circumstances in which our hearts have been splintered and broken in two. Our task is to find our way through the ruins so that we may, as the Zen saying goes, "allow our hearts to break open." It is here that one not only comes to love again, but also actually comes to love in a way that heals the entire world.

PRACTICE: THE STORY OF YOUR SACRED WOUND

Write a brief "woundology" biography, not from the perspective of your victimization but, rather, from the perspective of your strength to overcome adversity and your courage in the face of hardship. Identify the wounding that has since become your "Sacred Wound"—the wounding that is now your greatest strength and your contribution to others. Write about your Sacred Wound and the ways you now have the potential to heal and help others. Not just in spite of your wound, but actually in many ways because of it.

Bonus: Practice in Action

Call at least one trusted confidant today and share your "woundology" biography from the perspective of your strength and resilience. Share your heroism in the face of challenge, your bravery in response to profound disappointment, as well as the wisdom, compassion, and depth you've grown in response. Share with this person your Sacred Wound, and the contribution that you now have to offer others as a result of it.

From now on, I invite you to share your story from this perspective to ensure that you create relationships where you're encouraged to be strong, and that support you to grow yourself fulfilled, healthy, and happy.

Treating Yourself as You Want to Be Treated

Change your conception of yourself and you will automatically change the world in which you live.

—Neville Goddard

Though you may yearn to be treated with love and respect by "The One" that you love, the disappointing truth is that no one will treat you any better than you're treating yourself. I'm not necessarily talking about how often you take yourself dancing, or give yourself massages and pedicures, though I'm all for anything and everything that brings you pleasure. I'm speaking about something deeper than self-care. I'm talking about the actual ways you relate to yourself. The habitual ways you speak to yourself, the ways you respond (or not) to your own difficult feelings or unwanted needs, the commitments you make (or don't make) to fulfill your deepest dreams and desires, and the ways you honor (or fail to honor) your word to yourself.

Unless you've done some real work on this, the ways you treat yourself now as an adult are likely reflective of the ways you were treated by the grown-ups who raised you. It's called the "internalized parent," and it basically means that if you were raised by people who neglected you, abandoned you, or criticized you constantly, you most likely now treat yourself in much the same way. And you may now be suffering the maddening experience of being treated this exact same way by the very people who you hoped would help you heal from the painful experiences you had as a child. It's like some cruel joke of the Universe that no matter how hard you try to get away from the pain of the past, you somehow always wind up dating your critical mother or your abandoning father again and again and again.

When I met her, Anat was a fortysomething-year-old physician who had left her former husband ten years before because of his constant criticism and rejection of her. Although she desperately wanted to get married again, Anat reported to me that the men she met online who seemed to like her when meeting in person inevitably did not want to pursue a romantic relationship because they weren't sexually attracted to her. They all ended up saying those dreaded words, "I just want to be friends." Because she's slightly overweight, Anat believed that the extra pounds were the sole reason why these men found her so unappealing. However, I know many people much larger than Anat who have met wonderful people, fallen in love, and are now happily partnered, so I was suspicious. When I inquired about Anat's relationship with her own sexuality, her lips became tense and she replied in a venomous tone that she absolutely loathed her body and considered it to be her enemy, given her inability to lose the extra weight she'd carried since adolescence. Exploring this further I discovered that Anat's body was a battlefield between her mother and herself as she was growing up. Anat described her mother as a "full-blown narcissist" who constantly gave her the once-over, rejecting and punishing her with disdain for not being good enough. In response, Anat would try starving herself to lose the weight and please her mother. Yet ironically the moment Anat began dropping the extra pounds, her mother would then begin competing with her, again rejecting her, and covertly sabotaging her daughter's success. What I suspected was happening with the men Anat was dating was that they were picking up on the intense self-hatred that raged in her body, and intuitively avoiding getting entangled in that hornet's nest. Yet Anat was clearly such a likable, and even lovable, person that they did actually want to stay connected. Hence, their desire to be friends was actually sincere.

Love is not love
When it is mingled with regards that stand
Aloof from the entire point.

—William Shakespeare

It's easy to villainize Anat's mother for screwing up her daughter in the ways that she did. Yet if we let ourselves stop there, we'd be doing Anat a great disservice. Because even though we'd have insight into her heartbreaking relational challenges, not much would actually change in her love life. The leverage point for Anat's transformation was for her to take full responsibility for how she had become the rejecting, punishing, mean mother to herself. And help her to recognize that her relationships with others would always mirror her own relationship with herself. To help Anat graduate from this painful hall of mirrors was to invite her into a corrective practice of radical self-acceptance and unconditional self-love such that she would transform her relationships with men by first transforming her relationship with herself.

At first, upon hearing my prescription, Anat winced. Yet she was smart enough to understand what I was saying, and had had enough pain to inspire her to do whatever it would take to change this pattern. I'm happy to say that, as of this writing, Anat has been happily married to a fun-loving, intelligent, and emotionally generous man for several years now. A man who loves making love to her, as she does to him. And while she still struggles to keep her weight down, the number on the morning scale no longer defines her sense of self-worth, or dominates her intimate love life.

If you are someone who has had a hard time forgiving your parents for the unconscious or even cruel ways they treated you, I'm going to suggest that it's not because of what happened way back when. It's what just happened yesterday, when that same dynamic showed up on your doorstep (or worse still, in your bedroom) yet again. When we say, "Oh my God, I can't believe I'm dating my abusive mother or my rageaholic father yet again," what we're really saying is, "Wow, I've somehow created yet another relationship that's

> Friendship with one's self is all important, because without it one cannot be friends with anyone else in the world.
>
> —Eleanor Roosevelt

mirroring all of the toxic ways I've been abusing myself for years, due to the ways I've internalized the worst of my parents." While you're not responsible for the abusive ways your parents treated you as a child, you must be willing to be responsible for the abusive ways you've tolerated treating yourself for years now if you want your painful patterns in intimate relationships to change. As within, so without. There's no escaping it, really.

Rachael, a petite, pretty woman with long dark hair and big blue eyes, yearned to be in an intimate relationship. It seemed she had plenty of opportunities, as men found her extremely attractive. However, she was not satisfied with any of her suitors, clearly stating that she was unwilling to "settle" in her selection of a partner. Although this sounded good on the surface, there was something "off" about it. When I explored her criteria for "The One," Rachael described someone charismatic, creative, inspiring, and very much engaged in following his dream, whatever that may be. However, Rachael herself had been "stuck" for years in a high-paying job that she didn't actually like. She had a sense of what she'd rather do instead; but each time I encouraged her to pursue her passions, she had one excuse after another.

Finally, I suggested to Rachael that the real reason that the only men showing up in her life were the ones she'd have to "settle" for is that she herself was "settling" for a life that didn't inspire her. She gasped at the truth of my words. She began unpacking her attachment to staying in a job she disliked, recognizing her self-neglect was fueled by an addiction to the money and prestige her profession afforded her. Given that she grew up with a depressed, impoverished mother who "settled" for her lot in life and gave her daughter only small crumbs of attention and love, Rachael thought her way out was financial. Yet she suddenly saw that she'd simply re-created a life where she was continually depriving herself of those things that would create happiness, inspiration, and delight in her heart. In seeing this clearly, Rachael changed her priorities. She gave up working so hard, and began filling her time with that which nourished her heart and gave her a sense of happiness and hope. After several months of this radical turnaround, she met a very handsome and heart-centered man who loved those things that she'd come to love. They married the following year, and together moved halfway around the world to follow their mutual passions. They now have three daughters who are the light of Rachael's life, and she no longer has anything to do with the profession she once thought would save her.

What can't come through you, can't come to you. If you find that others are critical of you, instead of complaining and making them wrong, ask yourself if you're critical of yourself, and how you can start treating yourself with greater compassion. If you attract people who don't come through for you when it matters, take stock of whether or not you show up for you, and resolve to be a better friend to yourself. If your pattern is that others don't commit to you, ask yourself how committed you are to you, and start organizing your life around the realization of your own dreams and desires. In other words, get busy transforming your relationship with yourself as the key to unlocking the prison of this pattern. I once worked with a gifted spiritual teacher, Georgina Lindsey, who constantly reminded us of the Buddhist philosophy "There is no one out there."

> A loving person lives in a loving world. A hostile person lives in a hostile world. Everyone you meet is your mirror.
>
> —Ken Keyes Jr.

PRACTICE: TRANSFORMING HOW YOU TREAT YOURSELF

Take out your journal and list your primary caregivers. Caregivers can include an important older sibling, relative, grandparent, babysitter, or anyone whom you depended upon, and who participated in your day-to-day care when you were an infant, child, or adolescent.

Next, read through the following list to identify one to three negative ways in which each of your caregivers treated you while growing up. While you may identify with more than three on this list, choose those that were particularly wounding, and which now consistently show up as a theme in your adult relationships.

Abandoning	Critical
Abusive	Devaluing
Blaming	Diminishing
Bullying	Dismissive

Harsh	Pushy
Hateful	Rageful
Hostile	Rejecting
Hurtful	Shaming
Judgmental	Terrorizing
Lying	Threatening
Mean-spirited	Undermining
Negligent	Unsupportive
Physically Violent	Untrustworthy
Punishing	Withholding
Punitive	

Taking one of these qualities at a time, journal on how they tend to show up in your intimate relationships. Notice that it may not go just one way, but that you may now be the perpetrator of this quality upon others. *(For example, if your mother was negligent, write about how your lovers tend to ignore and neglect your needs. If your older sister was mean-spirited, journal on the ways that you are often attacking and mean-spirited toward your lovers when you get into a disagreement.)*

Taking one of these qualities at a time, journal on how you tend to treat yourself this way. *(For example, if your mother was chronically critical when you were growing up, write about your own tendency to be excessively self-critical. If your father raged at you for small mistakes, write about how you tend to rage at yourself when you fail to live up to your own impossible expectations.)*

In this holographic world, everyone is you and you are always talking to yourself.

—Debbie Ford

And finally, journal on how you might

begin to treat yourself with more respect and love. What new choices could you make, and what new actions could you take, that would demonstrate treating yourself the way(s) you would want to be treated? *(For example, if you've been self-abandoning, you could start attending to and honoring your own feelings and needs. Or if you've tended to speak to yourself in punitive ways, you could begin a practice of self-talk that builds you up rather than tears you down, such as self-encouragement and self-praise.)*

Bonus: Practice in Action

At least once today, make a conscious choice to treat yourself the way you want to be treated. Aspire to make this way of treating yourself your new norm by repeating it often. As you awaken your power to graduate yourself from toxic habits, consider forgiving your early caregivers who had internalized the negative ways their caregivers had behaved, then passed them on to you. Make a decision that the toxicity stops now, starting with how you treat yourself.

Suggested Study Guide for Group Discussion

1. What losses are you willing to embrace for the sake of love?
2. What empowering question(s) did you come up with this week, and what's opened up for you in living that question?
3. Whom, if anyone, have you forgiven this week? What was your part in the breakdown, and what amends will you make to yourself moving forward?

4. In which relationship(s) have fear, obligation, and guilt been determining your actions and what risks have you taken or will you take to evolve this relationship to a greater level of health?

5. What outdated agreements did you complete this week and what new agreements are you replacing them with?

6. Share your "Sacred Wound." What do you now have to offer others as a result of what you've been through in life?

7. How has your relationship with yourself been mirrored back to you by others, and how will you now begin treating yourself in the ways you want to be treated by others?

Transforming Your Love Identity

You are free to choose the concept you will accept of yourself. Therefore, you possess the power of intervention. The power which enables you to alter the course of your future.

—Neville Goddard

This week, we get to the heart of the matter by identifying, challenging, and evolving beyond your false Love Identity core beliefs. The goal is to awaken to a sense of yourself as more than worthy of happiness, love, and respect, and fully capable of learning how to keep yourself and others safe in an intimate union.

The work we engage in this week will hopefully be just the beginning of a whole new chapter in how you live and love, as you learn to relate from a healthier, and truer, perspective of who you are, and what's possible for you to both create and sustain in love.

This week, we will:

- Connect the dots between what happened (or didn't happen) to you way back when, and how love shows up (or doesn't show up) in your life today

- Explore the meaning you made of the wounds you endured while still forming a fragile and emerging sense of self
- Awaken to a deeper truth as it relates to these faulty perceptions of yourself and others
- Discover the new ways of relating to yourself, others, and life that will liberate you to create a different experience moving forward
- Step into a growth mindset to start cultivating the skills and capacities that will make it possible to create happy, healthy love
- End this period of profound self-examination with a Release Ceremony to cleanse away the hidden inner barriers you've struggled with and clear the way for love to enter your life

Connecting the Dots

The world breaks everyone and afterwards many
are strong at the broken places.

—Ernest Hemingway

Imagine, for a moment, your experience as a newborn. Unable to satisfy your own hunger, change out of soggy diapers into dry ones, quench your own thirst, move into a more comfortable position, or escape from a scary situation, you were completely at the mercy of those you depended upon. How these people felt about this responsibility, and how well they were able to perform it, was your initiation into the world of intimate love. Their ability, or inability, to respond to your limited capacity to express what you needed in any given moment determined whether the world was a safe place, or an unpredictable, dangerous one.

Willie was born into an alcoholic home. There were frequent fights and fits of rage as his parents sat each night for hours in the living room drinking, ignoring his cries from the next room. Even now, at the age of forty-two, Willie complains of a panicky feeling that has "always been with him" that he won't get what he needs from others. He has little trust that good things will come his way in life. His desperation becomes so great at times that, although he considers himself to be a good person, he admits to some white-collar criminal activity on and off throughout his adult life. Willie pines for romantic love but becomes so anxious and demanding when he meets someone that he likes, that he's just decided he can't handle it. He's been celibate for several years now.

Most of us carry scars from our formative years that are diminishing our ability to love and be loved in the present. Wounds that show up time and time again in the form of a painful pattern such as getting involved with those unavailable for a healthy, committed relationship, or finding ourselves entangled yet again with someone who's habitually needy, negligent, critical, abusive, or abandoning. Ancient traumas that play out in the present as an inability to sustain closeness over time—whether that be through the desperate neediness of love-addictive patterns, the unscalable walls of shut-down, push-away love-avoidant patterns, or some crazy-making combination of the two.

Holly and Javier fight constantly. Having moved to L.A. several months before to make it as an actress, Holly is far from home. She is straining with the burden of few financial resources and even fewer friends. She is living hand to mouth and is terrified each month that she won't make her rent. Enter Javier, struggling artist and actor himself. They fall madly in love and soon after, Holly begins telling Javier that she believes he should be taking care of her. He should move her into his loft, help her pay her bills, and provide the stability she is lacking in her life. Javier wants more than anything to do the knight-in-shining-armor thing, but he can't seem to get it together. He says he'll do something but then he forgets. He assures her he'll give her money, but then doesn't have any to spare. He supports her by going with her as she looks for a job, yet misses an important audition in the process. Now they're both angry.

The life they are creating together is just as volatile and precarious as Holly's has been for as long as she can remember. As a child, Holly's mother was an unpredictable rageaholic, unexpectedly flying off the handle with little provocation. Holly was constantly terrified. She spent her childhood grasping at straws in an attempt to feel a sense of safety and belonging, to no avail. Holly's desperate attempts to get Javier to provide her with much-needed stability have actually served to push him past his breaking point. His inability to meet her desperate needs are weighing upon him and "triggering" a fear that he is just like his father, who spent years unable to find consistent work to support his family. Javier finds himself behaving erratically, with less constancy than ever before. Intensely frustrated, he finds himself displaying frequent outbursts of temper. He has become Holly's worst nightmare all over again, as she is having difficulty distinguishing Javier's anger from the abusive anger of her mother. As for Javier, his worst fear in life is that he'll be a screwup like his dad and won't be able to do anything right—hence, his need to be a knight in shining armor in the first place.

This is a couple who are acting out their deepest dependency wounds together, unconsciously pulling on each other to play out a starring role in one another's darkest dramas. Though on the surface it looks like they're trying to help each other heal, the healing for Holly won't come by Javier's providing her a safe place to land. Nor will Javier's healing come from his ability to finally get it right and prove himself a worthy man by rescuing Holly. Their healings will come when each one turns their attention away from the other and instead look within themselves to identify and then challenge the core beliefs that are so desperately driving them. Until they do so, their ancient hurts will continue to show up in the present, and limit what's possible in love.

> You fell in love because your old brain had your partner confused with your parents! Your old brain believed that it had finally found the ideal antidote to make up for the psychological and emotional damage you experienced in childhood.
>
> —Harville Hendrix

While the sum total of who we are is not defined by the hurts we endured earlier in life, these wounds do tend to dictate our ability (or lack thereof) to create and maintain happy, healthy relationships. Relationships where closeness is a consistent source of comfort, support, and well-being, rather than a battlefield where we're constantly feeling disappointed or threatened, and endlessly trying to get out of pain.

Chances are, you're already aware of at least a portion of your own core wounds in the area of love. You've already begun to connect the dots between what happened way back when, and how love shows up or doesn't show up for you now. You may have even put in some time with therapists and healers trying to finally be free from these ancient hurts that are still wreaking havoc on your love life. You've identified your key "issues," like your tendencies toward codependence or your fears of intimacy. Or you've admitted you're a love addict. You've confessed your pesky little low-self-esteem problem, or your propensity to be critical and judgmental. Although it's good to have insights into how and why the past is still showing up in your present, it's important to remember, however, that understanding is actually a booby prize. It doesn't really change anything. To access the power to transform beyond these patterns, we'll need to understand the beliefs that lie beneath them at the level of identity as our first step in growing a solid, healthy sense of self that's an evolution from the wounded selves we formed in response to early relational traumas.

Children's talent to endure stems from their ignorance of alternatives.

—Maya Angelou

Developmental psychologist Erik Erikson distinguished several stages we must successfully pass through in order to arrive at adulthood fully prepared for life and love. Included are learning to trust others, as well as in the overall goodness of our lives; learning to operate as a separate, autonomous being; and developing a consistent personal identity that's congruent with having healthy relationships. In his book *Search for the Real Self*, psychotherapist James Masterson describes a "solid sense of self" as including the capacity to self-soothe, to express our thoughts and feelings authentically without the fear of either being engulfed (swallowed up!) or abandoned; the capacity to tolerate our own aloneness; a healthy sense of entitlement that life holds good things for us and we deserve to have them; the ability to assert our individuality and authenticity to others; and a stable sense of self. Meaning that you are who you are, regardless of whom you are with and what they feel or don't feel about you.

The core wounds we are exploring this week are those hurts that somehow stunted our development of a solid, healthy sense of self, as characterized by these qualities. And since solid relationships require solid selves, until we finish the unfinished tasks of our childhoods, we will forever be disadvantaged in love.

Luckily, you're a great learner, and there's never a better time than now to see the ways your past has become your present in order to evolve. Because, as author Ken Keyes Jr. said, "to see your drama clearly is to be liberated from it."

PRACTICE: CONNECTING YOUR PRESENT TO YOUR PAST

Take out your journal and complete the following sentences, answering as many times as you wish for each sentence stem. Don't censor yourself! Use your imagination and write down whatever comes to mind, even if it does not initially seem to make sense.

- The caregiving I received in the womb was:
- The caregiving I received as an infant was:

- The caregiving I received as a child was:
- The caregiving I received as a teenager was:
- How my mother felt about being my mother was:
- Consequently, how she treated me was:
- In response, I felt _____ and made it mean:
- The way(s) I see this showing up in the present in my close relationships are:
- The way(s) I covertly set up others to play out that wounding again are:
- How my father felt about being my father was:
- Consequently, how he treated me was:
- In response, I felt _____ and made it mean:
- The way(s) I see this showing up in the present in my close relationships are:
- The ways I covertly set up others to play out that wounding again are:
- The ways I now treat others that are similar to how my early caregivers treated me are:

NOTE: If you had a significant relationship with an older sibling, a foster parent, stepparent, or significant older relative or teacher, please do this exercise with that person as well. If you were adopted, you may want to do the exercise on your biological parents, even if you never met them and/or don't know who they are. Just use your imagination and trust your instincts about what was going on for them at the time. The point of this particular exercise is to access how you internalized your experiences, and not necessarily to uncover the exact facts of what actually occurred.

Bonus: Practice in Action

At some point today, do the following visioning meditation:

Sit quietly, centering yourself with your breath and stilling your body by releasing any tension you may find. Become present to "The One" who is soon to come to you. Feel this person sitting in front of you, offering you love. Soften your heart and open up to receive the love they are pouring into you. Notice how comfortable you feel with this person. How seen and heard you feel. Notice too how much you both enjoy caring for each other's well-being, how effortlessly you listen to and support each other, and how easy it is to laugh together, and to be your authentic selves with each other.

Allow yourself to deepen into the feeling of this experience, celebrating the joy of this union as though it were already here. Give thanks to the Universe for blessing you with such a beautiful love, and utter a simple prayer that you be guided in how you will now need to prepare and to grow, in order to manifest and sustain this happy relationship.

Repeat this experience often throughout the rest of the course.

Naming Your False Love Identity Beliefs

How do you take your woundings, your betrayals,
your "holes," and make yourself holy instead of battered?
This process involves the dramatic re-mythologizing
of yourself and your life . . . the gaining of
a very different perspective . . .

—Jean Houston

You have a story. About who you are, and what's possible or not possible for you in love. Your story doesn't necessarily live like words on a page. It's more like an obscure field of energy that encompasses you. As though you were imprisoned by an invisible fence or, as psychotherapist Polly Young-Eisendrath describes it, caught in your own little snow globe. Its subtle yet pervasive narrative quietly and covertly informs every decision you make, and every action you take in your relationships with others. And until you own this story, it unfortunately owns you. It dictates the limits you live with, year after year after year.

Your story is likely based upon the ways your early caregivers felt about you. If they were burdened by their caregiving responsibilities, you likely internalized their experience as a narrative about yourself that went something like: I'm a burden. Others are overwhelmed by my needs. I can never get what I truly need to be happy and well. If your caregivers were resentful about the new roles they were now expected to play as parents, you likely internalized their confusing feelings as a story that went something like: I'm bad. Others are always mad at me. I'm being punished just for existing. If your caregivers were too distracted by their heartaches and struggles in life to think much of you at all, you likely internalized their neglect as a story that went something like: I don't matter. Others matter more than I do. I am insignificant in this world. I call it your "Source Fracture Story"; the story you created in reaction to the original relational wounding you suffered, way back when.

Studies show that as far back as in the womb, we make decisions regarding who we are, what's possible or not possible in our relationships with others, and the nature of the world around us. Stories such as, "I'm not safe, others have ill intent and want to take from me, and love is dangerous," are often the conclusions of children far too young to understand that it is their caregivers, and not they themselves, who are in some way inadequate and deficient in their abilities.

Because these decisions were made so early in our lives, sometimes before we could even talk, they became pervasive in our experience of life and love. This is not because these stories are true. Though they usually feel true, which for some of us is enough to convince us that they are, due to how overly identified many of us are with our thoughts and feelings. Yet the real reason they occur to us as true is because we've spent so many years gathering evidence that validate them. Unconsciously showing up (or not showing up) in ways that have woven these narratives into the fabric of our lives, verifying them time and time again. It seems as though it's just our fate to live this miserable, tragic story, and we're unaware of ourselves as the actual authors of it.

Maria was born to a Mexican father and an Italian mother. Her father, a heavy drinker, regularly beat her mother until they were finally able to escape when Maria was four. She and Maria moved in with her mother's parents, who, according to her, were "basically good people." However, Maria remembers frequent comments about her Mexican blood, as her grandparents expressed their covert, and oftentimes overt, racism toward her. At the age of five, Maria did not know anything about racism. She did not know that her grandparents were being small-minded. She did not understand that there are many good people in the world who believe destructive and foolish things. All she knew was that, somehow, she was a "bad seed and less than others." She grew up feeling different, and inferior to other kids in the neighborhood. For many years, she struggled with deep feelings of inferiority and shame for who she was.

Consequently, as an adult, she tended either to get sexually entangled with men who she believed were beneath her and undeserving of her commitment and love, or to get hung up with those who looked down on her, and didn't believe she was good enough for them. Thereby, keeping her past alive and well in her present.

The traumas we internalized were either acute, such as the death of a parent, or developmental, such as being raised by a depressed or immature parent who constantly pulled on you to be the caregiver in your relationship, or what we therapists call the "parentified child." Yet the false beliefs we formed about ourselves were not limited to our own traumatic childhood experiences, but also subject to the inherited, unhealed traumas passed down through our lineage. In his book, *It Didn't Start with You: How Inherited Family Trauma Shapes Who We Are and How to End the Cycle*, my friend Mark Wolynn, director of the Family Constellation Institute in Northern California, reveals how the unresolved traumas of our parents and grandparents can be inherited and biologically and/or psychologically passed down through the generations.

Anna came to me confused and desperate. She was tortured that she was "still single" at the ripe old age of thirty-four. She described her humiliation at being the only single woman at the frequent parties she attended, where she struggled through the interminable evenings with deep feelings of embarrassment and shame. Though she was a size six, she complained of how fat and flabby she was. And though a raven-haired beauty with a thick ponytail cascading down her back, she described herself as "barely average." Her pattern was that whenever she met a man she liked, he would inevitably end up rejecting her, assessing her as somehow "not good enough." Predictably, the men who did want to be with her, she found lacking in some substantial way. In Anna's world, someone was always inferior.

Anna grew up in Beverly Hills, one of the richest and arguably most pretentious places in America. Her mother was a single mom raising two daughters on a modest salary. Her father left when she was in kindergarten, dropping their standard of

> If you look deeply into the palm of your hand, you will see your parents and all generations of your ancestors. All of them are alive in this moment. Each is present in your body. You are the continuation of each of these people.
>
> —Thich Nhat Hanh

living significantly. Anna remembers feeling deeply self-conscious about their low economic status, humiliated by her "cheap" clothes, her mother's "hideously old" car and their "ugly little" apartment on the wrong side of the city. By the second grade, she'd stopped having friends over. Anna spent her entire childhood trying to hide her shame as best she could.

Digging a bit deeper, I inquired into Anna's mother's life. It seems Anna's mother also suffered from feelings of inferiority that could be traced through the stories she shared with Anna about her own childhood. Born into a home with an alcoholic father who was unable to provide for his family, Anna's mother witnessed her own mother having to take "low-level jobs" like ironing to supplement the family's income. Initially, when she first met him at the age of 21, Anna's grandmother thought the young man who would soon become her husband was "a catch," given he'd gone to college and had a degree. Yet after they married and had children, little by little, his alcoholism worsened and the family had to move to a lower-class neighborhood. Eventually, Anna's grandmother was forced to do working-class labor to feed her children.

When Anna's mother married, she too thought she had found a husband who could lift her economic status. Hence, their move to Beverly Hills. Yet somehow the pattern tenaciously repeated yet again, and Anna grew up with many of the same feelings of being inferior that her mother had.

Most of us are familiar with the sad stories of our childhoods that have been getting in our way. Yet, in order to be free of the stubborn, painful patterns they breed, we must actually begin to decipher clearly the underlying automatic meaning we're making about who we are, and what is possible or not possible for us in love. The emotionally charged source fracture stories still living in our bodies as chronic frustration, non-possibility, and resignation. We must begin to notice how that meaning is then informing the covert, unconscious ways we show up in life that are actually generating evidence for that narrative.

What you think you are is a belief to be undone.

—A Course in Miracles

What's the story beneath your story? About who you fundamentally are? About how others feel about you? And about what's possible, or not possible, for you to have in love? These three beliefs that were born from the early relational traumas you endured, and which then crystallized as a sense of self. Your belief about yourself. Your belief about others. And your belief about life. All three of them making up the matrix that we're calling your False Love Identity.

Seeing this story clearly and challenging it is the single most important thing you can do to transform your love life. It's pretty much impossible to manifest a happy, healthy relationship if, deep down, you doubt your power to keep yourself safe in an intimate relationship, or doubt yourself worthy of having such a love.

PRACTICE: NAMING YOUR FALSE LOVE IDENTITY

Today we want to distinguish the erroneous beliefs and subsequent false identity you formed in your younger years in response to the disappointments and relational traumas you endured.

Take out your journal and write on the following questions:

- What was a significant disappointment I endured in my childhood?
- Where do I still feel that pain of that disappointment in my body?
- What did I make this disappointment mean about me? *(For example, that I'm all alone, that I'm not worthy, that I'm not wanted.)*

You can use the following list as a guideline if that's helpful.

- I'm alone. I'm bad. I'm a disappointment. I'm dirt. I'm disgusting. I'm disposable. I don't matter. I'm a failure. I'm a freak. I'm inferior. I'm a loser. I'm a mess. I'm not enough. I'm not important. I'm not loved. I'm selfish. I'm smelly. I'm stupid. I'm not valuable. I'm not worthy. I'm unwanted.
- Who else in my lineage, if anyone, may have shared this same belief? *(For example, my mom, my dad, my grandmother.)*
- What did I make this disappointment mean about my relationship with others? *(For example, that no one shows up*

for me, that others are more worthy than me, that others don't like me and will inevitably reject me.)

You can use the following list as a guideline if that's helpful.

- Men always leave. Women don't like me. Others want me around only because of what I can do for them. Others have ill intent. No one cares about me. Others don't want what I have to offer. No one chooses me. Others always reject me. Others matter more than I do. Others are always mad at me. Everyone is out for themselves.
- Who else in my lineage, if anyone, may have shared this same belief? *(For example, my mom, my dad, my grandmother.)*
- What did I make this disappointment mean about my life? *(For example, that I can never get what I need, that I will never have anything of true worth to call my own, that my gifts are not wanted in this world.)*

You can use the following list as a guideline if that's helpful.

- Love is dangerous. There's not enough to go around. My life is cursed. Life is hard and then you die. The other shoe is about to drop. Bad things always happen to me. Life is punishing me. I have to work twice as hard for half the reward. Life doesn't care about me. Love is for other people, not me.
- Who else in my lineage, if anyone, may have shared this same belief? *(For example, my mom, my dad, my grandmother.)*
- How old is the part of you at the center of this story? *(For example, "I'm really young, like two or three." Or "I'm ten." Or "I'm a forming fetus in the womb.")*

NOTE: The answer to this question need not be a fact, but more of a felt sense in your body. You may or may not recall exactly what was happening to you when you were younger.

Going back now to the original disappointment, what's an alternative interpretation of this experience? In other words, how can you now see what happened with your adult eyes, rather than interpret the situation through the eyes of a child who was too young to understand what was happening with any level of complexity or sophistication? *(For example, my parents were exhausted from working so much and had little attention to give. Or, my mother was grieving the loss of a child and couldn't tolerate opening her heart to me.)*

> In time, you will come to realize that the center from which you watch disturbance cannot be disturbed.
>
> —Michael A. Singer

Bonus: Practice in Action

Today is about increasing your self-awareness regarding the beliefs you are operating out of in any given moment. As you move through your day, remember to pause and ask yourself:

"What am I assuming is true right now?"

Notice how the assumptions you're operating from in any given moment are informing who you are being, and how you are relating to yourself and others: whether you are defended or open, asking for what you need or disappearing yourself, setting healthy boundaries or giving too much of yourself away.

Get into the habit of starting to ask yourself, "What am I assuming is true right now?" and then challenging your assumption by asking,

"What might be even more true?" or "What might be a more empowering way of seeing this situation?"

Waking Up to Your True Love Identity

*Transform does not mean to fix or make go away
whatever trauma and scars you may be carrying from childhood;
instead, you slowly develop a new relationship with your difficulty,
such that it is no longer a controlling factor in your life.*

—Phillip Moffitt

Carole's face was contorted into a knot. With her brow furrowed, her cheeks flushed, her nose dripping with snot, and tears gushing from her eyes, she rocked back and forth, wailing in a way that was both startling yet oddly invigorating to those of us sitting in the circle with her. Never before had she articulated her core belief that she was not wanted, and doing so liberated her to express the deep pain she'd lived with for as long as she could remember.

When she was finally able to speak again, she told the story of a mother who'd tried to abort her unsuccessfully three times, back before abortion was legal. Her whole life she'd lived with a vague, pervasive, and haunting sense of rejection. To declare it out loud, as it lived in her body, "I am not wanted. Everyone always rejects me. And there is no place for me in this world," was a welcomed, if not a somewhat shocking, relief.

More riveting, however, was what happened next. Rather than go further into the story of how much evidence she'd gathered over the years for all of the ways she was not wanted in this world, she instead leapt to her feet. As though able to turn to take on the beliefs head-on, she sneered, as if initiating a contest of wills. She began ferociously walking in a circle inside of ours, stomping her feet and flailing her arms as she loudly declared, "I AM DEEPLY WANTED BY ALL OF LIFE. I AM WANTED BY A GOD WHO CONSPIRED TO GET ME HERE IN SPITE OF MY AMBIVALENT MOTHER!" Once over the initial surprise of her unbridled and passionate self-expression, we too leapt to our feet and began cheering and celebrating this undeniable and joyful fact. It was one of the most victorious moments I've experienced in my teaching career, and it changed Carole's life forever. Almost immediately, the painful pattern of rejection, which had haunted her for decades, began virtually disappearing overnight. As though a magic wand had been waved over her head, she began getting coveted acting jobs (after years of auditioning to no avail), and quality men began showing up to court her. Something that had never happened until she claimed the truth of who she was: a woman who was deeply worthy of being wanted.

Many of us have worked for years trying to rid ourselves of these unwelcome and unwanted ways of seeing ourselves, with very little movement made. Year after year, we've suffered with a tenacious habit of defaulting to a shame-based, fear-focused internal experience of ourselves in response to a disappointment or hurt. Yet the goal is not so much to "get rid" of these parts of ourselves, as it is to change our relationship with them. To begin to challenge the stories that live in our bodies as the truth. To push back and reveal these constructs of self for being just that—constructs—and not at all the truth of who we are. In these moments, we must remember that who we are is far more vast than our ideas of who we are. Remind yourself that your original caregivers were not gods, and in fact were deeply, sometimes fatally, flawed. Just because your stepfather told you again and again that you'd never amount to anything, does not mean that this statement bears any resemblance to the truth. Just because your mother treated you like a handmaiden, does not mean you are unworthy of great respect and love. Just because your father left, does not mean that all men leave. In this shedding, our parents are revealed for the mere mortals that they are. So revealed, in fact, that we might even find it in our hearts to respond with pity and compassion for how difficult it

Only as one is willing to give up his present limitations and identity can he become that which he desires to be.

—Neville Goddard

must have been for them to try to give us what we needed, when they themselves were so clearly lacking.

Let me break it to you gently. Your parents, siblings, teachers, neighbors, and peers were very often quite off the mark in their assessment of you. They may have undervalued you, overpressured you, neglected to notice your strengths, ignored your unique abilities, failed to understand the blessed quirkiness of what it is to be you, or criticized you mercilessly for what they secretly feared was errant about themselves. That is no excuse, however, for you to then continue to shoulder the burden of their inadequacies. You must stop perpetrating the abuse against yourself that they originated by indulging these errant beliefs, day after day, year after year. For you are doing just that whenever you persist in treating yourself in the same destructive ways in which you complain your caregivers treated you. We can lament for years about the way our fathers neglected us, but until we stop neglecting ourselves it won't make one bit of difference.

The single most important thing you can do to break free of your old painful patterns, and begin living your version of happily ever after, is to ferociously challenge these narratives. To push back with such strength and conviction that you literally wake yourself up out of their trance. The old identity you created in response to trauma was fixed and never-changing. Inside of that "prisonality," as my friend, spiritual philosopher Neal Rogin, calls it, your painful patterns were predictable and inevitable. That is why you felt so resigned. To finally be free of this tenacious repetition, you must realign your consciousness, and internally anchor into your True Love Identity. Recognizing that you need do nothing to try to prove your value, and are deeply worthy of love just as you are. That you have the power to learn how to keep yourself and others safe in an intimate union. That it is your destiny to love and be loved. That you are wanted by all of life. That you are "a catch" who anyone would be incredibly blessed to have!

The greatest habit we must break is the habit of being ourselves.

—Dr. Joe Dispenza

Wake yourself up in ways that make healthy, happy love possible, and begin showing up in ways that are consistent with this newer, truer sense of self. For once you anchor into the deeper truth of who you are and what's possible for you in a way that you can feel in your body, you are liberated. Living from that possible self of your future—yourself as already loved, safe, supported, heard, seen, cherished, and deeply worthy of happiness—you unleash magic and miracles unlike any you have ever known. You literally compel the Universe to bring this great love straight to your doorstep.

> The bottom line for everyone is "I'm not good enough." It's only a thought, and a thought can be changed.
>
> —Louise L. Hay

PRACTICE: CLAIMING YOUR TRUE LOVE IDENTITY

Today, I invite you to read through the following practice a couple of times before you actually do it. This will give you the opportunity to connect with the story as it lives in your body, rather than try to do it from your brain. To start mentoring the "self in your body" that's been imprisoned in a false narrative about who you are, how others feel about you, and what's possible (or not) in the area of love. Today is about waking you up out of that trance! To do that, you'll want to begin by connecting with your wise, adult self that is holding resilience, strength, wisdom, and love. From there, leaning in to mentor the younger you that's been stuck in the old story.

1. **Become Still.**

    I invite you to put everything to one side, close your eyes, and take a nice deep breath as though you could breathe all the way down into your hips. Drop your awareness down into your body and become aware of all of the feelings and sensations in your body, releasing any tension you might be holding.

2. **Connect with a Deeper, Wider Center Within.**

    Connect with the part of you that is a wise, loving, and mature adult. Breathe the energy of yourself as a strong, wise, developed, and powerful adult all the way down into your hips, down into the earth, and out to the edges of the room and beyond. Place one hand on this deeper, wider center within you, making sure that it is lower on your body than where the emotional center of your False Love Identity resides.

3. Extend Love to Your Younger Self.

Taking some nice, deep breaths, extend love to the part of you suffering inside of that old painful story. Extend a sense of presence and care from your powerful and loving adult self. Compassionately tend to the part of you stuck in that old story of "I am" or "I am not." Simply witness that younger, tender part of yourself with deep love and compassion.

4. Explain to Your Younger Self What's Really True.

Take a wide-angle view on this limited story and begin challenging the conclusions you came to when you were too young to know any better.

Begin mentoring yourself to make more empowered and true meaning.

For example:

- To address the false belief "I'm not valuable," you might say: *"Sweetheart, what's true is that you're more than worthy of receiving great love into your life. You need to do nothing to prove your value."*

- Or to address the false belief "I'm alone," you might say: *"Sweetheart, you're not alone! I'm here with you! And the truth is, you came here to love and be loved. And you have the power to learn how to create happier, healthier connections that deepen over time."*

- To address the false belief "Others don't care about me," you might say:

    "Sweetheart, others might care about your feelings and needs if you took the risk to share them."

- To address the false belief "Others don't value me," you might say:

    "Sweetheart, some people will value you and some people won't. It's up to you to invest your energies in those who demonstrate that they do value you, and to lose interest in those who don't."

- To address the false belief "Other people get to have love but not me," you might say:

    "Sweetheart, you are blessed in love. Look around you! You have constant evidence that Life loves you deeply."

- To address the false belief "Love is dangerous," you might say:

    "Sweetheart, love is dangerous only when you lack the skills to create health and well-being in your relationships. You have the power to learn how to keep yourself safe in love."

Just speaking words of wisdom and truth to the younger you, fiercely standing to correct his or her false conclusions.

5. Create Your Love Power Statements.

From here, turn these mentoring conversations now into "Power Statements." Statements of truth that deconstruct the false meaning you've been inside of. Make sure you can feel these statements of truth in your body, deeper than where you've been holding the emotions of the false beliefs.

Create statements of such profound truth that they literally wake you up out of the trance of the old beliefs.

For example:

- *"I am more than worthy of receiving great love into my life. I need to do nothing to prove my value."*
- *"I came here to love and be loved. And I have the power to learn how to create happier, healthier connections that deepen over time."*
- *"I now choose to invest my energies in those who demonstrate that they value me, and to lose interest in those who don't."*
- *"I have the power to learn how to keep myself safe in intimate relationships."*

Write these statements down! Memorize them so that you are able to assert these truths the moment the younger self begins to make disempowering meaning of whatever is happening.

To download a free audio leading you through the entire "True Love Awakening" process, where you will be guided to identify your specific False Love Identity and awaken to your True Love Identity, please go to CallingInTheOne.com/TrueLoveAwakeningAudio.

Bonus: Practice in Action

Today, see if you can find the time to do an art project. You can use any materials you like, such as drawing paper and markers, paints and a canvas, or modeling clay.

Using your medium of choice, I invite you to create two images. The first embodies your old False Love Identity—that self-sense that you've defaulted to in relationships again and again and that has haunted your life for years. Do your best to capture the actual false beliefs about yourself in an image. Obviously, this isn't a literal interpretation, but simply a representation of what the belief feels like as it lives in your body, and takes over your relationships. When you're finished, see if you can name your figure.

The second figure I invite you to create is a representation of your True Love Identity—a figure that represents you as worthy, wanted, loved, safe, seen, heard, happy, and more powerful than the false identity belief you just created. You might want to actually write your Power Statements on this figure! Create a figure that is deeper, wider, and more powerful than the other figure you created. Again, name your figure.

Do these figures without concerning yourself with the artistic merit of your designs. Use your emotions to craft these two figures, allowing your feelings to lead the way. Use this creative adventure as an opportunity to experience yourself as having dominion and jurisdiction over your old beliefs, rather than the other way around.

Relating to Yourself and Others in New Ways

I think it took me until I got
diagnosed with breast cancer to figure out that
love is not something you tap-dance to get.

—Sheryl Crow

Inside of our False Love Identities—I'm too much, I'm not enough, I'm not loved, or I'm alone—we've habitually shown up in ways that have covertly and consistently generated evidence that our stories are "true." It feels like it's just happening to us. Yet if you look closely, you'll see that it's actually happening through us. Through how we're automatically responding to life inside of the interpretations we're making and the conclusions we're coming to that may or may not have anything to do with what's actually happening "out there."

For example, if you believe yourself to be invisible, you may assume that no one cares about your feelings and needs. That will make you less likely to express them, thereby making it impossible for anyone to demonstrate that they do actually care. Or if you're convinced that you aren't good enough to get what you want, you may settle for less. Which then locks in evidence of your inferiority. Or if you're emotionally centered in a story that you're all alone, you'll be on high alert the moment there's a potential conflict between yourself and others, assuming disagreement to be the beginning of the end. In response, you may twist yourself into a pretzel doing all you can to sidestep conflict. Yet in failing to engage key differences, you can easily find yourself alienated from your true feelings and needs. Given there is no real "you" there to love, you can all too easily become a shell of a person whom others can discard.

Once you begin unpacking yourself as the source of your painful patterns, you'll start seeing a multitude of subtle yet pervasive ways of relating born from the false beliefs you've been centered in. Ways of showing up or not showing up in how you've been relating to yourself and others that can't help but perpetuate the disappointing dynamics that have imprisoned you for years. Waking up to how you've brought your suffering upon yourself is both a sobering and somewhat shocking realization, and it may make you a bit sick to your stomach to see it clearly.

Angela, a stockbroker in her mid-forties, grew up in a small seaside town just outside of Boston. She knew she was a lesbian since the age of fourteen, when she developed a massive crush on the girl next door. They began an intense friendship that included secret sexual experimentation as they "practiced" kissing with each other. Yet when her friend started going steady with her younger thirteen-year-old brother, Angela felt devastated and betrayed. Humiliated by the rejection, she secretly concluded that who she was was somehow wrong and unwanted. Since she liked girls instead of boys, she decided that she would always and forever be rejected by the one she loved.

As an adult, Angela continued her unfortunate habit of befriending straight women who she secretly hoped would change. She'd spend years pretending to be someone's friend, clandestinely courting them, and waiting for them to finally see the light and recognize her as "The One." When I met her, she'd been alone and unpartnered for years. In fact, no other lesbian had even approached her romantically for the better part of a decade.

Initially, Angela was both confused and victimized by this pattern, blaming the world for not being more accepting of those who are gay. I empathized with her, as we unfortunately still live in a culture where heteronormative attitudes are indeed extremely prevalent. Yet I urged her to go deeper by noticing how she

> There are moments when one has to choose between living one's own life, fully, entirely, completely— or dragging out some false, shallow, degrading existence that the world in its hypocrisy demands. You have that moment now. Choose!
>
> —Oscar Wilde

> Until a person can say deeply and honestly, "I am what I am today because of the choices I made yesterday," that person cannot say, "I choose otherwise."
>
> —Stephen R. Covey

tends to show up in ways that validate the perspective that she is unwanted. How exactly was she relating to herself that set her up to be rejected in love? Who was she being with others that covertly set them up to not want her?

It wasn't long before she confessed her own internalized homophobia, and admitted her habit of internally shaming herself for any stereotypically lesbian characteristics she might display as being "too masculine," or "too butch." Angela immediately saw the connection between her own self-rejection, and the rejection she experienced from her straight friends. She also had to sheepishly admit the obvious. That chronically pining after straight women was a most certain structure for continual rejection. She could see too how she set up other gay women to dislike her by snubbing and dismissing them first, before she even knew much about them. Since most of us don't like people who don't like us, Angela was setting up these women to reject her as well. Yet another externalization of her own self-rejection.

We can talk about the traumas of our childhoods until we're blue in the face, but until we stop gathering relational evidence that validates the sad stories we crafted in response, nothing much can change. Our beliefs are relational in nature. They were formed in relationship to others, they're perpetuated in relationship with others, and they can change only in relationships with others as well. To evolve beyond them, we'll need to stop behaving in ways that pull on others to play out those disappointing dramas over and over again. We'll need to start showing up instead in ways that inspire others to mirror back to us the truth of our value and our power. For it is inside of gathering new relational experiences that our old beliefs begin receding into the background, and become a mere memory of who we used to be, and how life used to happen.

Intuitively, we know this. Which is why we've felt desperate for someone to come fix this for us. Yet this emancipation process must begin with us. We must first internally challenge the false conclusions that have been informing our choices and behavior ever since. Once we do, we will be free to start making different choices that can lead us to a brand-new life. Once Angela made the internal adjustment of owning her sexuality as sacred and worthy of respect—embracing rather than rejecting herself—she organically began making new choices. She stopped getting overly invested and involved with straight women who would never be capable of giving her what she needed, and instead began cultivating connections with other women who love women. She created a power statement affirming that there were many women in this world who'd be lucky to love her, and be loved by her. It was only a matter of weeks before she met her beloved partner Robin, and they've been happily building their life together ever since.

We are indeed the authors of our own experience, weaving into the manifest world a continual stream of proof for our own worldview. Rather than continually gathering data that perpetuates your False Love Identity, you'll want to now begin actively generating evidence for your True Love Identity instead. This means identifying new ways of relating that are consistent with the deeper truth of your own worthiness and power to create the love you desire, and having the courage to begin consistently showing up this way. Because evolution that can't happen through us, can't happen to us.

Now's the time for you to let go of who you've known yourself to be. To give up doing things because they're comfortable and familiar, and be willing instead to "try on" the you that you're becoming: someone who has good boundaries, who speaks up, who asks the right questions, who engages conflict directly, and who holds their own. As a person who listens to and honors their own intuitive knowing, who makes wise choices, who is less defensive, and more discerning of character. Who adequately protects themselves, who listens deeply, and who can tolerate disappointing others in order to stay true to themselves.

It sounds simple enough. Yet most of us have been so endlessly engaged in dissecting why we do the destructive things that we do, filled with the many reasons that explain why we are the way we are (usually some variation of a victimized perspective—what my mom, dad, or Uncle Arnold did or didn't do), that we may have forgotten to simply identify the new ways of doing things that could potentially create a different experience. As you've bravely been willing to see yourself as the source of your breakdowns, it's now time to start recognizing yourself as the source of your breakthroughs as well.

> The damage done to us during our childhoods cannot be undone, since we cannot change anything in our past. We can, however, change ourselves.
>
> —Alice Miller

PRACTICE: NAMING YOUR NEW WAYS OF RELATING

Take out your notebook and journal on the following:

1. **Identify Three to Five Specific Old Ways of Relating That Have Generated Evidence of Your False Love Identity.**

   Stepping into radical self-responsibility, see if you can name three ways you've been relating (to yourself, to others, or to life in general) that have generated evidence for your False Love Identity.

   For example, inside of believing I'm unlovable:

   - I've neglected my own needs.
   - I've settled for less than I deserve.
   - I've stayed in relationships with those who've treated me poorly for years.

2. **Connect with Your True Love Identity.**

   Write about what you've been discovering about the truth of your own value, power, and worthiness to love and be loved. As you do so, allow yourself to emotionally connect with your True Love Identity, anchoring into this center of truth and power.

   For example:

   I see continual evidence of how deeply I am loved by Life. And I'm learning to love myself, which is now being reflected in how others treat me. I have the power to start making choices that are self-honoring and self-respectful, and I'm committed to showing up this way from now on.

3. **Identify Three to Five Specific New Ways of Relating to Generate Evidence for Your True Love Identity.**

   Go over your list of your old ways of relating, and identify the new ways of relating that would be the opposite of how you've shown up until now. Notice that these new ways of relating are organic to being emotionally anchored into your True Love Identity. Once you identify a new way of relating, take it on as a practice, whether or not you are feeling it in the moment.

   For example:

   - I listen for, honor, and tend to my own needs first and foremost.
   - I raise my expectations to a healthier level of how I expect to be treated in my closest relationships.
   - I communicate with others how they'll need to treat me. If they're unresponsive, I lessen my investment in that connection.

4. **Identify the New Skills and Capacities You Will Need to Cultivate.**

   In order to make these new ways of relating your new "norm," you may now need to cultivate new skills and/or capacities. Identify what these are and look for at least one resource to get you started in expanding your repertoire of how you show up in your relationships.

   For example:

   In my pledge to listen for, honor, and tend to my own needs, I will now learn how to discern what my needs are. A good resource for this might be the Needs Inventory that's available online from the Center for Nonviolent Communication (CNVC.org /Resource/Needs-Inventory).

Bonus: Practice in Action

Take the risk of choosing at least one new way of relating today. For example, if you tend to close your heart and emotionally cut people off when you're angry, try picking up the phone to work it out instead. If you tend to martyr yourself to the demands of others, take the risk to simply say no to an unreasonable request, without overly explaining yourself. If you tend to talk yourself out of your own deeper knowing, take a chance on trusting your intuition by acting on it immediately.

Reclaiming
Your Disowned Self

Loving oneself is no easy matter just because
it means loving all of oneself,
including the shadow where one is inferior
and socially so unacceptable.
The care one gives this humiliating part is also the cure.

—James Hillman

The Sufi sage Nasrudin tells a story of two men. The first asks the other why he never married. The second man sighs deeply and confesses that he'd looked for years for the perfect woman. "Is it that you never found her, then?" asks the first man. "Oh, no," the second man replies sadly, "I did find her. It seems, however, that she was looking for the perfect man."

I recently had the good fortune of hearing psychotherapist Polly Young-Eisendrath speak on love. She suggested that the opposite of love is not hate or indifference, but idealization. The fantasy that someone's perfect enough to be worthy of our affections and commitment. Yet there's a certain childishness in assuming we have to find the perfect person before we can open our hearts to love. For perfectionism is actually the antithesis of love. Love, by definition, happens when it's safe to fall short in the presence of another. Think of those whom you've met in life who seem flawless to you. While we may admire or even envy these people, we rarely love them. It's not our perfections that make us lovable, but rather our very human vulnerabilities and faults.

Although the "shadow" was extensively explored by the great psychologist Carl Jung, it was psychologist Nathaniel Branden who popularized the term "the disowned self" back in the early 1970s with his bestselling book of the same title. In his book, he alerted us to the dangers of self-alienation—the turning away from one's own internal experiences. Judging whole parts of ourselves as unacceptable, unwanted, and unworthy of acknowledgment.

Candace, an artist who made beautiful pottery, was in her sixties when we first met at a *Calling in "The One"* workshop. Her pattern was to lose herself when in a relationship. She would organize so completely around the other person's needs and desires that eventually she'd get to the point where she had to leave to remember who she was. During the workshop, she recalled an experience she'd had as a young child. In response to being publicly reprimanded by her mother in front of other family members, she had the courage to stand in the middle of the room to announce in a booming voice that she had feelings about what had just happened. An older sibling turned to her and, in front of everyone, said, "Oh, yeah? Where are they?" to which Candace loudly replied, "Right here!" pointing to her chest, her face twisted in a scowl. Everyone burst out laughing, taken aback by her childlike authenticity. Years later, they would explain to her that they'd laughed because she was "so cute." Yet in that moment, Candace vowed to never again express her angry feelings to anyone, having internalized shame in response to being mocked, concluding it wasn't safe to be mad at others. Disowning her angry self, however, made it nearly impossible to negotiate for her own needs in an intimate relationship, and prevented her from engaging in conflict, which is necessary in developing healthy intimacy with another.

Many of the things we judge as unacceptable about ourselves are actually gifts, talents, or aptitudes, driven underground in response to being shamed, blamed, or taunted. Martina was born with a natural talent for leadership. Yet at the age of five, this propensity showed up as bossiness. As soon as she entered kindergarten, she began telling other kids what to do. The kids play-

> The biggest danger, that of losing oneself, can pass off in the world as quietly as if it were nothing; every other loss, an arm, a leg, five dollars, a wife, etc., is bound to be noticed.
>
> —Søren Kierkegaard

ing on the slide should let the little ones go down first, so the bigger kids could stay below to catch them. The kids playing house should have two moms, so the boy could be the baby like he wanted to be and didn't have to be the dad. Martina was gifted with the ability to see what was needed, and the capacity to problem solve in order to provide it. It would have been wonderful if her teacher had recognized her talents for leadership. Instead, all she saw was a nosy little girl who was getting into everyone's business. She took it upon herself to rein in Martina. It was an ongoing project, as little by little Martina internalized the constant chastising by her teacher as an idea about herself that she was "too much." By the time we met, Martina had been trying desperately to curb her tendencies to take over for years, internally shaming and berating herself for her organic big energy. When dating someone new, she'd do her best to dim down so as to "not turn him off." Yet in doing so, she ended up getting involved with those who were looking for a more retiring and demure partner. They weren't people who could contain her big energy. Nor could they support her to develop her innate talents for leadership. In fact, they showed up as an externalization of her own tendencies to silence and shame herself, thereby preventing her from developing those innate gifts and talents that would make her life most meaningful and fulfilling.

Most of us were taught to reject and disown much of who and what we are as we moved through the treacherous terrain of personality development. Little by little we sliced off slivers of our souls, trying to be like everyone else so we'd fit in. Hiding became a primary pastime as we began disappearing whole parts of ourselves in exchange for love. We obscured our genius, our vulnerability, our sensitivity, or our enthusiasm. We diminished our brilliance, our brightness, our badass fearlessness, or our love for that which wasn't "appropriate" such as ballet for boys or basketball for girls. So too were we shamed for that which was inconvenient for others, like our ability to put ourselves first, our organic sense of confidence, or our entitlement to more than our family had access to. And all but a few of us were shamed for our sexuality, and sent covert, sometimes overt, messages that disgraced, dishonored, and devalued us as sensual, sexual beings.

If you bring forth
what is within you,
what you bring forth
will save you.
If you do not bring
forth what is within you,
what you do not bring
forth will destroy you.

—Gnostic Gospel
of Thomas

Maya's mother died when she was a mere four years old. Her father remarried a woman who made it her mission to make sure that her new stepdaughter would not become a pregnant teenager, taking any and all opportunities to shame any attempt she made to "be pretty." When I met her, Maya was a highly accomplished attorney in her fifties who took little pride in her personal appearance, having never given much thought to dressing in ways that might enhance her natural beauty. She was confused about why no one had asked her out for close to two decades at that point, oblivious to the signals she was putting out that said, "I'm not interested in romance." Though an incredibly accomplished, intelligent woman, this had been a blind spot for Maya. Initially she was taken aback by my candor in telling her so plainly my own assessment of what was happening. To her credit, however, she examined how her disinterest in her appearance was a reaction to her stepmother's shaming, recognizing that she'd made it mean that she'd be a "bad person" if she put any effort into appearing attractive. Fortunately, she took my coaching and woke herself up from that story to claim the deeper truth that her sexuality was natural, good, and wholesome. From there, she was able to make a few simple adjustments in how she was presenting herself, rapidly attracting a handsome, successful man who was delighted he'd found such an accomplished, smart, and sexy woman to date.

If you want a true love to come into your life, then you must begin by becoming your whole, true self. For when you're willing to turn toward and embrace all of who you are—the beautiful as well as the bad, the noble as well as the notorious, the magnificent as well as the malicious—then you open yourself up to the possibility of being loved in the ways that you actually need to be loved. As well as become capable of offering this precious gift to the one you're calling into your life.

Our deepest fear is not that we are inadequate. Our deepest fear is that we are powerful beyond measure. It is our light, not our darkness, that most frightens us.

—Marianne Williamson

Jasmine, an actress in her late twenties, complained of a constant anxiety that others wouldn't like her. Although she's talented and has a large circle of dedicated friends, Jasmine often diminished herself by talking about how neurotic she is, how stupid she can be, or how she drives everyone nuts. Jasmine reported that her adolescence was marked by constant rejection by the girls at school. Her mother explained that the girls were just jealous. In response, Jasmine began putting herself down in the hopes that they would stop feeling so threatened. It worked. Little by little, the girls accepted her into their group. However, what worked then was not working now. Not only was Jasmine still anxious that others wouldn't like her, regardless of much evidence she'd gathered to the contrary (which was really based on the fact that she was creating all these "friendships" built on a somewhat false persona of who she was), but she also felt bad about herself. Her constant chatter of self-diminishment was taking its toll. Jasmine had to give up the habit of self-diminishment and take a risk to fully own her beauty and exceptional talents in order to grow. She had to stand in the center of what it was to have all that attractiveness, all that charisma, all that intelligence, and all that personal power. It was a lot to own.

I thought it interesting that Jasmine's main complaint when we first met was that she wasn't meeting any powerful men. I reminded her that she was the one who was disowning her power. It wasn't that there were no powerful men out there. It was that she was attracting people who were mirroring her own skewed relationship with power. I suggested that when she righted her own relationship to power, she would likely start meeting men who'd done the same. I recently ran into Jasmine and she shared that soon after making the decision to allow herself to be all that she is, she met a handsome, talented, and powerful man. A year into their relationship they're deeply in love and seriously considering marriage.

When we meet someone who we perceive has the qualities that we're disowning in ourselves, we'll tend to do one of two things. Either we'll judge them harshly, or we'll idealize them, assuming that they're superior to us in some way. Jerry kept dating musician-songwriters until he finally admitted his secret, lifelong dream of being one himself. He then gave himself permission to start playing piano again, after many years of ignoring his early musical training. Kathy was constantly drawn to men who made a lot of money until she finally figured out that it was the money, and not the men, that she wanted. She promptly took the risk of changing her career so she had the capacity to earn more money herself.

> If you admire greatness in another human being, it is your own greatness you are seeing.
>
> —Debbie Ford

We have to be careful that in throwing out the devil, we don't throw out the best part of ourselves.

—Friedrich Nietzsche

Sometimes it's not so much that we want that person, as much as we want to be that person.

Remember that in the history of the human race, there's never been, nor will there ever be again, another you. When you finally have the courage to accept and love the totality of who you are and give up trying to edit out whole parts of your humanity, you open up the possibility that someone else can do the same.

PRACTICE: CLAIMING YOURSELF FULLY

Take out your art supplies.

There are several ways you might choose to do this practice. Read through my suggestions that follow, and choose one to work on today.

1. **Draw or Paint a Self-Portrait Inclusive of All of Your Qualities.**
   Draw or paint a simple picture or representation of yourself in the center of a large piece of paper. It need not actually look like you. Allow yourself to be as a child, drawing or painting more for fun than the need to do it "right."

   One by one add the following qualities:

My power	My light
My beauty	My sexuality
My talent	My anger
My greatness	My love
My vulnerability	

2. **Collage Your Qualities.** Glue a photo of yourself in the center of a piece of paper or on a piece of cardboard. Look through maga-

zines for images that express the qualities. Glue them all around your photo. Write the name of each quality next to the picture as an "I am" statement.

3. **Create Dance Movements and/or Poses to Represent Your Qualities.** Put on some music that you love. Dance around the room by yourself to get your body flowing. Then use your body to create a "pose," a dance step, or a body movement of each of the qualities listed. You can use a mirror if that feels good to you. When you find a pose that expresses the quality fully and you "feel it" in your body, claim it with your voice by saying it loudly: I AM POWERFUL—I OWN MY BEAUTY—I AM TALENTED— I FEEL MY GREATNESS—I AM SAFE TO BE VULNERABLE—I FEEL MY LIGHT—I AM SEXY—I FEEL MY ANGER—I AM LOVE.

When you are finished, take out your journal and answer the following questions:

- What have I been turning away from in myself, reluctant to own fully?
- What parts of me have I been unwilling to express freely?
- What has it been costing myself and others to hide these parts of myself?
- How might I be projecting these disowned parts of myself onto others?
- What parts of myself do I want to turn toward and express more fully?
- What would I need to give up in order to do this?
- What might the rewards be for myself and others to express these parts of me more fully?

Bonus: Practice in Action

Do at least one thing today that represents a willingness to risk expressing more of your authentic self. For example, share an opinion when you normally would keep quiet; purchase an article of clothing that expresses a previously hidden aspect of yourself; sign up for dance lessons to recapture a childhood fantasy, etc.

Embracing
a Growth Mindset

Why waste time . . . hiding deficiencies instead of overcoming them?
Why look for friends . . . who will just shore up your self-esteem
instead of . . . challenge you to grow? The passion for stretching
yourself and sticking to it, even (or especially) when it's not going
well, is the hallmark of the growth mindset.

—Dr. Carol Dweck

Most of us have been compensating for, and tap-dancing around, our wounds and weaknesses for as long as we can remember. We unconsciously make vital decisions like staying single for years to avoid losing ourselves in another, hold on to unhealthy extra weight to try to avoid being approached sexually, chronically "date down" to avoid discovering we're not good enough for the one we'd actually want to be with, or get involved with married men or women who'll never really show up for us, just to avoid the possibility of being abandoned by someone we've come to depend upon. Yet rather than continue sacrificing our happiness trying to circumvent re-wounding experiences, how about we identify and begin engaging the necessary growth that would allow us to finally evolve beyond these undeveloped parts of ourselves? Like consciously cultivating the capacity to set good boundaries, learning how to say no without needing to overly explain yourself, building a more accurate sense of yourself as worthy of love, or growing a healthier sense of entitlement about what you should expect when opening your heart, and your bed, to another.

In her bestselling book, *Mindset: The New Psychology of Success*, my friend Dr. Carol Dweck, professor at Stanford University, distinguishes between a growth and a fixed mindset. A fixed mindset views who we are and what we're capable of as static and unchanging. Inside of this perspective, most of us will shrivel from the risk of doing things differently, and make our lives smaller in response to a challenge. Yet when we step into a growth mindset, we'll become open to challenge and more willing to be a beginner. More willing to make mistakes, and move forward without knowing exactly how it will all work out. Recognizing failure, breakdowns, disappointments, and delays as opportunities to grow in the direction of our dreams.

Tina sat with arms and legs crossed, indicating her resistance to what I was saying as I stood before the nearly one hundred people who'd gathered to hear me speak. At one point, she couldn't take it any longer. Her hand shot up with an urgency that compelled me to call on her immediately. "I get all of this stuff about not being victimized and taking responsibility for yourself," she said somewhat defensively. "But what about when you can't set boundaries? My dad used to rage at us whenever any of us tried to set boundaries when I was growing up, my mom included. So now I can't set any boundaries with the men I date, and they walk all over me. What am I supposed to do about that?" she asked, challenging me.

I answered by validating the pain that that must have caused her and her family, and by reassuring her that I was not suggesting she was responsible for anything that had happened to her as a child. Yet, I also dared to call her out on her powerlessness. As a grown woman, she was now responsible for the choices she was making in how she navigated her relationships. I invited her to try substituting the word "won't" for "can't." As in, "I won't set boundaries with the men I date because I am unwilling to risk them being angry with me like my father was." There was dead silence in the room as Tina internally tried on my suggestion. Slowly she began nodding her head in agreement. "You're right," she admitted. "I won't set boundaries because I'm unwilling to risk their rage."

"How long have you been alone, trying to avoid the possibility of someone either walking all over you, or raging at you?" I asked.

"Oh, only about fifteen years," she sadly replied.

When we're willing to give up being a victim—to stop laying blame and take full responsibility for our own patterns and experiences—we'll want to

I am still learning.

—Michelangelo, at age 87

look for the volitional aspects to how we show up in life. What choices are we making, and what's motivating us to make them? For once we own our own choices, a funny thing happens. The choice to do it differently suddenly appears.

It is no longer enough to know. We must now know how.

—Dr. Joe Dispenza

Yet the willingness to do things differently and the ability to do so are two separate things. I saw it in the perplexed look on Tina's face, as she grappled with how she might begin setting boundaries, given she'd never seen healthy boundaries modeled in her home, or had any previous experience with doing it well. Yet the good news is this: While she didn't yet know how to set good boundaries, she was, for the very first time in her adult life, finally open to learning.

My guess is that you have some ideas about those missing skills and capacities that have been troublesome for you in love. Maybe you don't know how to internally soothe yourself when you're upset. Maybe you're baffled about how to express difficult feelings in ways that would allow intimacy to take root between yourself and others. Maybe you shy away from conflict because you don't feel confident in your ability to respectfully argue in ways that deepen love, rather than destroy it. Maybe, like Tina, you don't know how to set limits, say "no, thank you," or draw boundaries that can keep love healthy and safe.

In today's world, where we now feel entitled to so much more than our grandparents ever did—a partner who's our best friend, our lover, our spiritual companion, and our equal in every way—we will constantly need to be growing ourselves psychologically, emotionally, morally, and spiritually. Having taken a stand for healthy, happy love, we're now challenged to live up to its demands. For more than a falling, love is actually a rising. A lifting upward toward the expansion of certain internal capacities, and progress toward a more evolved and elegant relational skill set.

PRACTICE: IDENTIFYING HOW YOU'LL NOW NEED TO GROW

While we all love the part where the happy couple rides joyfully into the sunset, the truth is that real love requires the development of certain skills and capacities.

When it comes to growing good relationship skills, there are two categories we will want to consider. The first are the "intrapersonal" skills, which are the growth of those internal skills and capacities required to have good relationships, such as self-awareness and self-soothing. The second are the "interpersonal" skills, which have to do with how we actually engage with others, such as having good boundaries, or being able to ask for what we need.

To help you identify at least one way you'll need to actively grow yourself healthier and stronger both intrapersonally and interpersonally, please read the lists that follow. Circle those that speak to you as skills and capacities you'll now need to learn to prepare yourself for love.

Sample of Intrapersonal Skills and Capacities

The ability to be:

- **Aware of Your Emotions.** This is where you are able to name and witness whatever it is you're feeling in any given moment. Where you can differentiate between your thoughts and your feelings. *For example, if I ask you how you feel, you might answer that you feel sad or hurt instead of saying, "I feel like he's being an idiot."*

- **Aware of Your Needs.** This is where you are able to name, witness, and value what you need to be fundamentally well, safe, and happy in life. Where you can distinguish between a healthy need and an unhealthy need that's coming from an unhealed younger place within you. *For example, a healthy need might be "I need my values to be respected," or "I need to know the truth." Yet an unhealthy need might be "I need to be the center of attention all the time," or "I need you to never care about anyone else other than me."*

- **Aware of Your Own Consciousness.** This is where you can examine your own assumptions and beliefs that are informing your feelings and needs. Where you can discern the lens through which you are perceiving and interpreting your experience, and that is driving you to take the actions you are considering taking, and to make the choices you are considering making.

- **Aware of and In Charge of Your Energy.** This is where you can assess the energy you are putting out there and make conscious choices to expand your energy or contract it, depending upon what it is you want to accomplish. If you have a pattern of overwhelming others, you may consciously choose to contain your energy more. If you have a tendency to disappear yourself, you may choose to expand your energy to be more visible to others.

- **Self-Defined.** You are the one who has the final say by defining who you are. If someone is projecting negative qualities onto you—criticizing you as bad, or treating you as though you are inferior or unworthy, you are open to considering who you've been being that would give them that impression. Yet ultimately, you are the authority on you, and you are not defined by anyone else's perspectives, choices, or actions other than your own.

- **Self-Disciplined.** The capacity and commitment to keep your word to yourself. To do what you promise yourself you will do, and by when, as a priority in your life.

- **Self-Mentored.** This is about your ability to engage a growth-oriented dialogue with yourself that is kind and encouraging, in ways that can help you make empowered meaning of whatever is happening in your life. This includes the ability to lovingly re-parent yourself in ways that help you learn difficult lessons, where you offer correction, wisdom, power, and perspective to the part of you that's upset.

- **Self-Motivated.** The ability to inspire yourself to become all that you have the potential to be.

- **Self-Reflective.** This is the ability to take responsibility for yourself, and to reflect on yourself as the source of your experience without going into shaming or blaming yourself. To admit your mistakes, unwholesome motivations, and faults honestly, while maintaining an underlying unconditional sense of respect, love, and high regard for yourself.
- **Self-Soothed.** This is your ability to de-escalate the intense emotions you're experiencing when you're triggered or upset. So that the actions you take and the choices you make can be made from the more rational, contained, and balanced part of yourself that has access to wisdom and can see what's occurring from a larger perspective.
- **Ready to Shift Centers.** This is the internal ability to dis-identify with the younger, tender self who has just been triggered, and emotionally shift into identifying with a more holistic, mature, wise, and well part of yourself in order to navigate life and love from there.
- **Tolerant of Difficult Emotions.** This is the capacity to hold whatever you're feeling from a deeper, wider center within you. Where you can simply breathe through difficult feelings without automatically turning to numb yourself or act out. To tolerate disappointing others, or being disappointed by others without going into a panic that you're now going to lose the relationship.

These are some of the ways you'll want to begin growing your relationship with yourself, in order to have happier relationships with others moving forward.

Sample of Interpersonal Skills and Capacities

The ability to engage in:
- **Active Listening.** The ability to mirror back what others are saying in ways that reassure them that you get them, and understand what they are trying to communicate to you.

- **Communication of Your Feelings and Needs.** To articulate your own inner experience in ways that allow others to find their way into your world. This includes asking for what you want and need in ways that assume the best in others, and offer them a chance to care for your feelings and to meet or negotiate your needs.
- **Conflict Resolution.** Learning to fight fair and in ways that can deepen love rather than destroy it, by growing understanding and building bridges between you.
- **Empathetic Listening.** To listen deeply to what someone is saying outside of your own agenda, as a good friend might. Growing your capacity to hear what's not being said, as well as what is being said, by attuning to the emotional tone of the communication being offered.
- **Setting Healthy Boundaries.** Setting limits that support you to maintain your personal integrity, while staying close to and connected with others.
- **Negotiating Your Needs.** The ability to advocate for your own needs and desires in ways that are win-win for yourself and others. To take into account that others have different reference points and agendas, and to stay open to hearing all sides before determining the terms of the relationship.
- **Relational Repair.** Recognizing the impact your behavior has had on another, intended or not, and discovering the art of making amends in ways that grow trust between you. Going beyond an apology by also making things right between you.
- **Respecting Differences.** Realizing that, while our shared humanity ensures many similarities, there are about as many ways to be human as there are people on the planet. We want to cultivate the capacity to not only tolerate differences, but also to be open, inquisitive, and reflective about our differing worldviews, values, and visions, coming to appreciate the diversity between us.

The doer alone
learneth.

—Friedrich Nietzsche

These are just some of the ways you'll want to consciously grow to realize the higher potentials your relationships hold for love, happiness, and well-being. Yet there are many ways to develop yourself to be capable of happy, healthy love. For example, learning to pace intimacy, read social cues, or match your facial expressions with your words are just some examples of the ever-emerging need to discover the art of great relating.

Now take out your journal. Write about the top three new skills and/or capacities you are going to take on learning, starting now.

Journal on what your limitations have been up until now, and how you've been compensating for, or tap dancing around these deficits. Write about what the future looks like once you've mastered these capacities, trying on the self of your future where you are already capable of showing up in these new, more empowering ways.

Bonus: Practice in Action

Go through your lists again, and notice those areas you're committed to growing to prepare yourself for love. Be curious about how you might now go about cultivating these capacities to sustain the love you call into your life.

Find at least one resource today such as a book, a class, or a video tutorial that will allow you to show up in healthier and more empowered ways of relating moving forward. Purchase the book, register for the class, or watch the tutorial to start your journey. As the proverb goes, the journey of a thousand miles begins with the first step.

Engaging a
Release Ceremony

In order to fly, you must give up the ground you are standing on.

—Elie Wiesel

One of the pitfalls of living in such a psychologically sophisticated culture is that we often have great insight about where our problems come from, yet have little power to actually change them. In fact, we'll often use our insight as an excuse to stay the same. "I don't do commitment well because my father left when I was four." While connecting the dots between what happened then with what's happening now matters, it's no substitute for starting to make different choices. As Werner Erhard once said, the essence of true transformation lies in the willingness to let go of who we've known ourselves to be, for the possibility of who we might become.

For everything there is indeed a season, and not all our problems will begin to disappear simply because we want them to or think they should. Some challenges must simply be lived with, and some simply lived through. Many, however, have outstayed their welcome and are long overdue for release. We continue to experience them, however, because on some level, they offer their advantages. In spite of our many complaints, we often perpetuate our painful push-pull relational dramas because, ironically, they help us avoid the true risk of love. Or maybe they leverage sympathy from family and friends. Perhaps they help us avoid growing up and taking full responsibility for our lives. Maybe we're hell-bent on making someone

> Spiritual life is about surrender, not understanding. Whenever that part of you that wants to figure it out, or know why, or know what for kicks in, kick it out.
>
> —Swami Chetanananda

wrong, and enjoy making them sit on the sidelines and watch us suffer year after year after year. And so, we've grown attached to the very things we bemoan the most. In fact, many of us have come to be overly identified with our drama traumas, and are buried under the mountain of false beliefs, arduous expectations, painful projections, and unresolved resentments that we've been carting around forever by now. Rather than see ourselves as innately capable of giving and receiving love, we've been frustrated by all sorts of burdensome habits and patterns of our own making that have kept it at bay. In order to break through to the possibility of happy, healthy love, we will therefore need to release all that stands in its way.

"How important is it to you to find love?" I asked the group of women who had gathered together for a workshop. "Very important!" came their collective reply, as one after another they each chimed in and nodded their heads in agreement. "What, then, would you be willing to give up in order to have it?" I asked, slowly scanning the faces in the room. "Would you be willing to give up your rigid criteria of what 'The One' is supposed to look like? How about your need to be right? Because letting go absolutely of whatever it is that is standing between you and love is what is necessary to create an opening for love."

We have such noble ideals of what we would do to find our one true love. Many of us would profess to lose it all—give up our social status and our precious possessions, forsake our family and friends, and move halfway around the world, if need be. Yet, ask us to give up our defenses, our habitual thought patterns, or our limited ways of perceiving ourselves and others and suddenly we are full of excuses and all sorts of reasons why we must stay the same.

The truth is, we simply cannot continue to invest our energies in our neuroses, our dramas, our resentments, and our fears and think that we are a space for love. We aren't. Our cup is either full or it's empty. You can't have water and air in the same space at the same time. In order to create an opening for love, we must first surrender those things that are blocking it in our lives. And it is here that we are confronted with our profound attachment to those very things that we whine about the most.

You are standing at the crossroads, and you must make a choice. You can either hold on to the comfort of your old ways, or you can jump off a cliff by letting go of who you've known yourself to be for the possibility of who you might become—to begin finding your way to the possible self of your future of love fulfilled. To challenge you further, you'll need to give up these things before you have any evidence that doing so will give you what you want. We can't let go with an attachment to receiving a particular outcome in return. The Universe won't bargain with us on those terms. Rather, our surrender must be absolute and unconditional. And so, you'll need to give up a relationship that doesn't serve you any longer, even though you risk being alone for the rest of your life. Or you must give up the comfort of an addiction even though you have no idea, at this point, how you're going to manage the difficult feelings beneath it. Or maybe you'll need to let go of manipulating others, even though you risk losing the only leverage you think you have to get what you want. Or you must give up punishing yourself, even though your circumstances have not changed, and may never do so. Perhaps you must give up the resentment you have toward your former husband, even though he's never apologized or taken responsibility for what he did.

Some people tell me that they would rather die than continue living without love in their lives. Yet trying to get them to shake up their routine, forgive someone who has clearly wronged them, or let go of old, outdated ideas about who they are and what is possible in their lives, and . . . it's . . . like . . . pulling . . . teeth . . . !

Having the willingness to let go absolutely is the one crucial key to transforming our lives. Hence the stereotype of "bottoming out" before one is willing to change, which implies that most of us are not willing to let go of our way of doing things until we've completely bankrupted ourselves. Ask yourself, Am I so stubborn that I must lose everything, and everybody who comes into my life, before I become willing to change? Am I so set in my ways that I would rather let loveless days turn into loveless weeks, turn into loveless months, turn into loveless years before I become flexible enough to try something new?

You must challenge yourself by asking, How

> Growth is a detox process, as our weakest, darkest places are sucked up to the surface in order to be released . . . often, it is not a change in partners but rather a change in perception that delivers us to the love we seek.
>
> —Marianne Williamson

willing am I to be inconvenienced? To be uncomfortable? To be wrong? How willing am I to surrender control? To follow directions? To take real risks where I might actually fail at something? Wherever you've answered with a resounding negative, or even hesitated just the slightest bit, is probably the exact place that you will need to go in order to expand your opportunities for love.

When we talk about "letting go" of our challenges, we are not talking about "getting rid" of them. Trying to get rid of a problem is like the compulsive overeater who goes on a crash diet rather than deal with the underlying grief and fear that is driving the addiction. That approach, however, is us trying to deal with the problem at the level of symptom, rather than at the level of cause. We must, instead, root out our false beliefs, and the underlying fears that motivate our behaviors. So while it's great to resolve that you are going to "give up drinking," for example, I encourage you to go deeper by adding, "I'm giving up destroying myself in order to try to control the feelings that I've been afraid to feel. I am now willing to feel what I feel and trust that I will be okay." Rather than stating, "I'm finally going to break it off with Gary," try going deeper by adding, "I'm giving up being run by fear that if I let go of Gary, I'll forever be alone and lonely. I'm willing to trust that I will find a better, more satisfying relationship, and that even if I don't, I will be okay as long as I am living with integrity."

If you are committed to calling in true love, remember that letting go of everything in its way is the appropriate way to channel your resolve. Be determined enough to release all that is fear-based, all that is limiting, all that is predictable, and all that is "safe." Surrender completely, remembering that growth is not so much a process of accumulation, as it is a process of release. Be resolved enough to embrace the courage it will require of you to start showing up differently: to speak up, even when you think someone else may be offended, or to set a boundary, even if you fear someone else may not like what you say. To forgive a mistake, even without an acknowledgment or apology, or to take the risk to open your heart, even if you can't be sure that your love will be reciprocated.

> Some people believe holding on and hanging in there are signs of great strength. However, there are times when it takes much more strength to know when to let go and then do it.
>
> —Ann Landers

PRACTICE: PREPARING FOR YOUR RELEASE CEREMONY

The work we've done in our past few weeks together culminates today, as we prepare for a release ritual designed to help you let go of all that has been blocking a happy, loving relationship from entering your life. You will need your journal, extra paper, a pen, and a highlighter.

Go back through your journal and review your writings. Highlight those things you are now ready to release from your life to make the space to receive a loving relationship into your life. Some of these things, like a false belief, you may feel completely ready to release today. Others, you may see as needing more exploration on your part as they are perhaps more pervasive and deeply rooted, such as resistance to getting help for the abuse you suffered as a child. Place a star (★) next to those things you feel ready to completely release today, and a heart (♥) next to those things you are now ready to explore further. Do this now.

Next, review all you identified as ready to release, and identify what you're willing to now embrace instead. For example, if you're releasing the hope that a former boyfriend will return, you might now embrace the possibility that you could find an even better match. If you're releasing disappearing yourself in order to not threaten others, then you might embrace speaking up and being visible. Write down all you are now embracing in your journal.

Now take out two extra pieces of paper. At the top of one, write "I Release." On top of the other, write "I Embrace." On your "I Release" paper, write down those things you are willing to completely surrender today (resentment toward a former lover, your mother's expectation that you be

> What has been full must empty; what has increased must decrease.
> This is the way of Heaven and Earth. To surrender is to display courage and wisdom.
>
> —Ralph Blum

married with children by a certain age, your belief that nothing ever works out for you, etc.). These are the things that you placed a ★ next to. Continue creating this list by also including those things that you placed a ♥ next to, as those things that you are going to actively explore further, perhaps with the assistance of a therapist, a coach, or a trusted spiritual adviser. For example, the pervasive push-pull patterns in all of your intimate relationships, or your chronic and destructive outbursts of temper.

On the paper with the heading "I Embrace," write down all of the new ways of being that you are taking on in place of all that you are letting go of.

If you have an altar, or a space in your home that is dedicated to sacred activities, put your lists in this place, in preparation for doing your ritual later today. Carve out some uninterrupted time, no less than a half hour, for the ritual.

Bonus: Practice in Action

NOTE: If you're doing the course with others, you may wish to do the following ritual together. If you're doing the course alone, you may wish to invite a trusted friend to be with you to serve as your witness. You will need your journal, the lists you wrote, a pencil or pen, scissors, a lighter or matches, and a place to safely burn papers (metal bowl, bathtub, large sink, burning pit at a beach, etc.).

There are many, many ways to perform a release ritual. If, for some reason, the following ritual is not appropriate for you (such as you have no place to safely set a fire), please feel free to modify this ritual to suit your particular circumstances. For example, you can rip up the papers and throw them in the garbage, or put the papers, one by one, on the ground, stomping on them, kicking them around, while verbally claiming your freedom. Feel free to be creative. There are about as many ways to perform a ritual as there are people on the planet.

RELEASE CEREMONY

I invite you to create a sacred atmosphere that is appropriate to performing a ritual such as lighting a candle, burning some incense, or putting on background music that you love.

Take out your lists. Make sure that for everything you've written down that you're ready to release, you have a corresponding thing you're also willing to embrace. For example, if you're releasing sexual shame, make sure to embrace celebrating the sacredness of your sexuality. If you're releasing blaming your parents, be sure to embrace forgiving your parents and taking responsibility for treating yourself the way you wished they had treated you. If you are releasing a desire for revenge toward your former partner, then embrace taking full responsibility for your part in what happened between you and the wisdom you've gained because of it.

If you are able to, stand up. Take both papers and, one item at a time, read aloud each thing that you are now letting go of, as well as the corresponding thing that you are now embracing instead. Read it as though declaring a vow to the Universe. For example, "I release the sorrow of my mother's life and I embrace full freedom to be happy myself." Go through your entire list, reading each thing you are releasing and each thing that you are embracing out loud. When finished, burn those things you are releasing. Then place all that you are embracing on your altar or in a sacred space. If you like, you can also post this list where you can see it each day as a reminder of your pledge to begin showing up in alignment with your future of love fulfilled.

When finished, take out your journal again. Write a list of actions that you are going to take, and by when, to support what you've just released. For example, "By Sunday, I'm going to write a letter to my mom letting her know that I've forgiven her," "I'm going to give myself a beautiful home by going out and purchasing a bedroom set for myself this weekend," or "I'm going to work on releasing compulsive overeating by going to the Overeaters Anonymous meeting near my house next Tuesday night."

Suggested Study Guide for Group Discussion

1. What connections did you make, if any, between the care you received in your early childhood or youth and what happens in your romantic relationships today?

2. What is your False Love Identity? When emotionally identified with the "you" of that story, how do you tend to show up that pulls on others to validate your beliefs?

3. What is your True Love Identity? When emotionally centered in the truth of your value and power, how do you tend to show up differently?

4. What, if anything, have you been hiding about yourself? What, if anything, did you do this week to begin expressing these disowned parts of yourself?

5. What are the new ways of relating to yourself and others that are reflective of your value and power? What skills and capacities will you need to develop to show up this way consistently? What resources will you use to grow yourself in these new ways?

6. Share your experience of doing the Release Ceremony, or actually plan a ceremony that you can all do together.

Setting Your Course

Life is a creation, not a discovery.
You do not live each day to discover
what it holds for you, but to create it.

—Neale Donald Walsch

Congratulations! Having released those things that have been blocking you from receiving love into your life, we are now at a place where you can begin consciously creating the relationship of your dreams.

This week, we will:

- Expand your perspective of what's now possible for you to create and sustain in love
- Standing in your intention, actively begin generating the fulfillment of that future in partnership with a force and field of Life greater than you
- Refine what you are looking for in a partner, by becoming clear about your sense of purpose and core values in life
- Awaken your intuition to help guide you along your pathway to the future of love fulfilled
- Establish personal integrity to create your best life and magnetize the best possible partner for you in this lifetime

Expanding Your Vision of What's Possible

The vision process is always self-examination. It's never, "God, I want this. Make this happen." It's always, "What do I have to become to live the vision, to manifest it, to reveal it?" The visioning process, then, is a process of transformation of the individual.

—Rev. Michael Beckwith

Several months after marrying Mark, I was flipping through some old journals when I came across an entry dated February 22, 1999. It read:

Good Morning, God:

What a golden morning—waking up at 5 A.M. to the rushing wind. Thank you, dear God, for weather in L.A. This morning I am going to write down my dreams and visions, to clarify and support them. My dream is to be a writer of significance—to write that which exalts and edifies the human spirit. I see a book ... out in bookstores around the country ... having a life of its own. Also, by my birthday, I see a beautiful engagement ring on my finger. It is reflecting a deep, rooted love between my husband-to-be and myself. He is my perfect mate. I like myself when I am with him. I feel supported and nurtured by our relationship. He is open to having children. I feel protected by him—loved, respected, held up—I love and am loved deeply and completely. I see this. I also see being pregnant with my husband's baby. We are thrilled. My breasts and belly are swollen. I waddle into the kitchen. He kisses my bare belly in bed. We are happy to bring this baby into the world. Thank You, God—Thank You, God—Thank You, God.

When I read this, I did a double take. I checked out the date at least three times before I finally believed that I'd written it a full six weeks before I met Mark for that magical third time. It sounded so much like my real life that I was stunned. At the time I wrote it, I had no prospects for a husband, I was forty-one and childless, and I'd never had a book deal or even come close to getting one. That's the power of standing inside of a vision and generating life from that possible future.

Years ago, Shakti Gawain, author of *Creative Visualization,* popularized the practice of visualization—a process that uses the power of our imagination to help us manifest what we desire to create in our lives. When we visualize, we create a picture in our mind of what it is we desire to manifest and then use our imagination to invoke, and feel the feelings that would accompany the having of this future. It is both a mental and an emotional process. There is a slight deepening of this process that metaphysicians call "visioning," that I'd like us to focus on today.

Christian mystic Florence Scovel Shinn distinguished between the two in her book *The Game of Life and How to Play It,* published in 1925. She wrote, "Visualizing is a mental process governed by the reasoning or conscious mind; visioning is a spiritual process, governed by intuition, or the superconscious mind." Whereas visualization can be limited by those things that can block our ability to see where we'd ideally like to go, such as low self-esteem, a lack of role modeling, or simply a lack of familiarity with what it is we wish to create, visioning is a process that can more easily bypass our "issues," and go straight to a whole new set of possibilities for our lives. For the impressions and inspirations we receive when engaging the visioning process usually live outside and beyond who we've previously known ourselves to be.

The writing I was doing that February morning was to reinforce and support a vision I'd had previously while sitting in a meditation. Since, for many years, I'd thought of myself as a struggling artist (broke, hip, creative, unsuccessful, and counterculture) who was basically alone in life (single and strong enough to be just fine without a man, thank you very much),

Hope is a waking dream.

—Aristotle

and a non-mother (having never even been an "auntie" by the age of forty-one), I was really stretching. The scene I was imagining had little to do with what my life looked like, or what was even logical, given my current circumstances. Yet it wasn't so much that I was trying to wrestle God into giving me some fantasy of what I thought I wanted, as it was that I was deliberately altering my consciousness to match and mirror the "having" of that future. Emotionally, I was trying this "possible" life on for size, and sensing into what it might actually feel like to be living it.

> Tell me what you yearn for and I shall tell you who you are. We are what we reach for, the idealized image that drives our wandering.
>
> —James Hillman

In order to manifest this vision, I realized that I was going to have to change who I knew myself to be. Just to demonstrate what a huge shift it was for me to experience myself as someone who's loved and successful, I'll tell you that the first time that Mark and I tried to go shopping for an engagement ring, I stood outside the store crying. I absolutely could not tolerate going into that store. I had been a poor artist and a struggling student for so many years that I simply couldn't conceive of the fact that this man was going to plop down several thousand dollars on a ring for me. A *ring*! I'd been shopping in thrift stores for so long, it was more than I could bear. We did not go into the store that day and, in fact, it took us more than four months to finally get the ring. (Lest you pity me too much, I'll confess that I have absolutely no problem spending money on myself anymore, as I finally figured out how to manifest financial abundance by doing what I love.) Holding a vision always requires us to adjust ourselves in some way to accommodate that vision. It's a discipline to practice living our lives inside of a vision. We are used to defining who we are according to our past experiences and by what is happening to us right now. Yet when you start living your life from your vision, you will be compelled to behave in ways that are foreign to who you've known yourself to be. Because how you normally show up, outside of any conscious effort on your part, is from the self that you created in response to your past. For example, if you were abused as a child by someone you depended upon, then no matter how much you want love, you may habitually put up walls against it, trying to defend against being hurt by someone you need yet again. Or if you were emotionally orphaned by negligent parents, then you're probably now codependent, and chronically overgive as a way to try to get someone to love you. Yet, consider how you might begin showing up differently if you started to allow yourself to be defined by a future of happy, healthy love instead. Someone who's anticipating being in a loving, committed union in the near future behaves differently from someone who is still dealing with a series of failed relationships and identifies as a person who has difficulty in intimate relationships. For it's the future you're standing for, and not your past, that determines who you are going to be, and how you are going to show up in life.

Your vision will always require you to expand your experience of yourself to accommodate the possibility of that future so that you are internally aligned with, generative of, and open to receive its fulfillment. My friend Rev. Michael Beckwith reminds us that "pain pushes until vision pulls." Once we begin living from a vision that is pulling us toward its fulfillment, we're no longer confined to suffering as our main catalyst for personal growth. Instead, our development begins to be inspired by a possibility. A possibility that influences us to make choices and take actions that can grow us in the direction of our dreams.

Years before writing a book, I held the seeds of a vision of myself as a teacher of love having a profound impact for good in our world. Yet at the time, I suffered from a terribly debilitating shyness that often prevented me from offering an opinion at a dinner party, let alone an entire teaching to thousands of people. One New Year's Eve, sitting with a group of friends, we went around the circle and shared what we were letting go of as we entered a new year. Although I didn't yet have a literary agent, let alone a book deal, the vision of this book that you now hold in your hands compelled me to say that I was giving up shyness. I knew I could no longer withhold my voice if I was going to fulfill my vision. For the next few months, every time I went to speak up, I'd have to acknowledge to myself that shyness was present, take a deep breath and simply let it go. These days shyness is no longer much of an issue for me. As a matter of fact, I sometimes have the opposite problem now of thinking too highly of my own opinions to the point where I'm not open to others'. So now I'm challenged to change myself yet again to become more open-minded and less invested in my own perspectives. Yet, because I am committed to living a life of deep relatedness and service to others, I'm willing to do whatever it takes to be in alignment with that vision.

The very center of your heart is where life begins—
the most beautiful place on earth.

—Rumi

Our task is to begin leaning in to and living from the possibilities we sense we hold for a happy and fulfilling future. Yet for those of us who've spent years feeling emotionally impoverished, or who've dimmed down our expectations of what's actually possible for us to have in love due to the disappointing experiences of our past, how can we even begin to discover a vision that has the power to start pulling us toward its fulfillment? The key is the reclamation of your desires—desires that are emotionally connected to your worthiness to receive their fulfillment, and centered in an awareness of your power to bring them to fruition. Then you will be free to fully embrace your hunger for love as a joyful act of co-creativity. To allow yourself to crave the experience of being seen, supported, and held in the sweetness of your beloved's arms. To surrender completely, and let yourself want what you want without apology or explanation. To hold your deepest desires as good, holy, sacred, and blessed.

Love is not frivolous, as some might suggest. It's as critical to our well-being as air, water, or food. Yet, if you've been emotionally centered in old beliefs that have assumed that you're doomed to live without love, then to survive you may have shut down, buried, or diminished your desires to prevent the pain that comes from wanting what you can't have. In doing so, you unknowingly also frustrated the creative process of life. For the beginning of new life is always desire. In fact, desire is what awakens and fuels a co-creative partnership with Life, as you learn to lean in and listen for your next steps to bring forth the fulfillment of all you yearn for.

Fortunately, you've had a chance to examine and release any old beliefs, agreements, resentments, and self-defeating habits that may have been preventing you from embracing your desires fully. Because when you were emotionally centered in a place of non-possibility, desire was agony. Who wants to want that which they're sure they can't have? Yet now connected to a sense of possibility, you're free to want what you want. Which is a very good thing. Because every time you embrace your desires—for what you yearn to experience, express, create, or contribute—it's like unleashing a stroke of the paintbrush on the blank canvas of your life. Your desires literally begin weaving the future that's now possible for you to create.

The only successful manifestation is one which brings about a change or growth in consciousness; that is, it has manifested God, or revealed Him more fully, as well as having manifested a form.

—David Spangler

Ultimately, we don't really have a vision as much as a vision has us. Rather than forcing our will upon the Universe, we open ourselves to catch a glimpse of what's now possible, then stick our foot in the doorway of that opening. We must turn our attentions and align our will toward the manifestation of that future. For, as those of us who are practitioners of metaphysics know well, whatever we focus on grows.

PRACTICE: VISIONING LOVE

We are going to do a visioning this morning. Find a quiet and comfortable place where you will not be interrupted. Make sure that your journal and a pen are nearby. I invite you to read through the instructions once or twice and then do them from memory as best you can. You can peek if you need to.

Close your eyes and take a few deep, relaxing breaths meant to center and focus you. Repeat your Power Statement(s) from last week silently to yourself, emotionally reconnecting with the truth of your worthiness to love and be loved. When you feel centered in your own value and power, ask yourself the following questions either silently or out loud:

- *"What do I desire to be experiencing with my beloved?"*
- *"What do I desire to express to my beloved?"*
- *"What do I desire to create with my beloved?"*
- *"What do I desire to be contributing to my beloved? And to the world as a result of our union?"*

If prayer is talking to God, then meditation is *listening* to God. Sit listening for the answers, savoring what comes to you. Allow the floodgates of your desires to open up. Welcome them all, naming them good and holy! Simply listen and stay present with yourself, without judging or assessing what comes to you. Just pondering the questions, and allowing yourself to imagine that you are experiencing these things now.

After a few minutes, open your eyes and write down in your journal the images, feelings, desires, and thoughts that came to you. When you are finished, move on to the next question.

NOTE: If a former lover comes to mind during the practice, look to discover the gifts that relationship held that you'd like to have again in your next relationship. Thank your former partner for reminding you of these qualities and then dismiss them, telling yourself that this person was not the source of these qualities. The Universe is.

- *"What would I need to give up or release from my life to allow this vision to come to me?"*

Again, sit quietly in the question and repeat the previous instructions. After a few minutes, write down the images, feelings, insights, and thoughts that came to you in response to the question.

When you are finished, move on to the final question:

- *"What will I need to embrace, and how will I need to grow to receive this vision?"*

Once more, repeat the previous instructions.

Bonus: Practice in Action

This morning, you were given information on what you would need to give up, or how you will need to grow to prepare yourself for the love you are calling into your life.

Take at least one action today in response to the second question you asked, "What would I need to give up or release from my life to allow this vision to come to me?" *For example, "I'd have to give up drinking and get into recovery" means that you might decide to attend an AA meeting; or "I'd have to give up hiding" means that you might sit in the front row of class and courageously raise your hand.*

Take at least one action today in response to the information you received to your third question, "What will I need to embrace, and how will I need to grow to receive this vision?" For example, "I'd have to grow my capacity to receive the love that others have for me" means that you might allow someone to do you a favor without immediately repaying it; or "I'd have to embrace my vulnerability" means that you might try being more emotionally undefended with someone you've been guarded with.

Acting on Your Intention

It was through self-examination that I found the root cause
of disappointment: not stating your true intentions very clearly
at the outset of any endeavor. When you fail to do that, and when
you fail to let everyone involved know exactly what it is you want,
chances are you will be disappointed.

—Iyanla Vanzant

Setting your intention is like planting your stake in the ground and declaring unto all of Life, "This shall be so!" It is a proactive, generative process. Meaning that our intention is only as viable as our willingness to roll up our shirtsleeves and begin actively co-creating the fulfillment of that future in partnership with the creative energies of Life, recognizing the power we have to cause a future that was never going to happen unless we stood for it.

Several years ago, forty-year-old Audre, a dynamic and attractive corporate trainer, courageously stood up in front of the room at a *Calling in "The One"* workshop to publicly proclaim her intention to open fully to receiving a great love into her life, and her willingness to let go of all of the barriers and blocks she'd built against it. One of her biggest internal obstacles, she confessed, was her rigid criterion of what she thought "The One" should look like. There, before a roomful of people, she took the opportunity to surrender her inflexible agenda and declare herself open and receptive to love, regardless of what it might look like.

A few months later, Audre wrote to thank me. It seems that soon after the workshop, she decided to re-create her online profile, taking out the exacting paragraph where she listed precisely what "He" should look like, as though she were posting a job description. Instead, she shared her musings on what their relationship might feel like for them both. A sacred home where they felt safe and happy in the company of each other. Where their mutual love of literature was a central part of their relationship, and where they enjoyed long walks through the woods together in a local park. It was not long before she met the wonderful man she would eventually marry.

She laughed when sharing that she would never in a million years have been open to him had it not been for the intention she set, for he was nothing like what she thought she was looking for. Ten years older than she is, with two grown children, Jose lived in a city hundreds of miles away from her home in Los Angeles. As if that weren't enough, she said with a sense of irony, she discovered rather quickly that he had only recently separated from his wife of twentysomething years. "Do you think that I had 'married' on my list?" she asked incredulously. Yet it was right—not just for her and Jose, but for all involved, including Jose's adult children and his former wife, who soon moved on to better circumstances as well. "It's funny," Audre said. "There's a lot of conventional wisdom out there regarding finding 'The One,' but then there's the mystery of what enfolds when you're simply standing inside of an intention, and a willingness to allow that intention to inform your actions and choices."

Rather than pleading for someone out there to give you love, you begin co-creating it from the inside out, allowing your intuition to guide your next steps in the direction of your dreams. Cultivating faith in the face of no evidence and continually holding space for a miracle, you faithfully move forward with the somewhat irrational belief that the fulfillment of your intention is actually possible.

Billie, an artist in her early forties, knew she'd cultivated an unshakable belief in the possibility of love when two of her good friends became engaged within a short period of time. She'd been visioning to find "The One" for a while by that time, and had a true feeling in her heart that finding her partner was both possible and probable. Because of this, she was organically overjoyed at the good fortune of her friends, seeing their success as evidence that she too would soon find love. She took their engagements as a chance to celebrate their happiness with the same enthusiasm as if it were her own, making herself a valuable part of their nuptial celebrations. In the past, she confides, she would

Consciousness precedes all matter.

—Albert Einstein

secretly have felt envious and threatened by their happiness and distanced herself from her friends, simply because she did not trust that love was on its way to her as well. Within just a few short months, I was not surprised when Billie herself met the woman she would soon become engaged to and marry.

In order to create accountability structures for yourself to act in alignment with your intention, you may want to share what you're up to with a trusted friend or circle of friends. People who can hold that vision *with* you, and *for* you. It's critical that we have these safe spaces to share what we're committed to in life in order to practice creating from our word. Most of us use language as though it were simply a descriptive tool, rather than a creative one. Yet speaking is a profoundly generative act. The prolific Vietnamese American poet Ocean Vuong wisely tells us, "The future is not so much in our hands as in our mouth. You have to articulate the future you want to see."

Hearkening back to my own story, when I miraculously called Mark into my life by telling my friend Naomi what it was that I was committed to, I essentially gave her permission to hold me accountable to be who I would need to be in order to fulfill my hoped-for future. My actions and choices needed to match my intention, and even become generative of its fulfillment. I could no longer flirt with unavailable men, or date those who weren't interested in being in a committed relationship, without Naomi asking me if I was being consistent with the intention I'd set. I will admit that, at times, I was completely irritated with her, rolling my eyes on more than one occasion. At other times, however, I was enormously grateful. Because sharing my intention out loud with another person obliged me to transform myself into the kind of woman who would actually be available to love another human being by my forty-second birthday. Because I understood that, I didn't stop with Naomi, but actually began telling most people in my life, including the men that I was dating, that I was committed to finding my partner. I tried telling them in a way that didn't seem like I meant that *they* had to be the one to commit to me and build a life together. Since I didn't feel needy in my quest for a mate, choosing instead to stand in a place of anticipation and possibility, they tended to relax, and some even began to explore the possibility that I might be "The One" for them. And although, through all of my many love affairs over the years, I'd not been proposed to since my high school sweetheart, I actually had one other proposal right before my first husband asked me to marry him. When you're ready, you're ready.

In her book *Soulmates,* psychologist Dr. Carolyn Miller tells a story about the celebrated actress Sophia Loren. As a child, Sophia was ruthlessly teased for being illegitimate, ugly, skinny, and poor. With such a disadvantaged beginning, Sophia attributes her success in life largely to her maternal grandmother. As a baby, Sophia's grandmother made up a song that contained words that affirmed that when she grew up, she would be happy, rich, beautiful, and adored. All of her dreams and aspirations would magically come true. Over and over throughout her childhood, Sophia's grandmother sang this song to her. By her early twenties, in spite of having a difficult and destitute start in life, every word of that song had come to pass.

The words we use serve as a sort of instruction manual to the Universe. I recall hearing a sermon from a minister who put it this way: "The whole Universe is genuflecting to you constantly," she said. "Yes, Boss, whatever you say, Boss. Be clear about the instructions you are giving." If you complain that "all the good ones are taken," then you'll likely meet only married or engaged people that you feel attracted to. If you complain to your friends that you'll never find the right partner, then my guess is that you'll probably be right.

When setting an intention like "My intention is to have a happy, loving, mutually committed relationship," you want to unleash a slew of coincidences, unforeseen opportunities, and unpredictable synchronicities. That's why it is critical to have integrity with our word. Because it "trains" the Universe to take you seriously. If someone is inconsistent with their word, it is like a child who lies continually. You stop taking them seriously. They could tell you the house is burning down, and you'd take your sweet time getting out. But if someone with a history of always speaking the truth told you the very same thing, you'd have a different response.

When I called my friend Naomi during my own initial *Calling in "The One"* process to tell her that I was setting an intention to be engaged by my birthday, I did so because I'd been successfully setting intentions in other areas in my life. Like an athlete who gets stronger the more she practices, I too was gaining strength in my ability to create with my word. I was getting better at it because I was getting better at being responsible for what it was that I had said. I had developed a certain level of consistency between what I said, and the choices I made and actions I took. It's like exercising a muscle. You get better at it the more you do it, and it's best

> Success depends on where intention is.
>
> —Gita Bellin

to build yourself up slowly but steadily. For those who run marathons, taking a ten-mile jog is not that big a deal. For me, you'd end up scraping me off the pavement after the third or fourth mile. Most of our abilities have to be cultivated and developed one day at a time.

We usually get what we anticipate.

—Claude M. Bristol

When you believe that love is possible for you and share your intention to manifest it, you open a portal of possibility. Yet, as the Good Book says, "Faith without works is dead." Therefore, you must deliberately begin weaving that future into the manifest world. Allowing the desires you felt in your meditation yesterday to inform how you show up today. If you yearned to experience joy with your beloved, look to actively create joy for yourself and others. If you yearned to create a beautiful home with your beloved, take time today to clean up the mess and beautify your home. Start showing up in ways that are consistent with the fulfillment of your intention, and refrain from doing anything that is inconsistent with your intention. This is the generative climate in which true love can "miraculously manifest."

Yet here's the challenging part. *We must take courageous, bold actions in the direction of our dreams, yet also remain completely unattached to the outcome.* In other words, *we must do our best to live 100 percent aligned with and generative of the intention that we set, without being attached to the results we are getting.* We simply cannot get caught up in trying to force the river of life to go in one particular direction. Rather, setting an intention compels our own healing and transformation. It's not so much that we force the hand of God, as we become willing to be who we need to be order to manifest the intention. We speak the word, take the actions, make the choices, and then let go—trusting that, as we do our best to live congruently with the intention that we set, whatever happens is perfect. Anthropologist and author Ralph Blum says it this way: "Practice the art of doing without doing: Aim yourself truly and then maintain your aim without manipulative effort."

PRACTICE: IDENTIFYING ACTIONS AND CHOICES IN THE DIRECTION OF YOUR DREAMS

Take out your journal, and begin by writing down your intention. For example, "My intention is to meet my life partner by the end of the year."

NOTE: Using a specific date adds a certain urgency that helps mobilize us to immediate action. However, if you feel too overwhelmed by doing so, I suggest you set an intention that you can completely own and align with, adding a "by when" time frame later on, if and when you feel ready.

Complete these sentences:

- My intention is:
- I am in integrity with this future when I:
- I am out of integrity with this future when I:
- With my beloved, I desire to experience:
- To generate this experience now, I can:
- To my beloved, I desire to express:
- To express this now, I can:
- With my beloved, I desire to create:
- To create this now, I can:
- For (or with) my beloved, I desire to contribute:
- To contribute this now, I can:

Bonus: Practice in Action

Call at least one close friend or confidant today who can stand with you in the vision of your intention fulfilled. Share with this person the intention that you set for yourself this morning. Give that person permission to provide coaching and to "lovingly confront" you if and when you are making choices inconsistent with your intention. If you are doing this course with a supportive circle of friends, share your intention with everyone in the group the next time you are together.

Take at least one action today that weaves the fulfillment of that future into the manifest world. For example: Set a boundary with a former boyfriend by telling him that you are no longer interested in sleeping with him; tell the woman you have been dating what you are truly wanting at this stage of your life; plant a garden in your backyard so that you can fill your home with fresh flowers.

Clarifying
Your Soul's Purpose

When love . . . [is] the context of your life,
what details cannot be reconciled?
When one knows north, all other directions are implied.

—Mark Austin Thomas

Most of us know at least one couple who appears to have it all—the money, the house, the kids—yet seems to lack certain magical qualities like delight, charm, and enchantment. Both partners appear to be moderately content. Yet when we observe such marriages, we know in our hearts that what they have is not what we're looking for. The trappings of what we might call a "successful" union do not necessarily capture the level of soul connection that many of us are longing for.

Often, I find myself reminding people that they could probably go out and get married within six months if that was all they wanted. The truth is, we've come to expect more from our unions than the economic advancement and social compatibility that our grandmothers were looking for. We now expect our intimate relationships to fulfill us at the level of heart, mind, body, and soul. It's a tall order.

Each of us enters this world called to fulfill a particular destiny. This calling usually lies just beyond our conscious awareness, and often beckons us with a sense of restlessness and dissatisfaction. In the past, those curious about this mysterious calling holed up in monasteries to ask questions such as "Who am I?" "What am I here for?" and "What is the meaning of my life?" However, more and more, these important questions are being asked and answered in relationship to one another.

Relationships that are able to graciously transition from the sexual-attraction/falling-in-love stage (which lasts anywhere from one to three years) to the attachment stage (which can last a lifetime) are often deeply rooted and organized around a shared sense of destiny, and the very best long-term partnerships are founded upon a common purpose.

Sakura came to me after being married for a relatively short period of time. Although she was a deeply spiritual person, Sakura married a man who is a professed agnostic. He lovingly supports her to pursue her spiritual practice while, at the same time, he eschews any particular path himself. Although that was fine for her when they were courting, she is now questioning her decision to marry him, particularly since she is considering going back to school to become a minister.

Sakura is in crisis. If she pursues her faith more fully, she risks alienating herself further from a husband who does not share her spiritual beliefs. However, if she does not pursue these goals, she risks sabotaging the fulfillment of what she believes could be her true destiny. The dilemma is an agonizing one.

I invited Sakura to explore with her husband not only what he does *not* believe in, but also what he actually *does* believe in, such as the need to contribute in some meaningful way. I am hopeful that they are able to locate a shared sense of purpose that goes beyond doctrine and didactic religious beliefs. This way, they can stand united in a shared vision. Unless they can locate something outside of themselves upon which to join, they could have a difficult time forging a thriving union. For many of us, finding our spiritual partner opens the gateway that leads to the fulfillment of our soul's destiny. That's why we are in such agony in that person's absence. However, the path to prepare ourselves to receive such a love can sometimes take

> An essential part of becoming marriageable is to be a maker, a person who cultivates a life of beauty, rich texture, and creative work. If we understand marriage only as the commitment of two individuals to each other, then we overlook its soul, but if we see that it also has to do with family, neighborhood, and the greater community, and with our own work and personal cultivation, then we begin to glimpse the *mystery* that is marriage.
>
> —Thomas Moore

> Joy can be real only if people look upon their lives as a service and have a definite object in life outside themselves and their personal happiness.
>
> —Leo Tolstoy

years. I suspect that's one reason that so many of us are waiting until we are older than our parents were before committing to marriage.

As with any journey, we must always begin from where we are. In this case, we start with ourselves. While we may yearn to find "The One" who can more deeply help us understand the value of our lives, the way we draw such a love toward us is by already being actively engaged in seeking and expressing our highest destiny. Unfortunately, some of us settle for a continual stream of crises that serves to distract and divert our attention, rather than challenge ourselves to engage in this more meaningful pursuit. Hence, our love life reflects this penchant for drama, which sometimes serves as a substitute for a true sense of purpose in life.

Eileen Caddy, co-founder of the Findhorn community, once said, "A soul without a high aim is like a ship without a rudder." Just as knowing your sexual proclivity promises to bring greater clarity to your love life, so too does knowing your soul's purpose. Everything comes into focus. Connecting with this "high aim" becomes your reference point—a primary directive from which all other decisions are made, particularly the decision about whom to create an intimate, loving relationship with.

It's not to say that Sakura married the "wrong person." But she would have been wise to explore the larger context in which both she and her husband were living, before taking the significant step of marriage. Now she has to backpedal and try to find a framework on which they can join so that she will not feel compelled to live a diminished and contracted life in order to stay bonded to him. In the old paradigm of marriage, it was common for people to live compromised lives that were ultimately less than what was possible. Yet in our more modern marriages, we look to form visionary and expansive unions that can support us in becoming all that we are capable of being.

Many of us confuse our jobs and our roles in life with our purpose. Yet Carol Adrienne, author of *The Purpose of Your Life*, tells us, "Our purpose . . . is not a thing, place, occupation, title, or even a talent. Our purpose is *how* we live life, not what role we live. Our purpose is found each moment as we make choices to be who we really are."

Our soul's purpose is always concerned with who we are for others. To bring hope, or to inspire, or to be a force for racial healing and reconciliation. Our purpose is deeply concerned with who we are *being*. Even more so than the specific things we might be *doing*. Doing is simply the vehicle through which your purpose is called to express itself in this moment. My soul's purpose is equally expressed in playing a silly game with my daughter, as it is in writing this book. Both are demonstrations of love toward another. Though I now get to be a teacher of love—a clear expression of my purpose—the truth is, I was consciously choosing to love back when I was a temp secretary and a waitress. These too were opportunities to extend care toward others. One is not better than the other. They are all equally elegant opportunities to be of service.

Discovering our soul's purpose is rarely an event, although epiphanies do happen. More often than not, it's a process that requires patience and perseverance. In order to discover it, you'll want to pay attention to what stirs your passions, lights you up, and just comes naturally. When you are living inside of your soul's purpose, you are often in flow. You lose track of time. You're not that concerned about how much money you are, or are not, making. You feel alive, useful, of service, and a part of all that is. The oft-quoted writing of George Bernard Shaw is worth repeating here:

> *This is the true joy in life, being a conduit for a purpose recognized by yourself as a mighty one; being a force of nature instead of complaining that the world will not devote itself to making you happy. I am of the opinion that my life belongs to the whole community, and as long as I live, it is my privilege to do for it whatever I can. I want to be thoroughly used up when I die, for the harder I work, the more I live. I rejoice in life for its own sake. Life is no brief candle to me. It is a sort of splendid torch, which I have got hold of for the moment, and I want to make it burn as brightly as possible before handing it on to future generations.*

Our soul's raison d'être is usually quite simple. We are here to help people. We are here to learn and to grow in wisdom. We are here to heal ourselves and others. We are here to help birth peace in the world. We are here to love and be loved. We are here to

Love, whether newly born, or aroused from a deathlike slumber, must always create sunshine, filling the heart so full of radiance, thus it overflows upon the outward world.

—Nathaniel Hawthorne

First, make sure you get into a relationship for the right reasons . . . I mean "right" relative to the larger purpose you hold in your life.

—Neale Donald Walsch

radiate kindness . . . or hope . . . or happiness. As you look to attract the love of your life, remember to first examine and explore the overall meaning and aim of this beautiful, unique journey called your life. For once you've located north, all decisions and choices will be that much easier to make, particularly the task of choosing your mate.

PRACTICE: DISCOVERING YOUR SOUL'S PURPOSE

Take out your journal. Write on each of the following questions:

- What do I love to do?
- What comes naturally to me?
- What do I feel passionate about?

Now complete these sentence stems with as many answers as you can think of:

> The times I've been happiest in life have been when . . .
> People have always told me that I'm good at . . .
> When I was a child, I always wanted to . . .
> The purpose of my life is . . .

- Fill in the blank:

    I am here to bring _____ to the world.

Bonus: Practice in Action

Do at least one thing today that expresses what you believe, at this point, to be your soul's purpose in the world. Make this action a demonstration of your intention to begin organizing your life more and more around this sense of purpose. This will usually entail seeking out others with a similar purpose to yours. For example, finding a church or spiritual group with similar values and aspirations; taking on a volunteer commitment with an organization that moves and inspires you; or joining a club that shares a passion that you have.

> The defining characteristic of soulmate relationships is shared purpose.
>
> —Carolyn G. Miller

NOTE: Don't worry about "not having enough time." When you're living congruent with that which matters most to you, life has a way of becoming more efficient and less frenzied, thereby leaving you with more time than you thought you had.

Receiving Inner Guidance

Intuition is the discriminative faculty that enables you to decide
which of two lines of reasoning is right.
Perfect intuition makes you a master of all.

—Paramahansa Yogananda

While we may be in the habit of asking our therapist, family, or friends for advice, it often doesn't even occur to us to seek our own counsel by going within. Often referred to as the "God Within" or our "Higher Self," this ever-present source of wisdom within is always available, just for the asking. Expressed frequently as a "gut feeling" or a "sixth sense," our deeper knowing lies in wait, whispering quietly in our hearts, and longing for us to finally turn our attentions toward its sage counsel.

All of us have access to wisdom beyond our years. It's the part of us that trusts intuition over logic, and instinct over knowledge. It's a timeless, alternative form of knowing that does not depend upon external proof, common wisdom, or current circumstances. Because of this, many of us consistently override its promptings. We doubt its validity and accuracy and, as a result, suffer painful yet preventable consequences.

When Chad met Janice, he fell for her immediately. She was beautiful, charismatic, and seemingly everything he had ever hoped for. Soon into the relationship, he began to feel uncomfortable with her relationship with her soon-to-be ex-husband, with whom she was in the middle of a long and grueling divorce. Although Janice insisted that the relationship was long over and told Chad repeatedly that she loved only him, he found himself feeling insecure and anxious whenever her ex-husband's name was mentioned. Chad's intuition told him to be cautious and to wait until he knew Janice better before surrendering himself completely. However, because Chad considers himself a "spiritual" man, he thinks that he *should* love with an open heart at all times. Therefore, he talked himself out of this feeling, assuming that he was wrong to feel mistrustful since, after all, "spiritual" people are *supposed* to trust others. Soon thereafter, Janice told Chad that she wanted to go into couples counseling with her ex-husband so that she could "work on that relationship."

Cease trying to work everything out with your minds, it will get you nowhere. Live by intuition and inspiration and let your whole life be a Revelation.

—Eileen Caddy

How many times have we plowed straight ahead, overriding our inner knowing with logic and reason? Almost every time I've done this, I've ended up regretting my decisions. I learned this big-time back in 2000, when the stock market fell fast and furious. I, like many people, lost thousands of dollars. My intuition had told me to sell all of my tech stocks right before they plunged in value. For days, I had a gnawing feeling that was absolutely nagging at me to sell the stock. However, because the stock had recently dropped in value by $500, I negated this inner prompting and decided to wait. I didn't think my inner guidance was accurate when it instructed me to sell my stock at a loss. Had I listened, I would have lost only $500 instead of thousands. It was an expensive lesson.

Whenever we do not listen to our inner guidance, our ability to discern between "two lines of reasoning" becomes more and more compromised. Our ability to trust ourselves devolves into an increasing dependence upon the opinions of others. When Janice was making false promises to Chad, against his better judgment, he became more and more dependent upon her to reassure him. He became consumed by an ever-increasing need for feedback and approval from his therapist, friends, and family. He was paralyzed to take any actions to protect himself because everyone he asked had a different opinion about what he should do. For every person who thought he was being foolish to open his heart to a woman whose divorce was not yet finalized, there was another who thought he needed to take a risk on what could be an extraordinary love. Because he was so dismissive of his own intuition, he began behaving with an intense desperation to have others tell him what to do. In situations such as this, where there really is no clear-cut right or wrong, all we have

You must begin to trust yourself. If you do not then you will forever be looking to others to prove your own merit to you, and you will never be satisfied. You will always be asking others what to do, and at the same time, resenting those from whom you seek such aid.

—Jane Roberts

is our intuition to guide and help us make a good, sound decision. How terrible, then, for Chad to be so estranged from himself and so thoroughly cut off from his ability to trust himself. Because of it, he was completely caught off guard, and utterly devastated for months after Janice decided to go back to her husband. Had he listened to and honored his intuitive knowing, he would have been more prepared for the choice she made, and able to recover from his disappointment more quickly.

One woman I worked with became so alienated from her ability to access her own inner guidance that she developed an overdependence upon her daily horoscope. She would not leave home in the morning without first consulting the newspaper. If her horoscope foretold a good day, she would feel hopeful and optimistic. However, if it forecast doom and gloom, she would become so anxious that she could barely get herself out the door to face the day. Her ability to connect with her own inner wisdom became weaker and weaker, as her dependence upon this external source of direction increased. Even though she could see how foolish her addiction was, she had little power to release herself from her obsessive need for someone else to tell her what to do and how to live her life.

While this might seem extreme, many of us look to astrologers, psychics, and "intuitives" to tell us if and when we will finally find love, as though they know more than we do. I had a student once who went to her psychic right before she began doing the *Calling in "The One"* process, desperate for reassurance that the program would work. He shook his head sadly while delivering the unhappy news that love was not in the cards for her in this lifetime. To her credit, she decided to do *Calling in "The One"* anyway, finding a way to hold possibility for herself in spite of her poor reading from this man. A few weeks into the process, she called him on another matter. When he went into a trance to provide her reading, he gasped. He said, "What did you just do? Your whole future has changed! Let me tell you about your husband." And indeed she did meet her husband within weeks of that reading. While I honor those who are gifted with these capacities and will often consult "intuitives" myself, don't ever give your power away to others to determine what life has in store for you. Don't forget that there is no fixed future, and people can only read what is already in your field.

While we often want concrete answers to questions like: When will I meet them, how will I meet them, where will I meet them—I will warn you that for the most part, your own inner guidance will be much more interested in helping you become who you'll need to be in order to be ready when love appears. Inner guidance is rarely concerned with specific bits and pieces of information, like a newspaper horoscope is apt to be. Although you might be tempted to call your psychic to desperately ask, *"But when will they call?"* your own inner guidance might lead you, instead, to release the panic and despair you feel over them not calling. It might invite you to let go of your attachment to them calling at all, thereby helping you to love and respect yourself more. This, in turn, eventually attracts more love and respect from others—but not necessarily from *that person.* And that has to be okay. Surrender is the beginning of wisdom.

Asking for inner guidance is asking for wisdom over knowledge. Whereas knowledge is generally concerned with separate and fragmented pieces of data, wisdom is apt to address the deeper integral meanings of our challenges. Its goals are not necessarily to get us what we think we want, as much as they are to cultivate and encourage our spiritual and emotional growth. When it comes to discerning which path is the "right" path to take, we let go of trying to control the answers that come to us. We don't try to force things to go the way we think they should. We give up trying to fit square pegs into round holes. Instead, we yield ourselves, trusting that, even if we do not like what we hear, we are safe to surrender to the larger context of our lives, trusting ultimately that all is well. Herein lies inner peace.

Wisdom is helpful in making the choice of who to open our hearts to and who to be cautious with. Wisdom helps us assess our own readiness to enter into an intimate relationship. Wisdom can instruct us on what needs to happen in order to experience greater intimacy and love with another person. Wisdom empowers us with a sense of how we might want to handle a difficult and potentially precarious situation in a way that has the potential to bless all involved.

> You know more than you think you do.
>
> —Dr. Benjamin Spock

How, then, do we access our intuition? How do we distinguish the voice of inner guidance from the voice of imagination or, worse yet, the internalized voice of the critical parent? How do we know that we are not simply making up an inner dialogue where we are imagining what our parents might say if we were to speak with them? These are the concerns I frequently hear from those who have not yet made this simple practice a daily ritual.

When I first began cultivating my ability to use intuition to guide my life, I wrote letters to Life (or the Universe) every morning. I asked Life (whom I call "God") about everything that concerned me. I'd write out all of the feelings I was having and then ask very specific questions about the situations I was in. No question was too small or insignificant. I asked about the relationships I was in, the work I was doing, the money I did or didn't have, and the plans I was making. I even asked questions about the food I was eating. I would always end my letters with the words "Dear God, please write through my pen. Thank you very much." Then I wrote a "Dear Katherine" letter back to myself. Before putting the words on the paper, I'd adjust myself to listen for them from within. Sometimes the words came quickly, sometimes slowly, but always they came. A whole new outlook, often one I'd never considered before, began flowing effortlessly through my pen. A depth of wisdom that I had rarely displayed in my life before began to show up. More important, perhaps, is that I actually began to act upon this new guidance that I was receiving.

After writing letters to God as a daily practice for about a year and a half, I began to get the guidance as soon as I asked the question in my mind. Eventually, I gave up writing the letters on a daily basis because I no longer needed to. I could hear the guidance immediately simply by asking a question within myself, then listening for the answer. For me, it has become a way of living that diminishes drama and disappointment and greatly enhances love and abundance.

In his book *Conversations with God, Book 1,* Neale Donald Walsch describes this process when he writes, as though God were speaking:

So go ahead now. Ask me anything. Anything. I will contrive to bring you the answer. The whole universe I will use to do this. So be on the lookout . . . The words to the next song you hear. The information in the next article you read. The story line of the next movie you watch. The chance utterance of the next

person you meet. Or the whisper of the next river, the next ocean, the next breeze
that caresses your ear—all these devices are Mine; all these avenues are open to
Me. I will speak to you if you will listen. I will come to you if you will invite Me.
I will show you then that I have always been there. All ways.

Several years ago, a group gathered in person for a three-day *Calling in "The One"* Breakthrough Intensive workshop. We had just finished an exercise where I invited people to write letters to God, then answer these letters by writing, as God, to themselves. It was a beautiful summer day and we were scattered on the lawn of a large Victorian house that serves as a Zen center in the heart of Los Angeles. Suddenly, two butterflies with magnificent bright yellow and black markings landed on the grass before one of the participants. Amazingly, the two insects were interlocked with each other as they proceeded to mate right in front of her. The woman was startled as she stared at the butterflies, who seemed unconcerned with her presence. The rest of the group began to draw themselves in a circle around the two butterflies, staring in wonder as they continued on together, seemingly unperturbed by the voyeuristic activity surrounding them. For a full ten minutes, we stood silently in a circle surrounding the butterflies, watching in awe. Finally, we left them and gathered again inside to share the meaning of this experience with one another. One of the participants reminded us that, in Native American teachings, butterflies represent transformation. We all agreed that the butterflies were a confirmation and a validation of the work that we had gathered to do that weekend and the experience was one of comfort and encouragement to all of us—like a kiss from God for all of our efforts.

Yoga teacher Erich Schiffmann says, "The moment you know that you do not know is the moment you open yourself to true knowing." Seeking guidance begins with an admission that you may not know the best course of action to take or the wisest decision to make. We then turn our attention within, ask a question, and listen. Be watchful. Guidance comes in many forms: creative ideas, insights, hunches, intuitive knowingness, premonitions, understandings, and even synchronistic occurrences. When it comes to calling in "The One," I encourage you to begin relying more and more upon the inherent wealth of information that lies within you, just for the asking.

PRACTICE: WRITING A LETTER TO LIFE

Today, I invite you to access a higher level of your own awareness through writing your own letter to God, whoever God is for you. You may wish to address this letter to "Life," "Universe," "God," "Higher Power," or "Higher Self." If you prefer, you can simply write a "Dear Wisdom" letter.

In your letter, write about the situations in your life that are difficult and challenging for you. Start by sorting through some of the feelings you are having and then move into specific questions that you have.

End your letter with the following sentence: "Dear Life/Universe/God, please write through my pen. Thank you very much." Then write a letter back to yourself from Life/Universe/God.

NOTE: The point of the exercise is not to get caught up in a debate over whether or not God exists, what you call God, or what your relationship is to a Higher Power. The point is to access a level of consciousness that is beyond our everyday, normal awareness. If the idea of writing a letter to God is difficult for you, try doing it simply as an exercise without getting too significant about it.

Bonus: Practice in Action

Throughout the day, practice going within and asking for guidance. Practice with the seemingly small decisions, such as what to wear or how to prioritize your tasks. This will allow you to get comfortable with the process so that when the big choices need to be made, such as whom to open your heart to or whom to begin a sexual relationship with, you are already familiar with how to ask, listen, and act upon inner urgings. You will be much more able to trust your intuition if you are in the practice of using it frequently.

As you move through your day, remember to turn your attention within and ask: What is the best choice I can make in this moment for myself and all involved?

Then trust what comes to you enough to act upon it. Do what you are guided to do, whether it is through a strong inner prompting, a creative idea, a sudden insight, or an actual external sign.

Establishing Personal Integrity

A double-minded man is unstable in all his ways.

—James 1:8

W hen we think of those who advocate for the cultivation of personal integrity, we often think of morally superior, holier-than-thou promoters of a particular religious ideology or philosophy. Most of us have at least one horror story to tell of someone who has taken a kind of perverse pleasure in pointing out our inconsistencies and faults. So it's not hard to see why we don't usually like being asked to examine our integrity. We think that it has something to do with judging and assessing our conduct according to the rules and tenets of others. So I want to make it clear that, when we explore this topic, we are not doing so from a moral point of view, but from the perspective of your personal power.

> Integrity is doing the right thing, even when you know that no one will ever find out.
>
> —C.S. Lewis

Roget's Thesaurus defines "integrity" as "the state of being entirely whole." Integrity is not as concerned with absolute truths (e.g., Murder is wrong), as it is with relative truths (e.g., If I say I'm a loving person, then I'm responsible for behaving in loving ways, both to myself and to others). A lack of integrity does not imply that one is a "bad" person. A lack of integrity simply suggests that one is being an inconsistent person—and an inconsistent person is a disempowered person, who is likely disempowering others as well. Whenever there is a contradiction within the self—a lack of wholeness and congruence—there is fragmentation and its resulting sense of angst. And when this happens, all sorts of symptoms appear that one might not, at first glance, necessarily attribute to a lack of personal integrity.

I once had a client, Manuel, who told me for two years that he was going to write a book. He felt that writing this book was directly connected to his life purpose and that once he wrote it, he would be given opportunities to speak and teach that he would not be given otherwise. When Manuel put his weekly sessions on hold, he told me that he was going to travel and write his book.

I did not hear from Manuel for an entire year. One day he called me and said that he was suffering from terrible anxiety and depression and that he must see me right away. It did not take long before I discovered that, although Manuel had done some traveling, he had not even begun to write his book. He thought about this book every day and every night and yet he filled his days with busywork and never seemed to "have the time" to sit down and begin it. I pointed out to Manuel that he was out of integrity with himself. I reminded him of the importance of writing this book in his life. We came up with a plan that had Manuel setting aside two hours every day to work on his book. Three days later, Manuel called to tell me that the anxiety and the depression lifted the moment he sat down to write. He had been feeling completely at peace for the past three days.

When you do not keep your word to yourself by taking actions you know deep down that you need to be taking, or when you are taking actions that are in conflict with your values or the future you're standing for, you will likely feel a tremendous drain of your personal sense of power. Smoking is a good example of this. Even though they may not even have said they would quit, usually people are at odds with themselves for continuing to engage in an addiction they know is doing them harm. There's an inconsistency between their commitment and their behavior and, therefore, they are in a weakened state.

Nadia, a thirty-one-year-old corporate middle-management executive, was longing to get married and

> Don't look for your dreams to come true; look to become true to your dreams.
>
> —Rev. Michael Beckwith

start a family. She knew in her heart that the younger man she was having sex with each weekend was nowhere near ready for a commitment. That was fine with her, she told me, because he wasn't someone that she would consider committing herself to anyway. He was "too immature, too selfish, and not successful enough." She rationalized their affair by saying that she was "just having some fun." However, when he didn't call one weekend, she became distraught. Her despondence was made worse by the humiliation she felt over her attachment to someone who clearly was "not good enough" for her. Nadia had been lying to herself about her capacity to separate her heart from her sexual behavior. She had to admit that, somewhere deep inside, she'd been holding on to a fantasy that he "would grow up and become the man she needed." Instead, he became another notch in the belt of her long list of failed and disappointing relationships. This, in turn, fed into her desperation and willingness to compromise.

When we lie to ourselves to justify behavior that is self-defeating, we become fragmented and discordant within. It's what we mean when we say that someone is "lost." They've lost the congruence of themselves from which to operate. This inharmonious relationship with the self is a breeding ground for addictions and all sorts of destructive, self-sabotaging behavior. The bottom line is this: When you are out of integrity with the future you say that you're committed to creating, you become a dumbed-down, diminished version of yourself. And that's no place to be standing when calling in the great love of your life.

Getting back into integrity with yourself and others is not too difficult. Mostly, it's about cleaning up the messes you've made and re-creating your life to be consistent with your word. In Nadia's case, she acknowledges that the future she's committed to is to create a loving family. While she sadly realizes that she cannot make this younger man love her and become the partner she needs in her life, she understands that she can always bring the love that is missing to any and all situations. Because she is committed to creating a life of love, she owns love as her North Star. Not

> Unfortunately, people almost universally justify or rationalize the mess in their lives resulting from their personal out-of-integrity behavior. They point to external causes of the mess . . . and never acknowledge that the mess arises from their own personal out-of-integrity behavior.
>
> —Michael Jensen

as something to get, but rather, as is consistent with what love is, something to give. She then gives love to herself by deciding to be rigorously honest with herself about her feelings, and to honor her sexuality as something that is sacred and not to be thrown about lightly. She then extends love to her young lover by releasing him fully to go his way, and live the life he needs to live. In her heart, she blesses his life and sets him free. She is complete; her integrity, restored. She is now living in a way that is consistent with her word.

> Personal integrity is one of the most important guardians of mental health. Put simply, integrity is the absence of contradiction between what we know, what we profess and what we do.
>
> —Nathaniel Branden

One of the biggest reasons we fail to honor our word is a resistance to owning our power fully. It's sometimes harder for us to own our power, strengths, and abilities than it is to admit our flaws and failures. As a matter of fact, we'll sometimes even bond with others over our mutual inadequacies and unhealed wounds. Rather than rise to the heights of our human capacity to cause a future that's not going to happen unless we stand for it, we'll instead define being human as a weakness. As in, "But, gee, I'm only human." Yet bartering away your power to avoid being responsible for your life is way too high a price to pay.

When you take a stand, then begin living in integrity with that possible future, watch out. The power your integrity will begin to unleash may be unprecedented in your life. All manner of miracles will suddenly start to occur. Synchronicities transpire, obstacles dissolve, and chance meetings magically happen. Trees blossom, flowers bloom, and hummingbirds begin dancing around your head. In other words, fasten your seatbelt. You're in for a ride.

Werner Erhard once called integrity "a mountain with no top." Meaning that we are always challenged to clean up the inconsistencies between who we say we are and how we are showing up. It is the daily practice of taking personal inventory and making constant self-corrections—righting our wrongs, telling our truth, making amends to clean up messes made, and bringing closure to that which is no longer appropriate. This daily practice of discovering and strengthening one's personal integrity encourages us to examine our cross-agendas

> It is the penalty of a liar, that should he even tell the truth, he is not listened to.
>
> —The Talmud

> And I know when I'm on track—that is, when everything is in a harmonious relationship to what I regard as the best I've got in me.
>
> —Joseph Campbell

and inconsistencies, like when we say we want love but behave in unloving ways toward ourselves and others, or claim to be ready for a mate while, at the same time, cling to self-protective and defensive ways of being. As a rudder steers a sailboat—never quite on target, but in a constant state of correction and adjustment—so we too continually engage the process of looking for where we are out of alignment so that we can restore our inner congruence, and therefore our power to create the miracle we are standing for.

PRACTICE: RESTORING YOUR INTEGRITY

Take out your journal and write on the following questions:

- What promises have I made to myself that I'm not keeping?
  (For example, I'm not showing up for my exercise regimen.)

- How can I clean this up and get back into integrity with my word?
  (For example, I can go for a walk today and schedule walk time each day this week.)

- What promises have I made to others that I'm not keeping?
  (For example, I promised my son's teacher I'd donate school supplies, yet never followed through.)

- How can I clean this up and get back into integrity with my word?
  (For example, I can call her to apologize for disappearing, and clarify what I can and cannot provide.)

- Where am I living out of alignment with my own values?
  (For example, I value forgiveness yet I'm indulging a resentment toward my sister and withholding my love by refusing to call her back.)

- How can I clean this up and get into integrity with myself?

  (For example, I can call my sister and engage my upset in an adult and self-responsible way.)

- Who else do I have unfinished business with that needs cleaning up?

  (For example, I never paid my last boyfriend back for the money he lent me.)

- How can I clean this up and get back into integrity with others?

  (For example, I can ask him to make payment arrangements until the loan is paid in full.)

- How could I begin showing up in ways that are in integrity with the future I'm committed to creating?

  (For example, I can start doing this course with more consistency and a greater sense of commitment.)

> *Few have the strength*
> *To be a real Hero.*
> *That rare man or woman*
> *Who always keeps their word.*
> *Even an angel needs rest.*
> *Integrity creates a body so vast*
> *A thousand winged ones will plead,*
> *"May I lay my cheek*
> *Against you?"*

—Hafiz, translated by Daniel Ladinsky

Now go back and review your list. Write a list of actions to take to restore your integrity with yourself and others.

Bonus: Practice in Action

Take at least one action today that restores integrity to your life. As you move through the course, continue monitoring where you are out of integrity and, without beating yourself up, simply do your best to clean it up and get back into integrity. Remember to take personal inventory on a regular basis to keep yourself light and clear. When your baggage in life is light, there is more room for love.

Practicing Prayer and Meditation

If I do not go within, I go without.

—Neale Donald Walsch

Most of us have very specific expectations about how we think our lives should go. The age by which we should be married, or how much money we're supposed to be making by now. We anticipate living long lives in relatively good health. We'll offer prayers of gratitude when things go our way, and prayers of petition for the things we *want* to go our way. Usually, along with those prayers is an attachment to what the answers should be. Then, if and when things don't go the way we think they should—we're still single on our thirty-fifth birthday, we don't get the promotion we were counting on, we lose money in the stock market, or go through the depressing experience of having a friend or loved one come down with cancer—we can get pretty cynical and resigned.

When I graduated from high school, rather than go to a regular university, I decided to attend Bible college instead. I never quite made it through the whole program and will often jokingly refer to myself as a Bible school dropout. Yet at the time, I very much wanted my life to be used as a force for healing and love in the world and it made sense to me to become a missionary. I wanted to help and serve people more than anything. So, for many months, I spent several hours a day in prayer and meditative contemplation asking God to use me for this purpose. Not long after I began this practice, everything in my life began to fall apart. The

> Anything you do
> has a still point.
> When you are in
> that still point,
> you can perform
> maximally.
>
> —Joseph Campbell

boy I'd dated all through high school broke my heart by marrying someone else, my best friend turned her back on me and took most of our mutual friends with her, and my parents completely stopped talking to me because I refused to go to a "normal" college like everyone else. As a result, the eating disorder that started when I was fourteen turned into a full-blown, raging addiction and I gained fifty pounds. For the next two years, I was extremely isolated and alone. Everything and everyone I thought I could count on had simply disappeared. I was terribly lonely. I was making minimum wage working at a daycare center and couldn't make ends meet. When I needed a root canal, I didn't have the $250 that the dentist charged, and so instead, I paid $30 for him to pull the tooth out just to be rid of the pain. To add insult to injury, the dentist tried to molest me as I sat drugged in his chair. I felt completely abandoned by God. Here I was, dedicating my life to serving Him, and everything that could go wrong did. I became so angry that I dropped out of Bible college and refused to pray at all for several years. I simply would not talk to a God who could betray me so completely.

A few years later, upon entering the twelve-step program Overeaters Anonymous to help me recover from my eating disorder, I was encouraged to begin using prayer and meditation as an important part of the program. As arrogant as it sounds, I had to actually "forgive" God before I was able to pick up these practices again. Little by little, I had to grapple with accepting the disappointments I had endured. In order to reengage a discourse with the Divine, which is basically what prayer is, I had to allow the tears to flow, and be brutally honest. Of all the prayer books I had contemplated, and all the sermons I had sat through over the years, none had prepared me to pray the prayers that I desperately needed to pray. "God: I don't even want to talk to You. I am so angry and disgusted with You. How *dare* You do that to me? I hate You. No, better than that. I don't even believe in You anymore. Even if You *were* real, I wouldn't want to know You." It wasn't pretty and it certainly wasn't "nice." But it was authentic. And because it was authentic, it was healing. My heart began to thaw, eventually freeing it again to love and be loved. Even though I pined for love, until I told the truth to myself and to God, I really had no room within myself to experience it.

Sometimes life is filled with such profound disappointment that we steel ourselves against it, just to make it through the day. We resist going into stillness because we can't bear to be face-to-face with the screaming in our psyches and the sadness in our hearts. We dread the possibility of being swallowed up by grief, fearing that, once we allow ourselves to start crying, we may never stop. Sometimes life can be like this. In response, many of us simply stop praying. We go on strike. We won't talk to a God who can appear to be so cold and indifferent. We desperately try to divert our attention away from inside ourselves. We turn on the television the moment we get home, and surround ourselves with demands and dramas designed to keep us as far away from our feelings as possible. Yet, what hope do we have for a loving, intimate partnership when we go to such lengths to avoid being intimate with ourselves? What hope do we have to trust another human being when we allow ourselves to become so mistrustful of God, however one defines God?

> To stay present in everyday life, it helps to be deeply rooted within yourself; otherwise, the mind, which has incredible momentum, will drag you along like a wild river.
>
> —Eckhart Tolle

I didn't fully comprehend the meaning of those years of heartache and loss until many years later, when I was in my mid-thirties. At the time, I was volunteering on Skid Row, facilitating songwriting workshops with men and women who'd been homeless and out on the streets. I had no formal training yet to become a therapist and was relying solely on my intuition to design the curriculum of the workshops. Sitting with a group of about twenty people who were all in recovery from various addictions or self-destructive behaviors, facilitating a process I'd created that was designed to help people heal from the most devastating of circumstances, I began to notice that I had a profound gift. As one miracle of healing after another began to happen, I saw that I had transmission of sorts. It was then that I understood. It wasn't that God had disregarded my prayers way back when I was nineteen, as I so fervently believed for so many years. On the contrary, He had answered them. I hadn't been abandoned at all. In that moment, I had an epiphany and realized that by entering a period of profound darkness, loss, suffering, and heartbreak, I learned what I would never have discovered at Bible school. How to build yourself back up, from the inside out, one step at a time, after suffering the most devastating of disappointments. How to let a broken heart catapult you into being a more kindhearted, compassionate person. How to forgive others after they'd done desperately hurtful things. And now here I was, helping others do the same as though it were as natural as breathing. I realized in that moment that it was precisely what I had asked God for all those years before, and I felt both deeply grateful and terribly ashamed that I had doubted so deeply.

Ralph Waldo Emerson once said that prayer was "the contemplation of life from the highest point of view." I've discovered that my students who pray for help and guidance tend to make much better progress than those who don't. It seems to allow them to view themselves and their challenges inside of a larger context. They feel less overwhelmed by their problems and more hopeful about possible solutions. Even those who do not necessarily consider themselves to be religious or "spiritual" will advance much more quickly once they begin to pray. I don't pretend to fully understand this phenomenon and yet, truthfully, I don't really need to. There's graciousness in simply receiving the gifts when they come and remembering to say thank you.

> *Cease looking for flowers!*
> *There blooms a garden in your own home.*
> *While you look for trinkets*
> *The treasure house awaits you in your own being.*
>
> —Rumi

I do have a theory, however, on just how and why prayer and meditation can have this profound effect upon our lives. Prayer and meditation connect us with what I'll call a "parallel reality" to the reality we are currently experiencing. It is as though we tune in to another frequency and can see what's happening in our lives from a completely different perspective. From our ordinary conscious mind, it might look like love is completely missing. Yet when we tune in to the situation in prayer and meditation, we suddenly see it as an opportunity to give love, or we remember a previously unnoticed act of kindness and compassion. So often, it isn't that love is missing in our lives as much as we missed it when it was there. Prayer and meditation plug us into the source of love and, therefore, render us much more conscious and aware of its constant presence.

Years ago, I saw the film *Fierce Grace*, a documentary about the late spiritual teacher Ram Dass. More specifically, the film was about Ram Dass's recovery from a stroke. In it, several people were interviewed about what it was like to be in the presence of Neem Karoli Baba, who most of us know as Maharajji, and who was Ram Dass's guru in India during the 1960s. It struck me that each one interviewed had had a similar experience of feeling a profound sense of love for themselves and others when they were with Maharajji. Without taking any of the psychedelic drugs that they'd been using before they met him, they were able to access a state of absolute affinity with everyone and everything, simply by being in the same room with him. So, for them, the experience wasn't so much that the Maharajji was extraordinary, as it was that they themselves were extraordinary when in his presence.

This experience of absolute love, peace, and affinity is what we are ultimately seeking to connect with when we pray and meditate. When we seek to commune with God, we do so not simply to be obedient to the dictates of religious doctrine. Rather, we do so in the hopes that we will be altered by the experience. That we will see our lives through a new, more optimistic lens, and be empowered to navigate life with a greater sense of hope and possibility. Many make this daily effort personally in service to the larger vision of our collective awakening. Such are the motivations to dedicate oneself to a daily spiritual practice.

While most of us know that we "should" make the time to pray and meditate, we may not see how it can help us achieve our goal of attracting love, and so we don't make it a top priority. Yet, scientific studies show that the emotional maturity that results from a regular meditation practice can greatly enhance one's ability to create healthy, happy intimate relationships. The ability to remain somewhat centered and balanced in response to a perceived threat (as opposed to becoming reactive and/or explosive), or to maintain a certain degree of calm in the face of disappointment (rather than becoming dramatic and defensive), is the mark of a person who is prepared to create a sustainable, loving, long-term relationship that can deepen over time. Those who know how to avoid becoming combative in reaction

What to do when you first awaken or before drifting off to sleep? Quiet your mind, lift up your heart, muse, mull over, make discoveries. Consider, conceive, create, connect, concede that it all starts within. Pray, read the Scriptures, sacred poetry or a meditation from an inspirational book.

—Sarah Ban Breathnach

to stress make better, more reliable partners than those who don't. It pays for us to actively cultivate these abilities, and one way to do this is through a daily practice of prayer and meditation.

So let's talk about the "how to." No one has the market cornered on the "right" way to pray or the "best" way to meditate, though personally I'm a big fan of Transcendental Meditation, or TM, as it is commonly known. Yet it's all about finding—and then consistently doing—what works for you. Praying—the act of talking to God—is as simple as that. Talk to God. Tell the truth. If you find it easier, write a letter. Sitting or kneeling, eyes open or eyes closed, whatever helps you focus on this discourse, just do it. Meditation, sometimes referred to as "centering," can be thought of as the listening component of this divine dialogue. We still ourselves enough to actually hear what Life is already whispering in the center of our souls. As such, meditation is really the act of becoming fully present, open, and available.

When we cultivate mindful attentiveness to the present moment, our driven need to do, do, do, and assess the value of our lives according to the list of our accomplishments diminishes. When we allow ourselves the space just to *be* (as in human *beings* rather than human *doings*), we reaffirm the unconditional value of our lives. We relax our racing minds, and slow down enough to become present and available to our hearts and our bodies. We decelerate the mental activity that so often usurps our intuition and our deeper feelings. We are less vulnerable to make our choices from the rantings and ravings of the "should" mind, and become more empowered to make choices from the totality of who and what we are.

When we talk of meditation, most of us think of the traditional methods of sitting still while observing and releasing our thoughts, and/or focusing on the breath in some way. However, there are many ways to come home to the center of ourselves. We can close our eyes and silently recite a mantra. We can rock ourselves gently to the rhythm of a Buddhist chant. We can take a mindful walk alone on the beach. We can put on some music and dance a plea to God, create a prayer in our journal, or speak sacred text out loud. We can paint love on a canvas, breathe in unison with a sleeping child, or sit quietly inside of a great cathedral, temple, or mosque to soak in its beauty and holiness.

Spiritual teacher Eckhart Tolle reminds us that "you 'get' there by realizing that you *are* there already." We must remember that, on some level, we are already profoundly connected to the forces of love. The more we go within to tap into this supply, the more equipped we are to come *from* there in our dealings. We can then actualize lives where love and affinity are as natural and commonplace to us as breathing.

PRACTICE: FOCUSED MEDITATION

Today, I invite you to do a simple meditation. Read the instructions once through and then do the meditation from memory to the best of your ability.

Sit up straight with your legs and arms uncrossed and resting easily. Close your eyes and relax your entire body. Starting at the bottom of your feet and working your way up through the body—your toes, ankles, calves, knees, thighs, etc., until you reach the top of your head—release any tension you find. Breathe in and out normally, without any effort, with your mouth slightly open and at rest. Feel yourself breathing but do not try to regulate your breath in any way.

Now, think of a quality you yearn to embody, such as Self-Forgiveness, Generosity, or Gratitude, and say this word silently to yourself on each inhale, drawing this quality deeply into the center of your heart. On the exhale, release anything that is in the way of being completely immersed in this quality. Stay with this meditation for at least three minutes, or until you feel a sense of peace wash over you.

Bonus: Practice in Action

In the New Testament, the Apostle Paul (after he was converted!) admonished us to "pray without ceasing," indicating that none of our concerns are too foolish or insignificant to bring before God in prayer.

Today, we're going to practice bringing our concerns to a Higher Power by making a "God Box." A God Box is any container—a shoebox, glass jar, wooden container, metal can, or paper bag—anything that you can decorate and put slips of paper in and take them out.

Sometime today, find and decorate a container that you can use as your God Box.

Make a list of those things that you are worried or anxious about today—your relationship to a particular person, your money, your health, your livelihood, etc. You may want to put "finding my life partner" on your list. Take a piece of paper and cut or rip it into smaller pieces. Write down each concern you have on its own slip of paper.

One at a time, place each concern into your God Box while saying a prayer, surrendering that concern to a Higher Power. Your prayer might sound something like this:

> *Dear God, Universe, Higher Power, or Benevolent Field of Life,*
> *I am giving this concern to You for Your keeping.*
> *Please resolve this issue in the best possible way for all involved. Thank you.*

Once you've given your concern to a Higher Power, you no longer have to worry about it. It's now God's (or the Universe's) concern. If you decide that you want to start worrying about that concern again, you literally have to go to the God Box, take out the slip of paper with that particular worry on it, and hold it in your own hands. When you are finished worrying, surrender your concern again by placing the slip of paper back into the God Box and repeating the prayer.

Making Wise Choices

Choice is your greatest power. It is an even greater power than love,
because you must first choose to be a loving person.

—Caroline Myss

Ever since the 1960s, when many of our social conventions were rendered up
for revision and review, we've had fewer absolutes from which to live. Discovering what's right for us, as opposed to what's right, period, has never been
a project of such ambiguous proportions. This is largely because, in all of recorded
human history, we've never dealt with as many moral and ethical uncertainties as
we do today.

Contrary to the way humans have been living for tens of thousands of years,
we of the twenty-first century now make choices about nearly every aspect of our
lives that, just a mere hundred years ago, would have been inconceivable. We can
choose to live the truth of our sexuality—gay, cis or straight, bi, fluid, asexual, or
polysexual (just to name a few)—and the gender we identify with: male, female,
gender neutral, gender fluid, nonbinary, or transgender (and more). We can choose
our religion, our profession, what kind of diet we want to eat, whether or not to have
children, and—of course—who, or even *if*, we wish to marry. Freedom is an awesome responsibility.

So, if you're feeling overwhelmed and confused about the enormous amount of
choice you now face on a daily basis, welcome to the club. We all are. But the one
place our anxiety is most acute is centered on what appears to be the absolute chaos
and total lack of predictability of our modern-day mating rituals. We respond to this
free-for-all with a profound need for someone who can tell us "the rules." We wish

> Think of your life as a canoe and your decisions and actions as your paddle. You'll get where you're going one stroke at a time with the decisions and actions you make.
>
> —D. J. "Eagle Bear" Vanas

that somebody would just explain to us how all of this is supposed to work. We want an expert—some book, talk show, or religious teaching—to provide us with a concrete structure to this madness called dating and mating in the twenty-first century.

Yet one of the realities of our time is that no such scaffolding exists. Not in the Western world, anyway. No absolute, agreed-upon collective "truth" can dictate our choices. Whereas once upon a time, everyone in the community could agree on how courtship was supposed to go, for many of us, that simply is no longer the case. And so, unless you are part of a smaller or more traditional community or culture where the rules of the game are clearly defined, you're pretty much left to your own devices. We must find our own way amid the rubble of our abandoned, ghosted connections, dashed expectations, wounded hearts, and ever-present ticking clocks. (And, yes, men have them, too.) There may be trends and statistical probabilities, but there are few absolutes anymore when it comes to the mating game. And that means that it's essential—*now more than at any other time in the history of humanity*—that we master the art of making good, healthy, discerning, wise choices, based upon an inherent esteem of ourselves and of others. As others are no longer making our choices for us, our destiny is now in our own hands. This is both a wonderful and terrifying charge. When we were in lack and limitation, there was little to choose from. Yet now that we are living in a state of abundant possibilities, life is a constant series of choices. Therefore, one of the goals we aspire to in life is to actually increase the number of choices we are faced with, and to become better and better at making wise ones.

On the most fundamental level, keeping your life free of the messes and entanglements that unwise choices create is actually one of the best things you can do to prepare yourself for love. Melissa, a twentysomething actress, came to me for counseling after a series of failed relationships. Melissa's pattern was to attract women who were unavailable for a long-term commitment. She was getting sick and tired of being sick and tired. She worked hard for many months to uncover some core beliefs that had kept her unconsciously choosing women who were not available for a committed relationship. She found two underlying beliefs that she had been dancing with for years. The first was a covert belief that she was unlovable, an interpretation she made as a four-year-old when her father walked out on her and her mother, without looking back. And the second was a fear that, if she surrendered herself to someone, that person would somehow begin to control and abuse her. This was also a belief that was formed in response to her father, whom she remembered as being excessively dominating

and bossy with both her and her mother. Armed with having made that which was unconscious now conscious, Melissa could challenge the beliefs and connect with the deeper truth of her own worthiness to be loved, and her own power to create safety in her intimate relationships. Having done this, she was hopeful that she would finally be free to attract a loving, committed union.

As is often the case, the first few opportunities for romance that Melissa encountered were with unavailable women. One was an actress who was on her way out of town to do a play in another city, with an anticipated long run. The next was a smart and savvy woman who, it turned out, was still living with her former husband. The third, Alison, was the "woman of Melissa's dreams." She was everything that Melissa had hoped for—charismatic, bright, funny, spiritual, beautiful, and extremely accomplished. Unfortunately, Alison also happened to be in a long-term relationship with another woman, and together they were co-parenting a child. He was only five, and Alison made it clear that they were committed to living as a family unit until he graduated from high school. Talk about a no-win situation. I wish I could tell you that Melissa wasn't tempted, but she was. It was hard for her to turn the first two down and sheer agony to say no to Alison. But, after a few topsy-turvy weeks, she made the difficult decision to avoid an avoidable drama and let Alison go. She did so, even if that meant that she would be alone in life. Two weeks after making this decision, Melissa met her partner, whom she now calls the great love of her life. Looking back, she shudders to think how close she came to missing the opportunity to be with her soul mate, for what would surely have been another heartache and disappointment.

Our fantasy is that, once we see our pattern clearly and make a definite decision to do things differently, our external world will change immediately. In lieu of meeting yet another unavailable person, we will suddenly start meeting only available people. Those ready to make a commitment. Instead of meeting more abusive people, we will suddenly start attracting kind and gentle souls who offer nothing but love and encouragement. This is rarely the case. What's more likely to happen is that, instead of immediately attracting a whole new kind of person into our lives, we find ourselves attracting exactly the same kind of person, or a person who at first appears to be different but isn't really. We're challenged with temptations that are similar to the ones we've faced in the past. Only this time we're wiser. This time we know exactly where a particular path will lead. We must make the more difficult choice by saying no to the enticement of doing the same thing while hoping for different results. We must choose to remain empty-handed rather than settle for repeating past mistakes. This temptation will generally happen not just once, not just twice, but several times. It's as though the Universe is testing us—are you truly finished replicating the familiar? Have you really given up the need to prove that you aren't worthy of love? Are you willing to stand in the void rather than compromise yourself again? These tests come our way whenever we declare we are ready to change. It is as though we are the protagonists of our own mythical tales, challenged to slay our internal dragons by making the right choices, based upon faith, and requiring immense courage. We are all searching for our own holy grail—the promise of falling into a sacred experience of eternal and transcendent love. Yet the Universe can do *for* you only what It can do *through* you. And that means that you are the one who needs to begin making different, and often difficult, choices in the direction of your dreams.

Most of us can point to a series of bad decisions and failed challenges. We suffer with regrets about our past choices, particularly given the severe consequences some of them rendered. *We knew better.* Yet we needn't beat up ourselves about the shoulda, woulda, couldas of our past mistakes. Rather, we need to accept the decisions we've made to date, and come to terms with the lost opportunities and losses we've encountered. When we see our lives as a series of challenges that offer us opportunities for growth, with the goal of growing in wisdom and compassion, then it's easier to accept our past errors of judgment. When we value life from the perspective of what we've learned, then failure is redefined. As there is no greater teacher than a missed opportunity and no

A sacred choice is one that does not seek to compensate for a wound, but to heal it.

—Rick Vassallo

greater lesson than the lesson of love gone awry, then those of us who've failed the most might also be the wisest and most compassionate among us.

Life is not so much about getting what we want when we want it, as it is about appreciating what we have when we have it. It's about learning to make choices that validate the value of the lives we have right now. Every decision we make, even the seemingly small and insignificant ones, have

> Like heroes in a mythic journey, we are meant to struggle to make the right choices.
>
> —Caroline Myss

weight and authority in the Universe to either create a life that we love, or one that is filled with compromise. Let's learn to value making the "right" choice, not because it's the right choice for others, not because it's the expected choice, the easiest one, or the path of least resistance. No, let's instead learn to value making the right choice because it's the right choice for us. Because it's the choice that is most true to who and what we are. Because it is the choice to live in integrity with our vision. Because we rise to the occasion of loving ourselves absolutely and reflecting this love in all aspects of our lives.

PRACTICE: LEARNING TO MAKE WISE CHOICES

Take out your journal and write on the following questions:

- What choices have I made in life that I regret most and why?
- What lesson(s) did I learn as a result of making these choices?
- What good came from each of these choices?
- What choices have I made based upon the values of others (parents, friends, advisers, teachers, etc.) rather than upon my own values?
- What were the consequences of these choices?
- What lesson(s) did I learn as a result of making these choices?
- What choices do I feel happy about and why?
- What lesson(s) did I learn as a result of making these choices?
- What good came from each of these choices?

- What choices am I facing today and how might I respond in ways that show honor and respect for myself and others?

Bonus: Practice in Action

As you move through your day, notice what you do each time you are faced with a choice. Do you look to others to try to second-guess what choice would please them, automatically responding the way you think you are "expected" to, or rise to the occasion of asserting what truly is best for you and others in any given situation? Wherever you find yourself automatically trying to please others at your own expense, or making a poor choice simply out of habit, try making a different choice than the one you feel compelled to make. For example, if your boss always expects you to work late at the last minute, try telling her that you aren't available to do so tonight; or if you are shy and normally avoid the limelight, try taking a risk to share your feelings with a group of people.

Before bed, take out your journal and write down the different choice(s) that you made today and what it was like for you to make them. Write also about any insights you had regarding your relationship to making wise choices.

Suggested Study Guide for Group Discussion

1. Share your vision of love fulfilled in your life. What would you have to give up or embody to manifest this vision?

2. Again, share your intention with the group. What actions have you taken or will you take, if any, to generate the fulfillment of your intention?

3. Share about your sense of purpose. What are you passionate about and what outlets do you have to express your passion in the world?

4. What is your experience of going within for guidance? What guidance, if any, did you receive this week?

5. Where has your integrity been out of balance and what have you done recently to clean it up?

6. What choice did you make in the past that you regret, and what valuable lesson came from that experience? What choice(s) are you facing today and how might you make a decision that is in alignment with your intention?

First Things First

The truth about intimate relationships is that they
can never be any better than our relationship with ourselves.

—James Hollis

W e've all heard it said countless times. "You have to love yourself before you can love another." But what does it mean to love ourselves? And how exactly can we do it?

This week, we will:

- Address the need to first make a commitment to yourself as the foundation for receiving a loving commitment from another
- Cultivate greater emotional intimacy with yourself to increase your capacity for emotional intimacy with another
- Grow your ability to give yourself the care you're needing as your foundation for giving to others
- Learn to tend to the part of you that gets triggered when disappointed or scared, and discover how to mentor yourself back to a more balanced center of health and wholeness within
- Mend your relationship with your body, and reclaim sexual wholeness to prepare for a union that will likely be physical
- Deepen your capacity for solitude, as preparation for the healthy autonomy required of all good relationships

Making Commitments

If I love myself I love you.
If I love you I love myself.

—Rumi

Thirty-nine-year-old Shandra had never been in a committed relationship. Although she complained that she always seemed to meet unavailable men, she eventually admitted that she was the one who was ultimately unavailable. Once she took responsibility for her reluctance to surrender herself fully to another person, Shandra met Anthony, a forty-nine-year-old widower who appeared to be looking for his new life partner. After several months of seeing each other, Shandra leaned in over dinner one night, took a deep breath, and asked Anthony if he would consider dating her exclusively. She admitted that she felt ready to commit to one person, and she was hoping that person would be him. Anthony paused for a long while before confessing that he didn't see a future for them. While he had grown to care about her and hoped that they would always be friends, he just didn't feel that she was the right life partner for him. For a few minutes Shandra felt hurt and rejected. But then she looked up and smiled. "I've just had a breakthrough," she said. "That's the first time I've ever been willing to commit myself to anyone. I'm disappointed that you said no but I'm damned proud of myself for asking." They laughed together and toasted to a new Shandra. Within the year, Shandra was happily, joyfully engaged to another man, and Anthony remains a good friend to this day.

Some of us have an almost paralyzing fear of making commitments. We're terrified of narrowing our options inside of an assumption that doing so will prevent us from realizing our own potentials in life. We're afraid of being swallowed up

> We know what happens
> to people who stay in
> the middle of the road.
> They get run down.
>
> —Aneurin Bevan

by the needs of another, assuming that ours will get marginalized in the process. We don't trust ourselves to set boundaries to keep ourselves and the other person safe if we get in too deep. We're convinced that someone will leave us as soon as we let them in fully. It's called being "love-avoidant," which is not an indication that you don't want a loving relationship. Only that you assume that having one would be dangerous. How would you know if you're one of these "commitment-phobic," love-avoidant people? Well, if you find yourself always entangled with unavailable people, as Shandra did, then that's probably a good clue. Rather than respond to these fears by deciding to grow ourselves healthy enough to set boundaries, tolerate disappointing others, or negotiate for our needs, we settle instead for the dramas and distractions inherent in a commitment-free life. Rather than learn how we could hold on to our own wholeness and autonomy when in a committed relationship, we either run as fast as we can, or we continually undermine the connection to destabilize it and prevent it from going to the next level. Yet in doing so, we land nowhere and belong to no one.

Our commitments are that which we organize our lives around. They are the sun we orbit around, and they feed us the ability to root down, and create lives of purpose and devotion. In order to create a life that is worth living, we must risk standing for someone, or for something, beyond ourselves and each passing emotion. I once knew a single man nearing forty who had a hard time making any commitments at all. Even arriving for our meetings on time was burdensome for him. He was completely engaged in whatever emotion he happened to be feeling at the moment, and any infringement on his ability to explore and express that emotion fully, disturbed him deeply. From a distance, his life seemed adventurous and even romantic. In reality, he was the prisoner of his emotions, tossed to and fro and unable to build any lasting or meaningful connections. Underneath his adventurous spirit, he was lonely to the core. He lived with the sadness that comes from continually disappointing those who wanted to love him. And he was confused much of the time because he had no center, no commitments from which to ground his life.

If you don't yet have your primary partner in your life, then give yourself to an ideal, a path, a cause, or a community. Many single people are in a lot of pain because they have no one to care about deeply and nothing to surrender themselves to fully. But there are millions in the world who need our care every day—animals, orphans, the elderly, or those disadvantaged in some way, who are withering away for lack of love and belonging. We can't be so selective, and still thrive in life. We can't say, "I'm just going to withhold all the love I have to give, until that one specific person that I deem worthy comes along," and think that life will feel worth living. That kind of stinginess will shrink up your heart, and hollow out your soul, and you might think it's simply because you don't have a lover.

Our ability to commit to others is, of course, predicated upon our ability to commit to our own lives. Without a fundamental pledge to our own health and happiness in life, we are limited in what we actually have to offer others. I remember the moment my entire life transformed. I was in my mid-twenties and living in a tiny eleven-by-eighteen-foot studio apartment in the Meatpacking District of New York City, years before it was a cool place to be. I was struggling terribly with an eating disorder I'd had since the age of fourteen, trying desperately to heal myself, but with little success. Week after week, month after month, I struggled to string together a few days of abstinence from compulsive overeating. As I stood discouraged at the corner the morning after yet another night of binge-eating, waiting for the light to change (what a great metaphor), I was having a silent dialogue with myself. I was trying to figure out what was missing in my attempts to stop hurting myself by my self-sabotaging behaviors. Tears began rolling down my cheeks as I realized that no one had ever fought for me in the way that I now needed to fight for myself. No one had ever gone to the wall to ensure my safety and well-being. No one had ever risen to heroic heights in order to make sure that I had a chance to thrive in life. Not my mother. Not my father. No one. In that moment, I made a commitment to me. I took a stand for my life. I would fight for me. I would go to the wall for me. I would be my own heroine. I would do whatever it took to get well so that I could be happy in life. And in that moment, the light turned green.

I have seen it demonstrated time and time again, first in my own life and then in the lives of others—that everything of substance you will ever have to offer to anyone in this lifetime begins with a commitment that you make to yourself. There's simply no skipping this step, particularly for those of us who had less than ideal parenting, in which the ability of our caregivers to give us what we needed was limited. Because I'd never experienced anyone being as committed to me as I now needed to be to myself, I was at a loss as to how to begin. I learned the value of putting one foot in front of the other in the direction of health, healing, and wholeness, one day at a time. I discovered that true self-love is not an emotion, but a steadfast devotion to realizing one's potentials. A fidelity to the promise of a bright and brilliant future that looks nothing like the wreckage of your past, and a willingness to generate this possibility, over and over again, no matter what. It's dedication to becoming resilient and unstoppable in the direction of your dreams. It's the tireless efforts to create a sense of safety, well-being, and happiness in your life. In other words, it's everything one might ever hope to receive from a soul mate who'd do anything and everything to make sure your life is beautiful.

And so, I learned what committed love with a partner might look like, by first committing to myself. Because in the context of lifelong partnership, love is not an emotion. Love is a course. An utterly steadfast, stable path that deviates not in the face of hardship or challenge. While we may look for a soul mate who is sexually attractive, makes us laugh, and makes as much money as or more than we do, these things are not the substance of true love. All of our criteria for a partner—they have to look this way, have that kind of job, dress like this, be hip, as well as fit—are all the superficial things that will disappear with time. All that will last is the devotion both given and received. True love transcends our ridiculously limited views of love, which have little to do with the most important aspects of love. Like loyalty, sacrifice, care, and devotion.

Commitment is the matter from which miracles are made. Many of us want proof that something is going to work out the way we want it to before we make a commitment to it. We want to know it's a sure bet, a good and solid place to invest our energies. Although this is understandable, there's a certain magic and synchronicity that reserves itself for when one makes a wholehearted investment of oneself that simply cannot be foreseen. The most miraculous of occurrences can come from a stand taken by someone in a moment of truth. It is equally as true that the most promising of possibilities can easily slip through our fingers simply because we were too cautious to commit fully to their fulfillment. This phenomenon is what German poet Goethe was addressing when he so accurately wrote:

> The more one forgets himself—by giving himself to a cause to serve or another person to love—the more human he is and the more he actualizes himself.
>
> —Viktor E. Frankl

Concerning all acts of initiative (and creation), there is one elementary truth, the ignorance of which kills countless ideas and splendid plans: that the moment one definitely commits oneself, then Providence moves too. All sorts of things occur to help one that would never otherwise have occurred. A whole stream of events issues from the decision, raising in one's favor all manner of unforeseen incidents and meetings and material assistance, which no man could have dreamed would have come his way.

PRACTICE: COMMITMENT CEREMONY

In service to supporting you to manifest a partner who is deeply committed to your well-being and happiness in life, I invite you to begin by making a commitment to yourself. The commitment I invite you to make to yourself—to cherish, love, and honor yourself, to grow in the direction of your dreams, to show up in the fullness of your power, to live in integrity with your own potentials—may be bigger than anyone has ever made to you before. If so, you are long overdue to make this pledge to yourself.

Read through the following instructions two or three times before doing it from memory.

Still Yourself. Close your eyes and take a deep breath, as though you could breathe all the way down into your hips.

Call in the Partner of Your Future. Imagine that the energy of your beloved partner-to-be is entering into your space right now. Step into the day of your commitment ceremony, whether that be a public wedding, an unofficial ceremony with your friends or family, or a private, sacred moment between just the two of you. Sense the sacredness of the day and the beauty of this moment. Without seeing what this person looks like, or what they're wearing, just feel into the field that's between you. Allow your heart to open and feel a river of love coming toward you.

Imagine Your Partner Committing to You and Your Relationship.
Now imagine your partner looking into your eyes, and speaking from their heart. Lean in to hear what they're saying: "I offer you my loyalty and my love. I pledge to do all I can to care for you, to protect you, and to keep you safe. I promise to do my very best to make you happy in life. I devote myself to supporting the fulfillment of your dreams and desires." As you imagine your partner saying this to you, listen. Breathe in their love, and open your heart fully to receive all they are offering.

Make These Same Pledges to Yourself. Now bring your attention home to yourself. Speak your own name, and make the same pledges to yourself that your beloved partner has just uttered to you. If you like, you can place your hand over your heart as, one by one, you say these things to yourself. They don't need to be exact. Just do the best you can to extend to yourself the same loving promises you just imagined your partner offering to you. "I offer you my loyalty and my love. I promise to do all I can to care for you, to protect you, and to keep you safe. I promise to do my very best to make you happy in life. I devote myself to supporting your dreams and desires." As you speak to yourself, do so with an open heart.

When you are finished, open your eyes and write your commitments to yourself down in your journal.

Bonus: Practice in Action

To live this lesson, I invite you to do one, two, or all three of the following:

Take at least one action today that demonstrates your commitment to yourself in action. Take a risk in the direction of your dreams, or let go of something you know isn't good for you.

Take an action today that demonstrates a commitment to others. For example, give $5 to a charity of your choice, or call your elderly neighbor to see if they need something at the store.

Take stock of those things you're doing but aren't really committed to. A good indication is that these things feel draining or burdensome. When you find it, make the decision to let it go, and do whatever it takes to complete that agreement, remembering that what you say no to will define your life as much as what you say yes to.

Developing Emotional Literacy

An inability to notice our true feelings leaves us at their mercy.
People with greater certainty about their feelings
are better pilots of their lives, having a surer sense . . .
about personal decisions from whom to marry to what job to take.

—Daniel Goleman

Rachel and Tyrell, both artists, have only been together for seven months now, although Rachel already sports a beautiful engagement ring on her finger. While all was bliss for the first few months, lately it seems that the relationship has been deteriorating fast. The couple has come to see me in the hope that they can find their way back to some sense of union and harmony or, at the very least, understand this recent turn of events between them.

The most glaring problem that I noticed almost immediately was Tyrell's very real struggle to articulate his feelings. To almost every question posed to him regarding his feelings, he would respond rather awkwardly, with a shrug of the shoulder and an "I don't know." The most he seemed to be able to say was that he felt "criticized" by Rachel. I tried to help Tyrell go deeper by explaining that, while I understood that he heard her questions and requests as criticisms, that "criticized" was not actually a feeling but more of an assessment that's based on his feelings. The feelings themselves might be "humiliated," "anxious," "threatened," or "ashamed."

Tyrell was also unable to understand Rachel's feelings when she tried to share them with him. In response to her disappointment and loneliness, he would look up and reply, "Love is a two-way street, you know." He seemed almost incapable of authentically empathizing with her emotional pain. Please don't think that Tyrell is a bear of a man. On the contrary, Tyrell is a soft-spoken, humble, polite, and very likable person. He simply lacks the ability to articulate his feelings, and is therefore unable to empathize with others in any meaningful way. This handicap, however, is seriously impairing the growth of a loving and lasting connection between them.

> It is only with the heart that one can see rightly; what is essential is invisible to the eye.
>
> —Antoine de Saint-Exupéry

Most of us are aware by now that the tenacious 40 to 50 percent divorce rate shows little sign of slowing down. Daniel Goleman, author of *Emotional Intelligence*, attributes this to the erosion of social pressures to stay in bad marriages, as well as the lack of economic necessity to do so. He asserts that because of these things, the emotional dynamic between a couple is that much more essential to the stability of the relationship. Emotional attunement and empathy are more acutely necessary now than ever before to ensure a successful union. Author and therapist Polly Young-Eisendrath adds to this by observing that never before have we aspired to a partnership of equals as we do today. Before this time, relationships had one dominant person and one submissive one. Today, we're uninterested in such unions, and insist upon equality across the board. As such, Young-Eisendrath notes that we're ill equipped to form such unions, as we're fundamentally lacking in the skills that would be required to live these ideals of love.

The ability to create an emotionally attuned, stable, healthy, and mutually respectful relationship, where both partners are capable of navigating their connection from the more mature parts of themselves, necessitates that they both share at least a moderate capacity for emotional literacy. Emotional literacy includes the ability to accurately read one's own feelings, then manage them by self-soothing or delaying impulsivity. Emotional literacy is also comprised of the ability to express those feelings in self-responsible ways, and to be somewhat self-aware of when you are projecting your own disowned feelings onto another. Also required is the ability to comprehend and respond appropriately to the feelings of others. We don't have to do these things perfectly. But solid relationships will require that we be able to do them at least reasonably well, as emotional attunement is the currency of all loving relationships.

Empathy, that crucial ingredient to a good relationship, is enhanced in direct proportion to one's ability to identify and be present with one's own emotions. Most of us collapse our emotions with our thoughts to one degree or another. In response to the question "How do you feel?" we might respond, "I feel like he's being a jerk!" rather than "I feel hurt, ashamed, embarrassed, or vulnerable." In her book *The Art of Emotional Healing*, psychotherapist Lucia Capacchione helps us identify our feelings by articulating for us nine "families of feelings":

Happy: Which includes blissful, delighted, enthusiastic, excited, glad, gleeful, grateful, and joyful.

Sad: Which includes discouraged, disheartened, down, gloomy, grieving, hurt, lonely, and melancholy.

Angry: Which includes agitated, bitter, enraged, exasperated, furious, irritated, mad, and resentful.

Afraid: Which includes anxious, fearful, horrified, nervous, panicked, scared, shaky, and terrified.

Playful: Which includes adventurous, childlike, creative, free, lighthearted, lively, spontaneous, and whimsical.

Loving: Which includes affectionate, compassionate, friendly, kind, nurturing, tender, trusting, and warm.

Confused: Which includes ambivalent, bewildered, conflicted, hesitant, perplexed, torn, troubled, and uneasy.

Depressed: Which includes burned out, dejected, despondent, helpless, hopeless, listless, weary, and withdrawn.

Peaceful: Which includes calm, contented, quiet, relaxed, satisfied, serene, and tranquil.

> Self-awareness ... [is] ongoing attention to one's internal states.
>
> —Daniel Goleman

There are other psychologists who distinguish between primary and secondary emotions. Which is simply a distinction between core emotions such as joy, sadness, or peace, and emotions that are a combination of two or more feelings such as frustration, which is a combination of irritation and impatience. Or reactive emotions—the emotions one feels about their emotions, like feeling angry in response to feeling vulnerable and hurt. It's a lot to be aware of. Yet our ability to recognize what we are feeling when we are feeling it is what Daniel Goleman calls the "keystone to emotional intelligence." That doesn't mean that we have to know "why" we feel the way we do, or whether feeling that way is "good" or whether it's "bad." The important thing is that we're able to identify what we feel, when we're feeling it, and, when appropriate, be able to share that with another in a constructive way that can help them find their way into our world.

Both analysis and assessment are less significant when it comes to being emotionally literate. In fact, they often thwart our ability to even know what we are feeling as we're apt to judge ourselves and cut off our inquiry if we don't like what we find. Rather than simply honor our feelings, most of us, in contrast, negate, repress, ignore, or stuff them down. We shame ourselves for feeling the way we do ("I shouldn't feel this way"), deny that our feelings exist ("I don't really feel this way"), or try to talk ourselves out of our feelings ("I need to stop feeling this way"). It's not even personal. Our whole culture is addicted to all sorts of distractions and quick fixes to help us escape our unpleasant or difficult feelings, and few of us have a sense of mastery over simply being with our own inner experience.

Some of us distance ourselves from our feelings in an attempt to be "more spiritual." This is a common but harmful mistake. Our "negative" emotions of anger, fear, guilt, and shame all have their role to play. Energy healer Karla McLaren writes about the benefits of *all* of our emotions in her book *Emotional Genius*. Anger, she assures us, is the keeper of boundaries, the emotion that helps us maintain healthy separation from others. When anger is repressed or ignored, she asserts, we will have difficulty honoring ourselves appropriately by setting limits, protecting ourselves from abuse, and/or avoiding unhealthy entanglements. Fear, the emotion we resist the most, has its place in our lives as well. The keeper of intuition and hyperfocused awareness, fear allows us to be fully present and alive in the moment. When fully honored and embraced, fear keeps us active, energized, and completely engaged in the world around us. The sister emotions of guilt and shame also serve a necessary function in our lives as the restorers of integrity when we've broken our own or someone else's boundaries. We need to learn to be fully present and available to all of our emotions in order to reap their benefits and learn from their

> Be open to your happiness and
> sadness as they arise.
>
> —John and Lyn St. Clair-Thomas

wisdom. My good friend Dr. Joan Rosenberg, professor at Pepperdine University and author of the wonderful book *90 Seconds to a Life You Love,* encourages us to grow our capacity to both name our emotions as well as simply track the somatic experience of each without resistance. Her assertion is that most difficult feelings last only about 90 seconds, yet our attempts to avoid them create monumental blocks to well-being, wisdom, and confidence, as well as undermine our ability to be happy and successful in life.

When Bobby met Charles, he pretty much knew from the start that he wanted to be with him. Although Charles was more ambivalent, he came around little by little. After a couple of years, when Charles moved from California to a beautiful home in the mountains of Colorado, he invited Bobby to join him. He was joyful at first. But because Charles had never really committed himself to the relationship, he continued to travel alone and for fun, almost as much as he had before he met Bobby. Bobby was alone and isolated much of the time and he became desperately unhappy.

When we first spoke, Bobby couldn't get out of bed, he was so depressed. However, he kept telling me why he thought he shouldn't be feeling the way he was. Charles was a great catch, he'd never promised him more than this, he should be stronger, more self-sufficient somehow. The more he told me why he shouldn't feel sad and depressed, the more I pointed out that, regardless of what he thought he *should* feel or not feel, he actually *did* feel sad and depressed. I asked him what sadness and depression were trying to tell him. Eventually, he gave himself permission to simply be with whatever he was feeling without judging himself so harshly. When he was able to honor his feelings in this way, they had an opportunity to heal him and guide him to make some much-needed changes. Bobby decided that he needed more from Charles and confronted him, being fully responsible for his part in creating the situation he was in. When Charles was unwilling to give him more, Bobby moved back to California and began a new life—one that honored his desire for close connection and engagement with others. He now uses his emotions to help guide his choices and he is finding life more rewarding and happier than ever before. Not surprisingly, Charles actually followed Bobby back to California and has recently proposed marriage. It's not so much that Bobby played the "unavailable" game. It's that in becoming fully present to and honoring of himself, there is now actually more of Bobby to love, and he began commanding more of Charles's respect, and capturing Charles's interest and attention more than he had before.

> When your emotions are allowed to take their proper place in your whole life, all healing is possible, because all energy is available.
>
> —Karla McLaren

When you know yourself, you don't need to defend against being known. We develop our capacity for intimacy by giving up our need to see ourselves a certain way. It's challenging to be authentic about some of our more self-serving emotions, motivations, and weaknesses. Who among us does not wish to think of ourselves as good, evolved, and loving people? Yet, truthfully, being human means that we have it *all* within us—greed as well as generosity, selfishness as well as selflessness, indifference as well as love. It's because we embody the whole spectrum of human possibilities, that our continual choice to choose love is so meaningful.

PRACTICE: WITNESSING YOUR EMOTIONS WITH LOVE

Today, I invite you to practice naming and simply witnessing your emotions, with a sense of unconditional self-acceptance and compassion. When we are willing to simply name and witness our difficult emotions, without needing to fix or change them in any way, we grow in our ability to listen and learn from each emotion. We also get to increase our ability to hear the unpleasant or difficult feelings of others without going into reactivity.

Still Yourself. Sit quietly for several minutes, and breathe deeply, as though you could breathe all the way down into your hips. Become aware of all of the feelings and sensations in your body. Notice where you are holding any tension, and as you find it, just let it go. With each breath, allow your awareness to drop deeper and wider until you connect with the part of you that knows you are being held and supported by a Force and Field of Life that loves you. Bask in the experience of being held and loved.

Connect with Your Wise, Adult Self. Connect with the part of you that is wise, resourceful, resilient, capable, and strong, and breathe this sense of yourself as a loving, mature adult presence all the way down into your hips, extending the energy of this center down into the earth and out to the edges of the room.

Extend a Sense of Presence and Love to Yourself. With a sense of deep presence and care, turn your attention to the "you" in your body and extend a sense of safety and compassion to this part of yourself from the deeper and wider center of your wise, adult self.

Witness and Welcome Your Emotions One by One. From a place of deep listening and care, ask yourself the following question, welcoming in with love whatever the response and mirroring it back with love.

Ask yourself: "What are you feeling?"

Listen for a Response. Be specific and clear. Give yourself time to name the exact feeling you're trying to articulate. *For example, "I feel apprehensive." "I feel hopeful." "I feel violated."*

Welcome in that feeling, resisting nothing.

For each feeling, silently say to yourself with a sense of acceptance and compassion, "I can see that you're feeling _____."

Notice the sensations in your body as you allow yourself to feel this feeling.

Breathe. Move on once you've allowed yourself to witness this emotion fully.

Do this several times until you've named all of the feelings present.

Listen for the Messages in the Emotions. Go through each emotion, one feeling at a time, to explore the message it might be holding for you.

*Ask each feeling: **"Is there something you're wanting to tell me?"***

For example, Excitement wants me to keep expanding beyond who I've known myself to be. Disappointment wants me to learn from my mistakes. Fear wants me to stay grounded and awake. Happiness wants me to continue doing what I did to get here. Sadness wants me to honor those I've lost by how I love those who are here now.

When finished, write in your journal about your experience of being fully present with your emotion(s), particularly the unpleasant ones, and any messages they had to offer.

Bonus: Practice in Action

Throughout your day today, pause frequently to simply be present with yourself.

*Ask yourself, **"Sweetheart, what are you feeling?"***

Witness your inner experience with love, extending a sense of compassion and care to the part of you experiencing that feeling.

*Mirror back to yourself what you hear by saying, **"I can see that you're feeling _____."***

Now add a question by asking yourself,
"Sweetheart, what are you needing?"

Witness your inner experience with love, extending a sense of compassion and care to the part of you experiencing that need.

*Mirror back to yourself what you hear by saying, **"I can see that you're needing _____."***

NOTE: For a guided audio leading you through this practice, please go to CallingInTheOne.com/Self-Love-Power-Practice.

Shifting
Where You're Centered

An old Cherokee man told his grandson,
"My son, there's a battle between two wolves inside us all.
"One is Evil. It is anger, jealousy, greed,
resentment, inferiority, lies, and ego.
"The other is Good. It is joy, peace, love, hope, humility,
kindness, empathy, and truth."
The boy asked, "Grandfather, which wolf wins?"
The old man quietly replied,
"The one you feed."

—Anonymous

There's good news and bad. I'll give you the bad news first. You will get triggered. Easily. The person you're dating will forget to call you back. Or you'll say something foolish. Or you'll gain two pounds. Or your bank account will get too low. You get the gist. It will happen, and it will happen quickly and as organically as taking a breath. When it does, you'll feel like you're back at square one. "See, I'll always be alone," or "See, I'm not good enough." In that moment, you'll assume that all of your hard work to transform your consciousness and connect with your True Love Identity will have been for nothing. Yet all that's happened is you fell back asleep, and you must now wake yourself up. The good news is, you can.

Disappointment is the biggest trigger of a false center. As life is full of disappointments, we need to get really good at "shifting centers." Noticing the automatic way that you're making meaning of what just happened, through the lens of your younger, traumatized self, and challenging it. Doing all you can to wake yourself up out of that trance to get yourself back into "power center." That mature, adult place within you that can see what's happening from a larger perspective and make more accurate and nuanced meaning. This is a critical skill to develop. Because wherever we are emotionally centered at the level of identity is where we are generating our lives from. And if you are in a false center, you can only create evidence for that sad story.

Andrea, an attractive, educated woman who owns her own home, came to a recent workshop and shared a story. While on a first date with a man she'd met on the Internet, Andrea mentioned that one of her specialties was homemade banana pudding. The man enthusiastically expressed that he *loved* banana pudding, and so she promised to make him some. He suggested that they have a picnic the following Sunday, and Andrea agreed. She was so excited that she purchased all of the ingredients the following day. However, when he hadn't called her by Thursday night, Andrea started getting nervous. When she hadn't heard from him by Friday, she called and left a message. He didn't call her back that night. Nor did he call on Saturday. Nor did he call on Sunday. Instead of taking the hint, licking her wounds, and letting it go, however, Andrea proceeded to make him the promised pudding because she "said she'd do it." She drove across town and knocked on his door Sunday afternoon, with a smile on her face and a big bowl of banana pudding in her hands. He answered the door, looking uncomfortable and unpleasantly surprised. Andrea could see that he had company—another woman who was glaring at her from across the room. Andrea sheepishly gave him the pudding, mentioning that he and "his guest" might enjoy it. Of course, she never heard from him again. And unfortunately, she lost her favorite bowl in the process.

This overattaching and giving away of ourselves to someone who has not yet displayed their intentions toward us is all too common among those of us who have early relational traumas that caused us to doubt our value. The disappointment of her date not calling triggered Andrea into a false center, filling her with the all-too-familiar sick feeling in her belly that, somehow, she again wasn't good enough. Now, on a conscious level, Andrea convinced herself that she was simply being generous. She told herself she was being a "postmodern woman" who could take the lead in moving a relationship forward. Yet she ended up feeling completely humiliated and devalued by her behavior. Upon reflection, she could see that she was overgiving as a strategy to try to get what she wanted. What initially appeared to be a charitable gesture on her part was really a covert attempt to get him to like her. She made that pudding and marched it over to his house because she was auditioning for the role of girlfriend. However, she was able to admit that that's not giving. It's manipulation. Manipulation in response to being internally triggered into an "I'm not good enough" false center, and filled with the anxiety that comes from allowing someone else's behavior to define who you are. From that center, her best thinking was to do something that proved that she was "good enough." Yet whenever we take action in response to being triggered into an old story like "I'm alone," "I'm not wanted," or "I'm not safe," all we can do is generate more evidence for that story. To her credit, she got the lesson. She is now much more conscious about overly attaching herself to someone she barely knows, who has not yet demonstrated a high regard for her. She understands that when she's disappointed, she should ask herself what she's making it mean. Then before she takes action, mentor herself back into an empowered center, where she's connected to the truth of her value and her power. Then, and only then, can she take an action in response to what just happened.

Some of us give, not because we're truly generous, but because we're strategists. Somatically centered in the old story, we give as a way to try to get others to like and value us. Or even better, to need us, because maybe then they won't leave. Giving becomes a kind of barter to belong—a bid for love, rather than an expression of it. Yet all overgiving ever does is demonstrate how little we value ourselves. This is how we train others to disrespect us.

You may have years of evidence for your old story that is causing you to feel hopeless about ever finding happy, healthy love. Yet if you do, it's not so much because it's true, but because you've been behaving in ways that convince others that it is. Your beliefs will have you show up in ways that pull on others to mirror that story back to you. It took Andrea weeks to get over the repulsed way that man looked at her when he opened the door. It was the

Your love should never
be offered to the mouth
of a Stranger
Only to someone who
has the valor and daring
to cut pieces of their soul
off with a knife
Then weave them into a
blanket to protect you.

—Hafiz

pain of realizing that she'd done that to herself that caused her to commit to never, ever overgive again to try to get someone to love her.

Good relationships are possible when we know our value, and can act from a healthy sense of entitlement, with the conviction that our feelings and needs matter. And that they should matter to anyone we allow into our lives on an intimate level. When we act from "power center"—the place within us where we are emotionally anchored in a sense of our own value and power—we train others to treat us with respect, consideration, thoughtfulness, and care. Some of us have spent years sitting in therapy trying to understand all of the reasons why others treat us so badly—why they're so narcissistic and just take, take, take; or why they use us sexually and then disappear; or why we always wind up betrayed and abandoned. Yet not much has changed. But the *moment* you start living from power center, and showing up in ways that are organic to that center, you will quickly start to see the truth of your value and your power mirrored back to you by others. It can be quite dramatic and startling to see how quickly the pattern can change.

Jennifer's pattern was that she was never the one chosen. In spite of desperately wanting a family of her own and in spite of being an attractive, accomplished person who'd make an excellent partner, somehow the people she dated always seemed to marry the next person they met after her. As she approached her fortieth birthday, she was beside herself with grief. She could trace the pattern back to her early experience of having two workaholic parents who never really seemed to want to spend much time with her, choosing work over her, time and time again. Yet knowing her wounding and changing the pattern were two different things.

However, when she looked at the pattern from a place of self-responsibility, Jennifer admitted that when dating someone she liked, she'd easily get triggered into an "I'm not wanted" story. Small things would start a cascade of insecurity inside of her: A text that took his attention away from her for a few moments, or a friendly, non-flirtatious conversation he might have with an attractive woman at a party. In response, she'd start to push. Suddenly, out of the blue, she wanted to know where the relationship stood, even though they were still in the early stage of getting to know each other. Or she'd start making him wrong for not making more of a commitment to their relationship, disregarding all the steps he'd made in that direction. Predictably, the person would run screaming from the room, grateful to be out of there. Yet once Jennifer was able to connect with, soothe, and mentor that younger part of her that so easily identified with the anxious "I'm not wanted" story, she was able to show up from a more empowered place. The power statement that helped her to emotionally stay connected with her value and power in these moments was *"I am a woman who is more than worthy of being chosen by the wonderful man who is proud to call me his wife."* This statement would wake her up from the trance of the old story, and calm her into a more adult center, and the truth of her worthiness to be chosen.

The next person she dated was a man she could have easily felt intimidated by, due to his many accomplishments in the world. Yet, rather than trying to win him over or get him to choose her, Jennifer instead stayed focused on being somatically connected to the truth of her value and her power while she was with him. Within three months he proposed. They have just started the delightful journey of getting pregnant, and are happily planning their lives together.

The fulfillment of your intention cannot happen from your old identity. When triggered, you must first take the time to internally shift where you're centered. For it's only when you are able to show up in alignment with the truth of who you are that you will be empowered to manifest the highest and the best that life and love have to offer. To me, this is the essence of what it is to love ourselves.

The rule of thumb is this: When triggered into a false center, take no action! Wait. Lovingly and fiercely push back against your old story, waking yourself up from its seductive trance. Patiently get yourself back into a place of power and value that you can feel within yourself, deeper and wider than your old story. Then and only then make a move. As you are the source of your experience, make sure that the "you" you're creating your relationships from is the true you.

PRACTICE: SHIFTING INTO YOUR MATURE, ADULT CENTER

I invite you to take on the practice of staying identified with and centered in your adult self. Notice when you get triggered and before reacting, pause to connect with your adult, mature self.

At some point today, notice if and when you start to feel anxious or depressed. Then pause to do the following:

NOTICE THE MEANING YOU'RE MAKING.

When disappointed, or "triggered," ask yourself, "What am I assuming is true?"

Notice the meaning you are making of what just happened.

Pause, take a deep breath, and ask yourself, "How old am I right now?"

Notice that you're now emotionally centered in a younger part of yourself.

See if you can also locate a more adult part of you that is observing yourself having this experience.

CONNECT WITH YOUR STRENGTHS AND RESOURCES.

Take an inventory of your strengths as an adult—your intelligence, re-sourcefulness, resilience, maturity, competence, and development. Notice that you have been cultivating skills and developing capacities for years and that you are a wise and loving person who shows up powerfully in many areas of your life.

For example, *You are a wonderful friend, a good parent, a competent professional, etc.*

EXTEND LOVE AND SUPPORT TO THE YOUNGER YOU.

Close your eyes and take a deep breath. Allow yourself to emotionally identify with your strong, wise, competent adult self.

Consciously anchor into your adult center by breathing the ener-gies of this self, down into your hips, down through the soles of your feet, down into the earth and out to the edges of the room.

From this deep adult center, extend love and support to the younger you who is inside of false meaning.

SPEAK WORDS OF COMFORT AND CONTAINMENT TO THE YOUNGER YOU.

Before allowing yourself to act from your feelings, try speaking words of comfort and containment to the younger you that is triggered.

ASSERT WHAT'S REALLY TRUE.

Remind the triggered, younger you of what's really true.

Speak your Power Statements gently but fiercely to wake yourself up from the trance of your old story.

TAKE ACTION FROM YOUR ADULT CENTER.

Now you can respond to whatever is happening from the wisest, strongest, most mature parts of yourself.

Bonus: Practice in Action

Today, consciously choose to practice walking in the world from your power center. Take your power statement and ask yourself, "How would I be walking down the street from this center? How would I be talking to this person, or eating this meal, or ordering my morning coffee if I were centered in the deeper truth of my own value and power?"

Giving to Yourself
What Was Missing

I dreamt last night oh marvelous error that there were honeybees in
my heart making honey out of my old failures.

—Antonio Machado

David, a competent, smart, and successful thirtysomething freelance writer, can't understand why, whenever he begins dating a man he likes, he starts acting out in obsessive, possessive, and overly dependent ways. In spite of his best efforts to do things differently, he becomes neurotic, needy, and insecure the moment he meets a man he hopes to have a relationship with. Like David, many of us who are functioning well in life, with good jobs and good friends, suddenly begin behaving as though we were starved for affection at the first sign of romance. Although David would be a catch by anyone's standards, the men he meets can't get away fast enough.

"Neediness" is a state of inner deprivation based on the unmet dependency needs from childhood. When we're needy, we're trying to get from someone something that was denied us in the past: validation, security, or approval. Unfortunately, though, many of these early unmet needs cannot adequately be filled in present-time, and particularly not with people we barely know. No one can ever make up for what our parents failed to give us way back when. Given the hunger that can so quickly consume us when we meet someone we like, how ironic it is that we so often

> Immature love says,
> "I love you because
> I need you." Mature
> love says, "I need you
> because I love you."
>
> —Erich Fromm

attract those people who are as lacking in their ability to love us as our early caregivers were.

Prisha, a petite woman in her mid-thirties, was raised by a mother who spent most of her time in bed with undiagnosed depression. Although Prisha believed that her mother loved her, she never felt loved by her. Rather, as a child, Prisha felt like a burden and an obligation. She consequently learned to make few demands. Prisha has been waiting all her life for Prince Charming to sweep her off her feet and passionately dedicate himself to making her happy and giving her all the love and attention that was missing in her childhood.

Prisha did meet a man that she liked quite a bit, and was hoping to have a relationship with. He, however, had an intrusive and demanding mother who expected him to "be the man of the house" at a very early age, due to an absent father. Because of this, he relates to the idea of being Prisha's boyfriend as though he will again be placed in the suffocating position of being overly responsible for a woman, and burdened by her excessive needs and demands. It's a big deal for Prisha to assert herself by telling this man what she needs from him. How awful, then, for him to respond as though her needs were a burden and an obligation. It's her mother all over again—her worst nightmare come true.

It's not that our needs are wrong. It's that we've been going about trying to get them met in the wrong ways. Even when someone wants to provide us with what was missing, unless we ourselves are actively giving to ourselves what we didn't receive, it will be like water through a sieve. For trying to get someone outside of you to fill up your empty holes without actively being engaged in healing your own hungry heart on a daily basis will be an exhausting and fruitless exercise. At some point, you'll just wear out people with the bottomless pit of your insecurities.

An endless supply of ardor can do little to alter the default of deprivation that one experiences when emotionally anchored in a false center. For that's what neediness is. Healthy dependency needs that are somatically anchored in an old false center such as "I can never get what I need" or "It's dangerous to let myself love someone." If you're centered in a story that you're somehow not safe to love, then no one will be able to reassure you enough that you are, without you first being willing to learn how to keep yourself and others safe in intimate love. You cannot get what was missing in your childhood from another person, *until you are actively engaged in doing all that you can to give it to yourself.* It's what we call "re-parenting" yourself.

Is it a trauma for a child to not be cared for properly? Not to feel loved and tended to with consistency, kindness, and adoration? Absolutely. Can the ravenous ache created by such a wounding ever truly be healed? Absolutely. Yet not from holding some poor soul hostage trying to make up for these gaping holes in our hearts. It's sad to realize that what we didn't get from our initial caregivers—attention, support, protection, and love—is water under the bridge. The understanding that you can never go back and undo that loss can feel tragic. As with any loss it must be

> The void Papa's death left in me became a kind of cavity. . . . My connections with men are all about trying to reach my father, about trying to fill a childhood void, about believing that such a man exists and getting angry at poor innocent men for not being that man.
>
> —Liv Ullmann

grieved, with the ultimate goal of acceptance. For it is our lack of acceptance that causes us to tenaciously cling to the fantasy that someone, somewhere will come and make it all up to us. Holding on to this fantasy creates chaos in our love lives. Because we aren't going into our romantic relationships as adults, but rather as children posing in adult bodies. Yet last I heard, most people are looking for someone to partner with, not to parent. Giving up the fantasy that someone is coming to rescue us from our miserable childhood is a true initiation, and a necessary passage to becoming an adult who's actually ready to enter into a loving partnership with an equal.

It's time to identify what was missing, and actively begin providing it for ourselves. Then we'll no longer be drawn to those who hurt us in the same ways we were hurt as children. Instead, we'll start attracting potential partners who are healthy and well enough to enter into an adult, loving relationship.

Ideally, early caregivers provide children with a reliable sense of unconditional love, emotional attunement, consistent and dependable nurturing, loving touch, and supportive encouragement that give them the courage to explore their environment, and an innate sense that they could trust themselves and the world around them. Caregivers also offer protection, and teach children how to both survive and succeed in the world, which includes managing finances. When these trustworthy qualities of parental love are consistently demonstrated, children internalize them.

> We all come to our relationships like hungry beggars saying, if not out loud, then in an unconscious whisper, "What are you going to do for me?"
>
> —Daphne Rose Kingma

They become part of a child's internal landscape—that which is commonly called "inner resources." If we did not receive these resources as children, we will most likely struggle in life and in love as adults.

Most of us suffered deficits in our early years that we've carried around since then. The problem is not, however, that these qualities were lacking as we were growing up. The problem is that they are lacking now. We don't care for ourselves in ways that are similar to how our parents didn't care for us. And so, we search for someone who will finally give us what once was missing. Like that little baby bird in P. D. Eastman's book who asked everyone he met, "Are you my mother?"

Yet it's not that no one "out there" has provided these loving qualities for us, as much as *we ourselves have been negligent in providing them for ourselves.*

I often see those who wish to find a partner but can't seem to keep away from the players—the ones who sexually use them, then never call, or keep coming back without giving much of themselves. These are people who come to take love, and offer little in return. Usually, if I inquire into the parenting these people received, I discover that they had an absent parent, or one who was neglectful or indifferent toward them. What was missing was the sense of being protected and cherished by someone who was committed to their well-being. For the most part, those who were cherished, truly seen, and protected by one or both of their parents do not wind up in these situations. Another example is a person who was not nurtured as a child. This person will have difficulties self-soothing when they get upset or afraid. This may even escalate to problems with addictive behaviors, since ritualistic conduct is often a substitute for the ability to self-soothe. The task for them, therefore, is to learn to nurture and soothe themselves.

It's time to start giving yourself that which your parents could not or would not provide. I know it might seem unfair that they should just "get away" with having treated you so badly. I once counseled a lovely woman named Jana who was angry when I suggested she do this. To her, it seemed so unjust that she would now have to make up for the cruel ways her parents behaved. She wanted someone else to pay for their sins. Now, Jana was a smart, successful woman. She knew what she was saying didn't make any sense. But the impulse toward fairness is a primitive one. And to Jana, it seemed unjust that she would now have to do all of this work on herself because of their mistakes. Week after week she'd come into my office and just sit on the couch with her arms crossed and her heels dug in. I'd like to tell you that she finally saw the light. She didn't. Instead, she died in a car accident before ever finding the freedom

> What lies behind us and what lies before us are tiny matters compared to what lies within us.
>
> —Ralph Waldo Emerson

to let love in. Moral of the story? Life is short. Let go of your stubbornness and mourn your losses. Get busy healing so that you can finally create the happiness that you deserve.

It's an affirmation of life to make the choice to love in the face of all that is not love. Perhaps your parents were doing the best they could. Perhaps they were not. What matters, however, is whether or not you find your way home to wholeness.

PRACTICE: IDENTIFYING AND FORGIVING WHAT WAS MISSING

Take out your journal, and write for several minutes on each of the following:

NOTE: I will use the words "mother" and "father," though I'm well aware that some had two mothers and some had two fathers, and some had only one parent, sometimes a mother or father, but sometimes a grandparent, aunt, or foster parent. Please modify the practice as you need.

- Describe your father's best, most supportive, and loving qualities.
- When did you feel safe with him?
- How often did he keep his word to you and others?
- In what ways did he let you down?

- Describe your mother's best, most supportive, and loving qualities.
- To what degree did you feel connected to her?
- When did you trust her to be fair and kind?
- When did you not?
- In what ways did she let you down?

Now write a list of what was missing for you in your childhood. Use the following list as a guide to help you identify what was missing:

Nurturing (soothing you when you were disappointed, loving physical touch on a regular basis, loving-kindness for no particular reason)

Basic Hygienic Care (washing of body, doing laundry, caring for your teeth)

Basic Life Skills (managing a checkbook, paying the bills, upkeep of the car and home)

Consistency and Dependability (kept their word, you knew what you could count on, life had a predictable rhythm, were able to earn a living)

Attention (spending time with you for no particular reason, noticing and responding to your moods, listening to you, understanding things from your perspective)

Encouragement of Your Talents (recognizing them, validating them, supporting them to grow)

Protection (from the hostile behaviors of: abusive siblings, the outside world, one another)

Being Cherished (delighting in and appreciating you, taking joy in your presence in the world)

Respect of Boundaries (honoring your privacy, protecting your right to say no)

Unconditional Love (loving you without needing you to "perform" in return, loving you without imposing their unfulfilled needs onto you)

When you have written your list, write or say out loud the following regarding *each* quality that was missing for you.

"I, _____, release and forgive _____ for failing to _____. I give up failing to _____ myself. I promise to do my absolute best to begin _____ myself from this day forward, and I claim _____ as mine fully and completely."

Bonus: Practice in Action

Take at least one action today that provides you with that which was missing in your childhood. For example: If you had an un-nurturing mother, take special care to prepare your favorite meal tonight; if you were never taught how to balance a checkbook, ask a friend who's good with money to schedule a date to come over and teach you how they do it; if you were always expected to say yes to the demands of others, try saying no in response to a request.

Preparing Your Body for Love

Being preoccupied with our self-image is like . . . coming upon a
tree of singing birds while wearing earplugs.

—Pema Chödrön

A sexual, romantic relationship is not just a union of hearts, not just a union of souls, but also a union of bodies. When we become lovers with someone, we offer up our body as a home and sacred resting place for them. As such, how we feel about our bodies has a huge impact on how open—or how closed—we are to forming such unions.

"It's odd," Samantha said, "but whenever I'm nervous about an upcoming date, my focus goes straight to the size of my thighs. Do I look too fat in these pants? Will he think my butt is too big? You'd think that, instead, I'd be more concerned with how I was feeling about going out with him or whether or not I thought I had anything interesting to talk about." The others in the group nodded in recognition.

It's all too common for us to transfer our insecurities onto the roundness of our bellies or the number on the morning scale. Being "too fat" has become the catchall for any feelings of self-doubt, shyness, or unworthiness we might suffer from.

Usually, when I ask someone if they love their body, they'll start telling me what they don't like. They're already so engaged in critical inner dialogue that's chronicling their physical imperfections and flaws, that it's nearly impossible for them to not respond with a list of things they'd like to improve. But imagine, if you will, calling up a dear friend ten, twenty, thirty times a day to tell them how fat and physically flawed they are. How long do you think they'd tolerate that before putting a stop to it? How long would you? How is it, then, that so many of us put up with this loathsome dialogue within ourselves day after day after day?

We want to be five pounds thinner, two inches taller, have bigger breasts, thinner thighs, or more defined abs. We want to firm up and pare down and we want to do it yesterday. Yet, it's very hard to change anything about ourselves while engaging in a diatribe of self-criticism, as most of us do. That would be like me trying to get one of my kids to change something about themselves by telling them everything that's wrong with them, and all the things I don't like about them. Yeah, right. They'd likely respond by digging in their heels and doing absolutely everything in their power to stay exactly the same. (Don't ask me how I know that.) Until my kids know that I love and accept them absolutely 100 percent as they are, they are not going to be willing to comply with my demands that they be any different.

We're all like this. The more you tell yourself that your body is too this or too that, not enough this and not enough that, the more you'll likely stay the same, or become even more of whatever you're criticizing yourself for. That's why a lot of diets fail. Because we start them on the basis of how much we hate how we look, or because we'd just as soon die before we'd let anyone see us naked this way. Many diets are just another self-punishment—another way we get to disparage ourselves. They're like being put on a strict budget after a naughty spending spree. It's only when we alter our eating habits out of love and respect for ourselves, as well as an optimistic possibility of what could be, instead of what has been, that lasting change has any real chance to take root in our lives.

While most can acknowledge the massive amounts of body shame in our culture, we'll go on indulging our right to measure ourselves according to extreme and superficial standards. This form of self-abuse isn't a once-in-a-while phenomenon. Self-loathing is rampant. It's actually considered "normal" for us to dislike our bodies. It's "normal" for us to assess our self-worth according to our current pant size. It's "normal" for us to condemn and judge ourselves in punitive, harsh, and disparaging tones when it comes to our physical appearance.

I frequently remind people that, in some parts of the world, female circumcision—

A woman watches her body as though it were an unreliable ally in the battle for love.

—Leonard Cohen

the cutting and mutilation of the clitoris—is also considered "normal." In many remote villages in India, bride burning remains a common and "normal" practice. In some areas of the Middle East, forbidding the education of women, with its resultant poverty for themselves and their children, is, once again, a "normal" phenomenon. There's now even a movement in place to challenge the "normal" practice of circumcising boy babies, which many consider to be an insensitive and even cruel practice. Just because something is "normal" does not mean it is not also deeply destructive. Similar to how it is throughout the world where these rituals are common, we ourselves are often the ones to perpetuate the abuse by passing these "normal" practices down to our children. And on and on it goes, until people wake up from the trance and begin to consider another way.

From the age of nine, when Isabella entered the early stages of puberty, her weight-obsessed, obese mother began a constant commentary on Isabella's size. By the time she was a teenager, Isabella hated her body and loathed going shopping for clothes. Although she was only slightly overweight at the time, her image of herself as obese, like her mother, grew with each passing year.

I met Isabella when she was in her late forties, years after her mother had passed. Although she was only slightly larger than the average woman, her image of herself remained fixed in adolescence. She believed that she was "too fat" and, therefore, unattractive. She blamed her weight for the many disappointing experiences she'd had with men, and felt angry and resentful toward her body for "betraying her." This antagonistic relationship with her body caused her to relate to herself as though she were a talking head, ignoring herself almost entirely from the neck down, which is actually what *I* suspected was more at the root of her difficulties with men. I mean, really, if Isabella is hell-bent on rejecting herself, what chance does anyone stand with her?

When she came to me, Isabella was struggling with a multitude of health issues. Over the years, she had tried so hard to uninhabit her body, that I wasn't surprised she was having these problems. As a matter of fact, I was amazed that she'd been as healthy as she was for as long as she had, given she'd had such a hostile relationship with her body for so many years now. As a neglected child might begin getting into trouble in order to draw attention to herself, so too did Isabella's body begin getting sick to demand attention from her. Isabella was forced to tend to herself with gestures of loving-kindness and self-care. Little by little, her body began to respond to her attempts to heal, but only in direct proportion to Isabella's willingness to re-create her relationship with it.

Does my body make me look fat?

—*New Yorker* cartoon

It was difficult for Isabella to give up her malevolent attitude toward herself. She wants to lose weight as a precondition to accepting herself. I keep telling her that it's the other way around—that she has to accept herself exactly as she is, and start acknowledging the miracle that her body is, as the precondition for transformation. Sometimes we hold on to the very things that are causing us pain. As of this writing, Isabella is still struggling with her tenacious attachment to the idea that she's "too fat to love." She's hauling the burden of her mother's self-hatred around like a monkey on her back, even more addicted to the negativity that bonds her to her dead mother, than she is to the food. It always amazes me how we'll fight tooth and nail to defend the right to live compromised lives.

When our relationship to our own body is adversarial, we'll do things such as over- or undereat. We'll make poor food choices, abuse drugs and/or alcohol, and engage in promiscuous and/or high-risk sex. We'll smoke cigarettes, exercise compulsively, and deny ourselves water. We'll forget to rest. We'll relate to our bodies as a series of things that need to be improved upon and/or fixed. We'll fracture and fragment ourselves, objectifying our bodies as much as we complain that others objectify us. We'll reduce our value down to the number of calories consumed that day.

If you are operating under the assumption that who you are before the surgery, underneath the hair dye, and without the makeup is unacceptable, then you are relating to your physical self from the "I'm not good enough" false center, and acting out that story in your relationship with yourself. From this consciousness, you might do one of two things. Either be driven to find someone who meets your "perfect" criteria—someone who has the "right job," the "right look," and is from the "right family," as a way to compensate for what you consider to be your own inadequacies, or you might "date down." Meaning, you'll take the risk of getting involved with only those who relate to you as superior to them, in order to avoid the possibility of being rejected and exposed as "not good enough" by someone who has more to offer. If this is you, then the answer is not in trying to "get to the bottom of your self-loathing," but to get on top of it! To rise above by making the conscious

> Self-love is the only weight-loss aid that really works in the long run.
>
> —Jenny Craig

decision to transform how you are relating to yourself. To begin honoring your body as the miracle that it is. To tend to your temple—whatever its form, with gratitude, awe, and love. To see perfectionism as the enemy of love, and begin a zero-tolerance policy on any disrespectful internal dialogue that diminishes your ability to stand strong in your value.

Opening our hearts to ourselves with all of our quirky physical imperfections—wrinkles that are "too deep," chins that are "too weak," thighs that are "too fat," and feet that are "too flat"—is a powerful preparation for love. For when we take a lover to our bed, it's about opening ourselves to the experience of being loved and adored for exactly who we are, and exactly who we are not, as well as being willing to extend this sweet state of grace to another.

One of the most important things we can accomplish in this lifetime is true self-appreciation and self-acceptance, whether or not we see the number that we want on the morning scale. Until we develop the capacity to love and appreciate ourselves *just as we are*, we will go through life with our noses pressed up against the glass. No matter what externals we manage to manifest, in spite of ourselves—right livelihood, the "perfect" mate, healthy children—we will always feel just a little on the wrong side of happiness.

Our bodies are the hosts of our great spirits and the home of our grand souls. They house the vastness of the life force that moves in and through us, and grant us the gift of life itself. To relate to them as anything less than this miracle is a distortion of who and what we are.

PRACTICE: HEALING YOUR RELATIONSHIP WITH YOUR BODY

We're going to do an open-eye meditation. Please read through the instructions once or twice and then do it from memory as best you can.

Take off all your clothes and sit or stand comfortably in front of a mirror with your hands relaxed and resting by your sides. Take several deep breaths, relaxing your entire body as your lungs expand and release, expand and release. Do a full body check for any tension you may be holding, beginning at the top of your head and moving down through the bottom of your feet.

Now start with the top of your head. Notice any judgments you have about your hair or the size and shape of your head. For each judgment you find, talk to the part of your body that you have been judging.

Take the following three steps with each and every judgment you find:

> The body is a sacred garment. It's your first and last garment; it is what you enter life with and what you depart life with, and it should be treated with honor.
>
> —Martha Graham

1. Ask that part of your body to please forgive you for being so harsh and unloving toward it.

2. Consider something you can truly appreciate about that part of your body.

3. Thank that part of your body for something and mean it in your heart.

Here's an example:

Judgment: "I hate how frizzy my hair is." **Step 1.** "Please forgive me, hair, for telling you over and over how ugly you are." **Step 2.** "I really appreciate how curly you are. I also like your color and texture." **Step 3.** "Thank you, hair, for being so full and wild when it rains."

Go through your entire body, doing this process with each judgment you find. For those parts of your body you have no negative judgments about, simply do Steps 2 and 3.

NOTE: If you have a particularly critical and fractured relationship to your body, you might wish to do this meditation on a regular basis until all judgments are neutralized and appreciation is restored.

Bonus: Practice in Action

Watch the judgments you make today about your physical appearance. Each time you notice yourself being critical toward yourself, for any perceived physical flaw, silently take Steps 1 through 3 within yourself.

Healing Your Sexuality

Your desire for a new beloved needs to be addressed to the spirit
of love. . . . and to be broadcast to the four corners of the earth,
reaching out across time and space to the unknown partner who
is waiting for you. Then all the possibilities are open and the magic
can unfold in its own mysterious and unpredictable way.

—Margot Anand

There was a time when I was so confused about how to get my needs for close-ness met, that I thought I had to go out and "get" myself a lover. I looked for this person as though I were shopping for a new coat. They had to be the right size, the right shape, and have the right kind of style. Most important, they had to look great on me. I tried on more than a few good people, but took them off just as fast. Without really meaning to, I created a lot of hurt feelings. It wasn't in-tentional. I just didn't have much wisdom when it came to taking a lover.

We all have our stories to tell, although many of us would prefer not to. Nowhere have we created more drama for ourselves and others than in the bedroom. We've misidentified lust as love, and chemistry as connection, more times than we'd care to admit. Decisions that seemed just fine at midnight looked anything but by the morning's light. We've used poor judgment, acted out of desperation, been con-fused, and made mistakes. In the process, most of us have, at one time or another, been pretty badly burned by the flames of our own passions.

Sexual energy is a vortex of power. At its most exalted, our sexuality is nothing short of evidence of our God-like status. Entrusted with the ability to create life, and blessed with the capacity to breathe healing, hope, and vitality into the heart of our lover, we are bestowed with a sacred gift. Our desire for sexual bonding illuminates our need to immerse ourselves fully in the forces of love, and merge with that which lies beyond our individual selves. The loss of separateness that happens during sex—the tangling and twisting of legs and limbs, saliva and sweat—is reminiscent of the one time in our lives where our merging was absolute. It's about as close as we'll ever come to returning to the oneness we experienced while still in the womb. As such, sexual union can be likened to a return to source energy, and it is the deepest affirmation of life there is.

Yet, as we all know, there's a shadow to this story. As with all powers, sexual energy is also often abused and tragically misused, and many of us have suffered unspeakable pain because of it. At its most debased, sex is the assertion of dominance. A thief who steals power from its prey. Ask any survivor of rape, incest, or sexual abuse what it's like to have one's innocence and sense of safety ripped away in this most terrible way. For many, it is an initiation into the underworld, where years can pass as one struggles through the maze, trying to find their way home again.

All of us wish we had a magic wand that could take our broken, crooked places and make us whole again. We want the sorrows and the shame to rise up and out of our bodies, leaving in their place only the lessons learned and the wisdom gained. For we intuitively know that we need to reclaim the sacredness of our sexuality in order to unleash the full power of who we were born to become. Sexual energy lives in the second chakra, which is the center of our creativity in life. When we're not in full possession of our sexual energies because we're either shut down, or holding shame, hurt, defensiveness, or rage in this part of our bodies, we're operating at a deficit. It's like trying to talk with laryngitis. Our power to generate what we're here to create is compromised, whether that's birthing a project, a baby, or a loving, nourishing relationship.

It's not just those of us who've suffered sexual abuse who are vulnerable to feeling disconnected from our sexual centers. Many of us were raised in religions that separate sexuality from spirituality. Even in progressive, New Thought communities, we may find ourselves praying and meditating upon the Divine from our hearts up. Moving our attentions upward through the tops of our heads, as though the God we worship lives somewhere in the sky. We rarely include our bellies, our hips, our genitals, our thighs, and our feet in

> Hindsight is always twenty-twenty.
>
> —Billy Wilder

our daily practice. In this way, our sexual center is split off from the holy energies of the Divine. I mean, when was the last time you included your genitals in your conversation with God? Our sexuality is generally considered off-limits to spiritual practice. It's basically a heart-down phenomenon, if you're healthy enough to have your heart connected to your genitals, at all. Because our wild sexual passions are basically considered to be part of that which debases and defiles all that is good, holy, and sacred.

Given all this, is it any wonder that so few of us trust ourselves fully when it comes to making good, sound sexual decisions? Many of us don't even know our own sensibilities or values. "Is casual sex okay, or do I wait until we're committed?" "Should I ask what we need to know up front [for example, 'What does this mean for us?' 'When was the last time you were tested?' or 'Does this mean we're monoga-mous?'], or simply cross my fingers and hope for the best?" Given that intuition and wisdom come to us through the sixth (the "third eye") and seventh (the "crown") chakras, and that sexual hunger lives mostly in the first (the "root") and second (the "creative center"), how do we know which center within us to seek for answers to our own pressing questions? It's not just the players who don't know which part of their bodies to think with anymore. It's most of us.

> Not having tasted
> a single cup of your wine
> I'm already drunk.
>
> —Rumi

Most of us harbor at least a small amount of shame for past sexual indiscretions—choices that we wish we'd made differently. Our transgressions stay with us somehow, soiling some secret part of our soul, as though something precious and irretrievable has been lost or, worse, stolen from us. We all need to forgive ourselves for some lack of judgment we displayed at one time or another. Years ago, when I was still in private practice, one man had been with me for a year before he dared confess an incestuous incident he'd initiated when he was ten with his little sister, who was seven at the time. Having finally admitted his horrible sin (for that was what it was for him), after carrying it in secretive shame for nearly twenty years, he was able to make amends with his sister. She was both touched by his grief and deeply healed by it. She assured him that she'd long ago dealt with it and had come to forgive him, knowing what a good person he is. Their relationship became stronger and he, free for the first time, felt as though a great burden were lifted from his shoulders. He had confessed with remorse and humility and, in so doing, was free to denounce the role of "perpetrator" by committing himself to becoming his sister's "protector" and "provider," and, consequently, filling that role for all of the women in his life. Not long after, he became engaged and is now very happily married. He attributes his availability to creating a loving relationship with his wife to having healed this sexual wound, which had been seriously eroding his regard of himself as a good and honorable man.

Not all violations are so easily erased. Statistics indicate that nearly one-quarter of us (one-fifth of all men and one-third of all women) were sexually assaulted in childhood. Sexual abuse in childhood can have severe consequences, made more acute because the perpetrations occur at a time when one's personal boundaries are only in the rudimentary stages of formulation. At least when we're adults, we know when we're being violated and we understand that our road of recovery must include reclaiming our sense of power and protection. Children, though, rarely understand what is happening to them. The very people they are supposed to trust suddenly turn on them, infecting them with dark and disturbing forces. They know intuitively that something is very, very bad, but they can't comprehend what it is in any substantial way. This was made even more confusing for some, as they enjoyed being given special attentions and affections. For those who have undergone such an ordeal, I don't have to tell you that surviving childhood sexual abuse is a spiritual path unto itself.

Sexual woundings, and the ways they influence one's life after the fact, don't just go away by themselves. I've met people who twenty, thirty, forty years later, still find that guilt, shame, and mistrust are again re-triggered in situations that include the possibility of closeness and love. Some assume that they have to heal these wounds fully before they can find happiness in love. They don't. The truth is that you may be working with this particular wounding for years to come, learning to push back against the sense of unworthiness, fear, or powerlessness that gets activated either when someone gets too close or when they disappoint you. You may need to learn how to

> Experience is the name everyone gives to their mistakes.
>
> —Oscar Wilde

turn toward that younger part of yourself, from the part of you that's holding wisdom, discernment, and self-compassion, so that you can make empowered meaning of whatever is happening that is triggering you.

When you don't feel safe with another person, remind yourself that *you* are the source of safety. And that you're safe with you, and learning how to keep yourself safe with others. Many people tell me, "I don't trust others," or "I don't trust love." But what they're really saying is "I don't trust myself to keep myself safe when allowing myself to be close to someone." If you are a survivor of sexual abuse, one of the things that happened in that experience, particularly if it was ongoing, is that you stopped learning how to negotiate your boundaries, speak up for yourself, ask the right questions, or even discern motives—yours and theirs. In other words, you stopped learning the nuts and bolts of how to keep yourself and others safe in your close relationships, which is something that we must all learn to do in order to have happy, healthy love. Without this development, you'll have a tendency to do things like be intimate too quickly, or overly invest your heart in someone who's not reciprocating your affections, not negotiate the terms of the connection before taking off your clothes, or show up in inconsistent, somewhat confusing ways that make others feel unsafe, which then puts them on the defense, which then validates that others can't be trusted.

Sometimes people get confused about how to heal from the sexual abuse, and assume it's simply a matter of deconstructing their walls to dismantle their defenses and start being more open with everyone. When someone tells me this, I beg them *not* to do this! The walls are a crude way of keeping you safe that were constructed in the absence of having concrete skills like good pacing, or discernment, or negotiation for your needs, or knowing what boundaries to set. These are the skills that generate safety between ourselves and others. If I asked you the question "Is it safe to cross the street?" you'd have to admit that it's safe only if you know how to look right and left before you step into the crosswalk. So before just dismantling the wall, ask yourself what new skills you are now going to practice in order to grow safety between yourself and another. Then take the risk to be a beginner, and get busy learning how to do this. And if you've been abused and have never really looked at it too deeply, do yourself a favor. Make an appointment with a therapist who's trained in sexual abuse recovery. Either that or call a rape hotline, even if the incident happened a long time ago. At the very least, they'll be able to tell you where to go for help. Healing sexual abuse can and does happen when you know how to work with this particular wounding, and there are many exceptional practitioners and resources available to help you on your journey.

There is an argument to be made for abstinence during this period, to begin focusing your energies on the partner you are calling into your life. However, rather than make that a hard and fast rule, I encourage you to stay connected to the integrity of your path, and use good judgment. Just as not all committed sexual encounters are healthy ones (I recall a student who'd been repeatedly raped by her husband), not all noncommitted sexual encounters are "unhealthy." I suggest that you make a commitment to yourself that all of your sexual choices will be self-honoring. Ask yourself what you need to know *before* taking your clothes off. Stay present and conscious to how you feel and what you need when making your decisions. Give yourself permission to change your mind if you become uncomfortable. Make sure you're safe and that your expectations are realistic. Many of us use sex as a way to try to bond the relationship prematurely—to sort of slip through the backdoor in the hopes that this becomes something, and it usually winds up to be yet another disappointing experience. If you're going to have sex with someone without a clear commitment, please do yourself a favor and don't expect sex to solidify the deal. I believe that many of us have learned that lesson one too many times.

Culturally, we have reduced sexuality to its most primitive function—that of a physical act between body parts. In doing so, we have omitted the subtleties of such a soulful encounter, and the inherent power dynamics involved. Much of our focus on sex has to do with how to have more of it, and for longer periods of time. Yet, sexuality extends far beyond penises, anuses, and vaginas. Sexuality can include many things we don't ordinarily think of as sex. My vibrantly creative and beautiful friend Lora, an actress and talk-radio host, has been holding the high watch for her man for well over a year. A highly sensual woman, Lora loves to dance. Every Sunday afternoon, she puts on her tights and her dancing shoes, and spends hours on the dance floor, dancing freestyle. Sometimes she dances alone, sometimes with a partner, sometimes with a group of people. She is in one moment soft and sensual, in another primitive and wild. At times she is light and playful, then she'll suddenly become heavy and sad. Through all of her moods and emotions, she connects deeply with her body, and allows herself the luxury of self-expression and surrender. She feels the gazes of admiration and desire from the men around her and yet she knows that she is there for herself and herself alone. Contrary to many other areas of her life, Lora's dancing is one place where she doesn't have to perform. In essence, she is there to make love to herself.

Sensual pleasures such as dancing, eating, gardening, or creating art flourish in the lives of the celibate, and rightly so. Our sexuality transcends whether we have a partner at this particular point in time, or not. Sexuality need not always be literal, and surrendering to passion is not always about orgasm. Massages, rubbing scented oils into your skin, working with clay, kneading bread, lovingly primping and preening yourself are all ways to be sensual during this period in your life without actually going to bed with someone. We are not simply waiting for someone to show up before we allow ourselves to express the lover that we already are. What I finally learned through all my trial and error was this: that it is far more important in life to *be* a lover than to *get* a lover. In the words of Sufi poet Rumi: *Lovers don't finally meet somewhere. They are in each other all along.*

> *You arouse me with your touch*
> *although I can't see your hands.*
> *You have kissed me with tenderness*
> *Although I haven't seen your lips.*
> *You are hidden from me.*
>
> —Rumi

PRACTICE: SEXUAL CLEARING AND VISIONING

Take out your journal. We are going to begin with a meditation. Read it at least twice, then do it as best as you can from memory.

Get Still. Sit comfortably, close your eyes, and take a deep breath, as though you could breathe all the way down into your hips, genitals, and thighs. Become aware of all of the feelings and sensations in your body. Notice where you're holding any tension and let it go.

Exhale Release/Inhale Reclaim. On each exhale, breathe out any energies of former lovers (or anyone with whom you've had a sexual encounter) that you've been holding on to with regret or sorrow. Release any shame, hurt, or anger that you've been holding in your second chakra (your genitals and lower belly). With each inhale, reclaim your wholeness and power, retrieving any portions of your body, heart, or soul that you either gave away or feel was taken from you. Continue to breathe this way until you feel clear and free in your second chakra, or until you feel ready to proceed. Give yourself as much time as you need.

Call in the Soul of Your Partner-to-Be. When you're ready, call the lover of your future into your meditation. Imagine them before you, lovingly gazing into your eyes, and allow yourself to feel safe and loved. Feel your heart open in response to their love. Lovingly offer your body to this person as a home and a sacred resting place. Feel them receive this offering as they, in turn, offer their body up to you with the same level of love and devotion. Begin to imagine what the touch of your beloved will feel like. Imagine what it feels like for them to stroke your hair and your face gently. Feel your beloved kiss your neck, your chest, your belly, your inner thighs. Now allow yourself to touch and kiss your beloved in the same way back. As you do this, feel the intense love and attraction that exists between you. Notice that you feel very safe with this person. There is a sense of complete trust and surrender that is both natural and joyful.

When you are ready, open your eyes and write about this sensual, loving relationship from the perspective of how it feels to actually *have* it. What is the experience of being held and loved by someone you trust, and who turns you on?

I believe in the flesh and the appetites,
Seeing, hearing, feeling are miracles,
and each part of me is a miracle.
Divine am I inside and out, and

I make holy whatever I touch or am touched from,
The scent of these arm-pits
aroma finer than prayer, this head more than churches,
bibles, and all the creeds.

—Walt Whitman

Bonus: Practice in Action

Allow yourself to have a highly sensual day today—dress in sensual clothes, wear a sensual scent, move in sensual ways, eat sensual food, make sensual art, listen to sensual music, write sensual poetry, etc. All day, continue to express and enjoy your own sensual energy.

Cultivating Solitude

If you want to become full,
let yourself be empty.

—Tao Te Ching

I once had an affair with a married man. I did the classically cliché thing of think-ing he would leave his wife like he said he would. One night, when I really needed him and he wasn't there (yet *again*), I paced the floors of my apartment, face to face with a dreaded loneliness I'd been avoiding for years. Not knowing what else to do, I began to shout and dance its pain in my body. I howled its aching cry as I lay despondent and sobbing on the floor. It wasn't so much that I was crying over the guy, as it was that I was crying for the thousands of times in life that I'd felt abandoned, unloved, and deserted. The affair was just my latest attempt to avoid feeling (and *healing*) those feelings. Yet rather than helping me run away from these feelings, my relationship with him had caused me to run right smack into the center of them. I don't know how long I carried on that way but in the morning, when I woke up, I was at peace. I called my married friend and broke it off with him. It was the first time that I had enough of myself to be that strong. I had faced down the beast and I had come out whole.

All sins are attempts to fill voids.

—Simone Weil

Poet Marianne Moore once wrote, "The best cure for loneliness is solitude." While loneliness is an aching sense of separateness, sometimes in the company of others, solitude is the experience of being deeply connected to, and in full possession of, ourselves. Loneliness is not the enemy. Alienation from ourselves is. We are never lonely because we've lost contact with others. We're lonely when we lose contact with ourselves.

Most of us understand, intellectually anyway, that we should be cultivating a certain capacity for solitude before entering into a relationship. It makes sense that solitude would give us the chance to develop a more solid sense of self, so we have more to offer our soul mate when they arrive. Yet I'm not sure we understand just how important it is to develop a sense of autonomy and sovereignty within, as the foundation for happy, healthy love. My dear friend and bestselling author Melanie Tonia Evans coined the phrase "self-partnering" that actress Emma Watson kicked into the lexicon, much like Gwyneth Paltrow made my phrase "conscious uncoupling" known throughout the world. Melanie and I recently had a good belly laugh about it, grateful to positively impact culture in these ways. Basically, Melanie describes self-partnering as feeling whole within yourself, without needing another person to complete you. It's the ability to keep one's own counsel, to know one's own mind, to tend to one's own needs, and to soothe one's own emotions. We're happy that Emma made her phrase known, particularly as it erases much of the negative stigma of being single. This time of turning inward to grow a healthy, supportive, and nourishing relationship with yourself is essential to having good relationships with others, as most of the toxic relational dynamics we struggle with like codependence, narcissistic abuse, or push-pull patterns, are all the result of an undeveloped capacity for it.

Particularly now, when so much is happening in our world that's pulling our attentions outward—deeply distressing stories in the news; constant texts that have us responding as though each message were a crying baby; social media that fills us with fake "facts"—it's tempting to marginalize the need for such development. To find our way home to the center of ourselves in the midst of such a consistent onslaught of external interruptions is a deliberate act of self-love. Yet without taking this on, we're vulnerable to repeating dysfunctional patterns in our intimate connections. How often have we sold ourselves short by becoming entangled with people we knew were wrong for us because we tired of being alone? How many times have we let fear keep us in relationships

> Go placidly amid the noise and the haste, and remember what peace there is in silence.
>
> —Max Ehrmann

> Enter into the stillness
> inside your busy life.
> Become familiar with
> her ways. Grow to love
> her, feel [*her*] with all
> your heart and you will
> come to hear her silent
> music and become one
> with Love's silent song.
>
> —Noel Davis

long after they have fulfilled their purpose? In what ways have we sacrificed ourselves to avoid the risk of sitting in our own silence? It's time to face our fears and transform our aloneness into a source of strength.

For weeks after the affair was over, I began to actively cultivate the practice of solitude to help me heal. Each day, I made sure to spend some time alone, and in silence. I turned off the TV, shut down the computer, silenced the phone, and refrained from listening to music. I even put down my books, my journal, the newspaper, and any creative project I was working on. I just sat. Or I walked. Or I watched my breath. Sometimes I was bored. Sometimes I wasn't. But it did not matter. I did it anyway. For the longest time, there was an all too familiar sadness present. Yet, I stopped being afraid of it and, instead, did my best to make a companion of it. Invited it in for tea, so to speak.

These minutes of solitude became the foundation for what I would call my "down days." These were days when I would take an entire twenty-four hours in silence. I would let those closest to me know that I was doing this, so they wouldn't panic when I didn't answer my phone. On these days, I allowed myself to read, write, pick up my flute or guitar, and occasionally listen to soft instrumental music, but that was it. Otherwise, I rested, petted my cat, did yoga poses on the floor of my bedroom, and listened to the quiet. Sometimes I went for a walk to look at the trees. But all the time I watched my breath, and listened to my heart. We became good friends.

And then one day the sadness was gone. In its place was a sense of peace and stillness that seemed to follow me through my days. I still wasn't thrilled to be single, but somehow the pain of it was gone. I was content to simply be with myself. Today, with a thriving teaching career, the delight of singing, writing, and recording music, an amazing international group of friends to keep up with, and a family of my own to care for, I miss the time when I could simply decide to be still and then just do it. What a luxury to have those long stretches of hours

> The self must know
> stillness before it can
> discover its true song.
>
> —Ralph Blum

to just be. That's why it's important to appreciate where we are in life and what we have when we have it. I remember someone telling me once that I really could have it all—I just couldn't have it all at one time.

> Just to be is a blessing.
> Just to live is holy.
>
> —Rabbi Abraham Heschel

This is a special time in your life. Don't miss out on the opportunity that it presents by wishing you were somewhere else. The secret to being happy in life is to choose what you have. What better time to cultivate solitude than when one is single? It's a gift. Don't waste it.

PRACTICE: BE STILL

Spend five to fifteen minutes this morning sitting in stillness. No TV, no journal, no book, no phone calls, emails, or texts, no social media, no activity. Just be still.

Begin now.

Then take out your journal and write about that experience.

Spend three to five minutes each day in stillness and solitude, if you can manage it.

Bonus: Practice in Action

Schedule time in your busy life for a "down hour" or a "down morning" or a "down day" this week. Any amount of time you can commit to will be fine. Just make a date with yourself to go within and spend some time with your most intimate of companions—yourself.

Suggested Study Guide for Group Discussion

1. What commitments are you making to yourself and your own life, in preparation for receiving a commitment from your beloved?

2. What is your experience with turning toward and welcoming your own emotions? When you do this as a regular practice, what begins to open up in your relationships with others?

3. When were you triggered this week and how did you respond? Were you able to get yourself back into power center and act from there? How do you show up differently from each center, and what does that generate?

4. Share about the experience of awakening to the goodness and beauty of your own unique physical self.

5. How are you expressing your sensual, sexual self in safe and nourishing ways?

6. Share what's waking up in you in the moments of stillness and solitude that you've given yourself this week.

A Life Worth Living

You cannot have a happy ending to a miserable journey.

—Abraham Hicks

Happy, healthy relationships require a certain level of maturity and generosity of spirit—those same qualities that improve our overall satisfaction in life, with or without a partner. Now is the time to consciously grow yourself in the direction of your dreams by actively taking on becoming who you'll need to be, to be ready for love when it appears.

This week, we will:

- Practice generosity, particularly toward those we've been blaming or making wrong, to further expand our capacity to love and be loved
- Awaken to an unconditional sense of happiness, joy, and well-being in life
- Courageously start to show up in new, healthier ways with others that are reflective of our value and power
- Deepen our ability to both listen and speak in ways that create greater closeness and connection
- Improve our communication skills to create more meaningful and resilient connections with others
- Identify new choices and new actions to take with others to finally graduate you from old painful beliefs

Being Generous

Marriage is no way of life for the weak, the selfish, or the insecure.

—Sidney Poitier, in *To Sir, with Love*

The Dalai Lama was once asked if he was ever lonely. "No," he answered simply. When asked what he attributed this to, he replied, "I think one factor is that I look at any human being from a more positive angle; I try to look for their positive aspects. This attitude immediately creates a feeling of affinity, a kind of connectedness." The Dalai Lama has what we might call a "generous listening" for others.

We tend to like those who are generous with us, allowing us to make mistakes and be imperfect without holding it against us. When people are generous, we feel like we can breathe around them. We feel like we can be more authentically who we are. Generosity is a spacious phenomenon.

Yet, most of us are pretty stingy. Rather than looking for and appreciating people's positive traits, we assess them, instead, through the filter of who we think they should be that they're not. Instead of extending ourselves with open, unguarded hearts, we enter the majority of our encounters defended and closed. This withholding of ourselves is so common that we just think it's normal.

In his beautiful book *The Untethered Soul*, bestselling author Michael Singer tells us that the secret to being happy has little to do with what we've acquired or accomplished in life, and everything to do with liv-

> The most effective way to achieve right relations with any living thing is to look for the best in it, and then help that best into the fullest expression.
>
> —J. Allen Boone

ing with a heart that is open and tender toward others. I took a weekend seminar once that was about developing the capacity to love others more fully. Most of us in the room thought of ourselves as fairly evolved in this regard. After all, we had paid good money and given up an entire weekend to learn more about how to be a loving person. Who does that, except someone who is pretty far along the path already? But the facilitator challenged our notions of ourselves by asking, "How long do you think you could keep your heart open if, after confessing your deepest passion and adoration for someone, they made it clear to you that your love was not reciprocated? How long do you think that you could continue to be generous with your love in the face of such a rejection?" Most of us had to admit, not very long.

Yet, what better opportunity to give love than when one is not getting what they want? It's easy to be generous and loving toward those who are generous and loving toward us. However, to extend ourselves beyond what's easy—to give in a way that compels us to let go of something that we are attached to—that is where true generosity begins.

Our more frequent response of reflexive defensiveness creates for us an emotional vacuum. When we hold back our love and care for any reason, we end up feeling hungry for love ourselves. In her book *Enchanted Love*, Marianne Williamson writes, "To the extent that love has dried up in my life, it was always because I became miserly with my expression of compassion. To the extent that love has blossomed in my life, it was always because I expanded my willingness to express the love that often cowers like a child in a corner of my heart." In our reluctance to extend ourselves in love, we create an intense craving for love in our hearts. Our drive to find "The One" is intensified as a kind of compensation for the love that is missing in our lives.

In her book *In the Meantime*, Iyanla Vanzant reminds us, "We go into a relationship looking for love, not realizing that we must bring love with us." Rather than look for someone to get love from, we need to also focus more on finding someone we can give love to—someone who inspires us to expand beyond the limitations of our own self-absorption. This requires that we be skilled in the practice of giving love, even when it's the hard thing to do.

> It always boils down to the same thing—not only receiving love but desperately needing to give it.
>
> —Audrey Hepburn

It's important you stay steady in your resolve to expand your capacity to love and be loved to ensure you're ready when love appears. This capacity to tolerate not getting what you want without closing your heart is one of the keys to a union that can root down and grow over time. Healthy relationships require each person to tolerate being disappointed by the other, without punishing them by withdrawing love. The choice to steadfastly continue to love someone in the face of being let down by them is indeed an act of generosity. Granting someone the right to say no in order to honor themselves, and knowing that you too have this right, is the hallmark of happy, healthy love.

Generosity is an act of abundance, and an affirmation of life. Yet not all self-sacrifice is a kindhearted gesture. Sometimes our "generosity" comes with a covert agenda to manipulate another person into being who we want them to be. Yet we'll dress up our selfishness with altruistic words and sacrificial gestures, trying to pass ourselves off as something we are not. You know. You've probably dated that person. The one who gave to you in the hopes that they would get something in return. Maybe you've even *been* that person. The one who's sweet, and kind, and goes out of their way to understand. Until, that is, you get it that the person in front of you is in *no way* going to be able to give you what you want. So often, when I was dating, I had to keep reminding myself that, even though the man I was dating was completely unable or unwilling to give me what I wanted, that didn't mean that he was wrong. It just meant that he was wrong for me.

There is a Native American custom that judges a person's wealth, not by what they have, but by what they give. In order to continue giving without an attachment to getting something specific back, one must be connected to an inner source of wellness and wealth. Buddhist nun Pema Chödrön says, "The journey of generosity is one of connecting with this wealth, cherishing it so profoundly that we are willing to begin to give away whatever blocks it. We give away our dark glasses, our long coats, our hoods, and our disguises. In short, we open ourselves and let ourselves be touched."

When we find ourselves wondering why we don't have more love in our lives, we would do well to consider more ways that we might extend it. Love that can't get out has a hard time getting in as well.

Although it can feel almost counterintuitive to

> Real generosity is doing something nice for someone who'll never find it out.
>
> —Frank A. Clark

look for ways to give love when one is feeling deprived, to do so is as though we take a stand for our lives, demonstrating a commitment to have love in our lives. In *The Prophet*, Kahlil Gibran calls those who have little, but give anyway, "the believers in life," assuring us that "their coffer is never empty." That's because life always has a way of balancing itself out. In his essay "Compensation," Ralph Waldo Emerson encouraged us to live with such profound generosity that the Universe Itself would be compelled to reward our efforts. Advising us to "love, and you shall be loved," he believed that "all love is mathematically just, as much as the two sides of an algebraic equation." Therefore, he admonished us to "put God in our debt."

It feels good to be a big person—the one to forgive, to apologize first, or give up saving face in order to save the relationship. There is always that initial "But I don't *want* to!" However, once you take a deep breath and give up the need to be right, to look good, to punish someone for hurting you, or to make someone wrong, then you're free to experience a profound love that becomes a way of life.

> Even after all this time
> the sun never says
> to the earth,
> "You owe me."
> Look what happens
> with a love like that.
> It lights the whole sky.
>
> —Hafiz

Being generous in how you listen for the good in others, or in how you grant people space to be exactly who they are and who they aren't, or in keeping your heart open and soft in response to not getting what you want or need in that moment, is a spiritual discipline. The more you practice it, the stronger you become. While developing your "generosity muscle" might appear to be optional for you at this point, your very future most likely rests upon your ability to practice the kind of self-control required to love another human being for the long haul. It takes bigheartedness to love someone beyond

All those happy in the world are so because of their desire for the happiness of others.

—Shantideva

the initial attraction and falling in love period. Some of us aren't used to stretching ourselves so. To give up *having* to be right, *having* to prove someone else wrong, *having* to have the last word, *having* to be understood—that is the mark of a person who is ready to create a loving relationship that can last and flourish over time.

PRACTICE: BEING GENEROUS WITH YOUR LOVE

Take out your journal. Write on the following question:

Who in my life am I making wrong?

Now choose a person from your list and write on the following question:

What is _____ wrong about?
       (person's name)

Once you've gotten it all out, now turn your attention to yourself by asking:

How has my certainty about this caused me to withhold my love?

(For example, am I punishing? Shaming? Have I closed my heart to punish this person?)

Now switch hats and pretend that you *are* this person. Completely surrender yourself to standing in their shoes and try on their point of view. Don't worry. You're not giving in. You're simply stretching to see the situation from a more holistic perspective. In this exercise, you might just discover that, as philosopher Ken Wilber suggests, "Everybody's right about something," and that there's room for more than one perspective.

Complete the following sentence stems as though you actually *were* this person. Write for several minutes, exploring various reasons why, from their perspective, they might actually have a point.

I am right because:

What _____ *doesn't understand about me is:*
　　　 (your name)

Now come back to being you again, and answer the following question:

Understanding their perspective (which doesn't mean I agree with it, per se), how can I now choose to be more generous with them for the sake of our relationship?

Bonus: Practice in Action

Take at least one generous action today. This could include, but does not have to, telling the person what you wrote about this morning, that you understand their point of view. Other generous actions might be apologizing to someone, forgiving someone, giving up being right in the midst of a conversation, or simply choosing to focus on the good in them. This letting go of your judgments is not a begrudging resignation. It is a deliberate act of enlargement on your part. If you've truly been generous, you won't have a feeling of self-righteousness or superiority, but rather, you will feel as though your soul has expanded and grown larger. This is you being the biggest person you are capable of being. Go ahead and stretch yourself.

Choosing to Be Happy

Most folks are about as happy as they make up their minds to be.

—Abraham Lincoln

Years ago, while attending Overeaters Anonymous meetings to help heal the eating disorder I'd had since adolescence, I became familiar with the above-mentioned quote. It both annoyed and intrigued me. How, I wondered, am I supposed to be happy when coming home alone each night to an empty apartment? How can I be happy when I'm still so overweight and out of shape? How can I enjoy life when I have so little money? I'd wanted to dismiss those words as irrelevant to my life, spoken by a man who understood nothing about the kinds of challenges most of us face today. However, the more I understood Abraham Lincoln as someone who experienced many bitter disappointments and failures, the more I couldn't just dismiss his words as some Pollyanna philosophy spoken by a person who knew nothing of how hard life can be.

In my early thirties, I went through a prolonged period where I felt sad and deeply disappointed over what I believed to be my failed singing career. At the time, I'd just ended a three-and-a-half-year relationship and I was working as a temp secretary, something I loathed and was ill-suited for, to say the least. In response to my constant whining, a good friend would simply smile and say, with a gleam in his eyes, "The secret to being happy, Katherine, is to choose happiness for what you have." Once I got over being completely irritated with him for what seemed to be a total lack of sensitivity on his part, I began to consider his words.

Even though I was totally miserable, I was also tired of my defensive posturing on why I had a right to be so utterly unhappy. It seemed pathetic, even to

> Can you tolerate happiness? If we don't believe ourselves worthy of happiness, we won't allow love to take root in our lives. It's outside of our beliefs about our lives and we'll sabotage love.
>
> —Nathaniel Branden

me, to be defending my victim position, and I grew weary of hearing myself complain. I began thinking of myself as one of those "feverish little clod(s) of ailments and grievances, complaining that the world will not devote itself to making you happy" that George Bernard Shaw was talking about in his famous quote. I became curious about this idea that one could simply be happy by choosing to be. As a spiritual challenge, I decided to take on cultivating the quality of joy, thinking, "Well, if I can be happy now, under these conditions, then I can be happy anywhere, at any time." So, instead of trying to change my circumstances, I began accepting them and blessing them as they were. I began to consider the possibility that life could be cherished and accepted on its own terms. I began relating to disappointment and struggle as an opportunity to deepen and expand myself to include the totality of the human experience in my definition of what makes a worthwhile life.

The disappointment and deep sorrow that I felt didn't go away. Nor did the fact that I was a complete disaster at being a temp secretary. However, my overall sense of humor and well-being kicked in. And, lo and behold, I began enjoying my life, as lopsided and puzzling as it was. I gave up resisting the circumstances I was in and began instead surrendering to them. I did this by simply accepting all that was happening and, even more important, all that wasn't. I even began saying prayers of thanks for everything almost as an experiment, to see if I could alter my experience without altering my circumstances.

Although we tend to believe that happiness exists as some sort of reward for having successfully mastered all the particulars of our lives, nothing could be further from the truth. Call it one of the biggest lies of all time, which we've completely bought into. We're not unhappy because we don't have enough of what we think we want. We're unhappy because we're resisting and rejecting what's in our lives as unworthy of appreciation, and we're frantically caught up in trying to fix something that we perceive to be broken. That's an awful lot of pressure. That being said, I recognize that some of you may suffer from clinical depression and that for you, finding happiness is not simply a matter of choosing to feel better. For those of you dealing with a serious depression, please know that I have endless admiration for all you do to stay strong and generative of health and well-being in the face of it. I have seen firsthand that dealing with depression does not have to prevent you from creating a loving union with a wonderful person who gets you, and accepts the totality of who you are and all you struggle with, including depression.

> Everything has its wonders, even darkness and silence, and I learn, whatever state I may be in, therein to be content.
>
> —Helen Keller

I went back to graduate school to become a psychotherapist a couple of years later. Not having much money, I rented a small one-bedroom apartment in a funky part of the renowned beach town of Venice, California. Being single and broke at the age of thirty-five was not exactly what my mom had in mind while raising me, and it was difficult for her to understand. She tried to be supportive by being careful to say all the right things, but I'd watch her eyes dart back and forth over my neighborhood when she visited. Even though she wouldn't say it, I knew how disappointed she was.

When she flew out from New York to attend my graduation, I was grateful that she'd traveled three thousand miles to be with me. We were excited as we spent the day before the graduation ceremony preparing for a party we were having the next day. As we were going from store to store, she began discussing my future plans, which, as she saw it, now included getting out there and making some *money*. The frustration she'd felt all those years while I delayed marriage and family to pursue an unprofitable singing career, followed by more years as a starving student, followed yet again by a charitable music project to lift those who were living out on the streets, coated each word she spoke. I began feeling really pushed and pressured by her dissatisfaction over my life. After a while, I lost it. Standing in the kitchen while cutting up vegetables, waving a knife around like a lunatic, I cracked. "Mom!" I shouted. "What if I never have a lot of money? What if I never have what you think I'm supposed to have? Maybe this ratty little apartment is as good as it gets! Maybe this moment is the absolute pinnacle of my life!" And I stormed off to the one room that I could actually slam the door shut to, the bedroom.

My poor mom. Her feelings were pretty hurt. After all, she'd come only to support me and let me know how proud she was of me. And she was basically just doing that thing that moms do by wanting more for their daughters than a single life filled with financial struggle and hardship. Upon reflection, I realized that I was not reacting to *her*, as much as I was to the constant internalized pressure that *I* felt. I was the one who thought that: (1) something was very wrong with my life (i.e., I *should* have a husband and lots of money by now), and (2) things had better change soon, because I was definitely not okay the way I was. What I was essentially declaring to my mom, but really to myself, was that I was no longer going to be on some treadmill trying to get my life to fit anyone's expectations of what it was supposed to look like, including my own. I was going to accept who I was and what I had as enough, even if it meant that I lived alone in that silly little apartment for the rest of my life. My relief was palpable and that incident became a defining moment in my life. I had finally stopped resisting my life.

We cause our own unhappiness by refusing to accept life on life's terms. And unhappy people tend to create unhappy relationships, or none at all. We've heard of the studies that indicate married people are happier than unmarried people, and seen this as evidence that being married makes you happier. However, we've also got to consider the possibility that happy people are more likely to attract love into their lives than unhappy people are. And creating happiness begins with accepting, and surrendering to, the life you have right now. As is. Failed expectations and all. Complete with disappointments, struggles, and heartaches. All of it. As it is right now.

Often we become attached and driven to getting married because we are invalidating the lives we are living without a partner as inferior and second-rate. The desperation we can feel comes from an unwillingness to accept the possibility of being on our own. It comes from the belief that you must marry in order to have your life be valid and worth living. Another lie we collectively perpetuate.

What makes life worth living is being actively engaged in becoming the finest, most delicious human being you can possibly be in this lifetime. What makes life worth living is finding people and projects that you can love and stand by and give yourself to completely. Too many of us long for relationships where we can hide out. But that isn't a soul mate experience, that's a survival experience. Living your "best life," as Oprah calls it, is now, in this moment, under these

> We have no more right to consume happiness without producing it than to consume wealth without producing it.
>
> —George Bernard Shaw

circumstances, whether or not your experience includes intimate love at this point in time.

You must be able to create a life that lights you up whether or not you have a lover, a great career, a lot of money, a great house, a healthy child, or a hit song. Part of creating this magnificent life may include being actively engaged in the pursuit of such blessings. However, to place the burden of validation of your life upon the achievement of such things is a terrible encumbrance.

Joy is an unconditional experience that is not attached to circumstances. It is a choice one makes to cultivate a consciousness of unconditional acceptance and appreciation of what is. You may not like what's happening right now, but you can be with it. In giving up your resistance, you allow yourself to be present with your more difficult emotions. In so doing, you free yourself to also feel contentment, happiness, wonder, and gratitude. Joy is the by-product of being emotionally fluid in life. It comes from the simple appreciation of being alive—and *not* in response to getting what we want in life.

In my life I find that I usually get what I want but rarely when I'm feeling desperate to have it. That's how it works and it's why people say you'll find your soul mate when you aren't looking. It's not the "not looking" part that allows your soul mate to come to you; it's the nonattachment part that does it. Usually those people who "aren't looking" will allow only loving and healthy people into their inner circle, because desperation isn't driving them to compromise themselves. If they have to be alone for the rest of their life, they'd rather do that than create destructive, dramatic entanglements. They don't lose years of their lives entwined with people who treat them poorly or don't love them. They set about making their lives worth living by pursuing things that capture their interest, good friends and meaningful activities. It's not necessarily that they weren't looking. It's that they were busy enjoying their lives, with or without a partner.

Years ago, when in my mid-thirties, I had a funny experience that taught me a good lesson about how things come to you when you're no longer desperate to have them. When I was ten years old, I had a friend named Cathy Swift. Each day after school Cathy and I used to meet at my house and put on Monkees records at top volume. We would then proceed to sing and

> Men who are unhappy, like men who sleep badly, are always proud of the fact.
>
> —Bertrand Russell

> Life has no other discipline
> to impose, if we would but
> realize it, than to accept life
> unquestioningly. Everything we
> shut our eyes to, everything
> we run away from, everything
> we deny, denigrate, or despise,
> serves . . . us in the end. What
> seems nasty, painful, evil, can
> become a source of beauty, joy,
> and strength, if faced with an
> open mind. Every moment is a
> golden one for him who has the
> vision to recognize it as such.
>
> —Henry Miller

dance our way through the house. We pretended that Davy, Micky, Peter, and Mike were singing to us. We were madly in love with each of them, changing off one for another each week. One week I loved Davy and she loved Peter. The next week I loved Peter and she loved Micky. I would have gladly given my right arm to meet any one of them.

Fast-forward twenty-five years. Having met a guy at an informal Saturday-afternoon gathering, we made a casual date to meet later that night to see a play together. Peter seemed nice enough, but he certainly didn't look like he had much going for him financially, although I believe he was kind enough to pay for my ticket. But he did talk a lot about being in show business in a way that confused me. He struck me more as a struggling actor, yet he spoke intimately about having a great deal of success. Right before the curtain went up I said, "I'm sorry, should I know you? Have you done something that I would know about?" He smiled rather shyly and said, "Well, if I told you, it would ruin our date." With that, the theater went black. Suddenly, I got it, and gasped. I was out on a date with Peter Tork! I nearly fell on the floor! My friends Leo and Bill teased me for weeks, calling my answering machine to sing, "Hey, hey, we're the Monkees!" while giggling hysterically. See, that's how life works. It's when you're no longer attached that all good things come to you.

PRACTICE: CULTIVATING UNCONDITIONAL HAPPINESS

Take out your journal and write on the following question. Begin each sentence with "I must have . . .":

What do I think I absolutely must *have in order to be happy?*

Now go back and circle those things you can see that you are attached to having. (*Hint:* Whatever makes you angry, depressed, or upset to think of *not* having is probably something that you are attached to having.)

One by one, go through each thing you've circled and say this prayer:

Dear God/Higher Power/Universe/Life:

I believe I must have _____ to be happy. However, I am willing to release this attachment now, knowing that my life is good and beautiful exactly as it is, with or without this blessing. I accept that it is possible for me to have a sense of joy, with or without _____, and I fully surrender myself to what is currently so in my life today. Thank you for all that I do have in my life today. Amen.

Do this with everything on your list.

Bonus: Practice in Action

Practice unconditional acceptance of your life today just as it is, and make a conscious choice to be happy whenever possible. Every time you feel yourself frustrated, disappointed, and restless today, give thanks for your life, exactly as it is and exactly as it is not. Affirm the goodness of your life whether or not you are getting what you want at any given moment.

Owning Yourself as Cause

Many of us treat life as if it were a novel. We pass from page to
page passively, assuming the author will tell us on the last page
what it was all about.

—James Hollis

I knew a woman once who was about thirty pounds overweight. She complained about her weight all the time, blaming her chronic boredom and loneliness on her dress size. No matter how many diets she tried, she could never seem to rid herself of the extra pounds she was carrying. Finally, she confessed to me that she was afraid that if she lost the weight, men would find her attractive and she wouldn't be able to keep them away. "So, lose the weight but don't bathe," I somewhat mischievously suggested, in the hope of reminding her that she was the one in charge of her own body.

Most of us go through life as though we were a pinball, bouncing off everything and everyone who tries to touch us. Tender beings that we are, we are constantly in reaction to someone or something. If we look at what we *do*, instead of what we *say*, we will see that, ultimately, most of us are more interested in protecting ourselves from the risks of love than in the actual experience of it. We go to extraordinary lengths to avoid the possibility of being hurt, regardless of the hunger in our hearts. We rarely own outright how often we sabotage love by admitting, "I am more interested in being safe than I am in being loved." Instead, most of us will pretend to be looking for love while covertly doing all that we can to kill off any possibility of it. We may yearn for deep and meaningful connection, but we'll react as though any gesture of advancement from another were potentially a full-on attack. Perhaps, on some level, it is.

> Thoughts crystallize into habit and habit solidifies into circumstances.
>
> —Brian Adams

Nicole and Nancy came to see me when I was still in private practice. Although they had been together for only a few months, they were highly reactive and volatile with each other. Their pervasive communication style was to blame each other for the flaws and failures of their relationship. Rather than listen respectfully to each other's complaints in an attempt to increase love and affinity between them, they listened, instead, for leverage. How can I make the other person wrong? What can I blame on my partner? In what ways can I best defend my position? Unfortunately, this narrow, contracted way of relating is what some of us call "being in love." But it is the shadow side of passion, and the underbelly of ardor. In this highly reactive environment, all that's beautiful about love is cast aside and, ultimately, sacrificed in service to the need to protect oneself.

Dr. David Burns, associate professor of psychiatry at Stanford University School of Medicine, conducted an intensive study with 1,500 people to differentiate between what was happening with partners in a thriving, contented intimate relationship from those in a disappointing, miserable one. He found that "[o]nly one thing emerged as having a causal impact on long-term satisfaction: blaming your partner for the problems in your relationship." In other words, the *one* disparity between happy, flourishing partnerships and unhappy, failing ones was whether or not, and how intensely, they played the "blame and shame" game.

When we are having a hard time being responsible for ourselves as the cause of what is happening to us, it is generally because we have confused and collapsed "being responsible" for "being wrong." For some of us, owning our part in the creation of a situation is likened to admitting guilt and/or complete defeat. Nicole and Nancy both have the same source fracture wound of being shamed by a highly critical parent. As children, each of them was frequently blamed and made wrong with little provocation. Therefore, taking responsibility for what was happening in their relationship, on some level, equated to admitting guilt and was accompanied by deep feelings of shame and self-reproach. They could not acknowledge responsibility for what was happening without also agreeing that they were fundamentally bad people. They could not own how they were each covertly, unconsciously showing up in ways that set the other up to fail, or how they were misinterpreting what just happened and then reacting in ways that were causing the breakdowns between them.

All relationships are handicapped to the extent that we are unable to be responsible for what we, ourselves, are creating in that relationship. This goes for relationships with friends, family, co-workers, and acquaintances, as well as with lovers. Whenever we blame others for the current circumstances in our lives, we abdicate responsibility for our own choices and actions, and we reinforce our own impotence. We construct an "either/or" world—either I am right (and someone else is wrong), or I am wrong (and, therefore, deeply shamed). In this world, we are preoccupied with blaming ourselves or blaming others, believing that we *have* to be right to be worthy of the air we breathe. Yet whenever we play the blame and shame game, no one wins. Because shame stunts development. It literally stops any growth from occurring. In becoming preoccupied with listening to gain leverage to prove ourselves right, we have not only alienated those who love us, but we've also thwarted our own ability to grow in healthy ways in response to whatever breakdown we're dealing with.

In her book *When Things Fall Apart*, Buddhist nun Pema Chödrön states, "Blame is a way in which we solidify ourselves." She talks about our resistance to giving up our way of conceptualizing life as a right/wrong proposition by being willing to enter the "middle way" where we are "sitting on the razor's edge, not falling off to the right or the left." She continues:

> *This middle way involves not hanging on to our version so tightly. It involves keeping our hearts and minds open long enough to entertain the idea that when we make things wrong, we do it out of a desire to obtain some kind of ground or security . . . Could our minds and our hearts be big enough just to hang out in that space where we're not entirely certain about who's right and who's wrong?*

True love feels safe to explore and admit one's weaknesses, because doing so is not an admission of guilt or inferiority. In a high-level love relationship, we have the freedom to admit our shortcomings and our erroneous assumptions because we aren't afraid these confessions will then be used as ammunition against us. There is a sense of re-

I'd rather be happy than right.

—Hugh Prather

lief in being able to freely admit our faults without the fear of being judged, just as there is a sense of relief in being able to grant another person the right to also be flawed without using their flaws against them. In this atmosphere, there is little talk of who is right and who is wrong. Both partners are constantly engaged in an inquiry of how they can better understand themselves and each other. The growth they are each committed to feeds into genuine interest in how they are each personally responsible for whatever is occurring between them, in order to heal and evolve. In this atmosphere, hearts blossom, love deepens, and relationships thrive.

I once had a spiritual teacher who admonished me to take on being 100 percent responsible for the quality of my relationships at all times. We like to think of good, solid relationships as being a 50–50 proposition. However, the best relationships are really 100–100. Because when I am only 50 percent responsible, then I am always at the effect of what the other person does or does not do with their 50 percent. Now, I'm not suggesting that if someone is being disrespectful or even blatantly abusive toward you, you should hang out and tolerate it because you think that taking 100 percent responsibility means you now have love enough for both of you. What I am suggesting is that, if and when someone is being disrespectful toward you, then you consider asking yourself how it is that you gave someone else permission to disrespect and abuse you, because that's *your* part in what's happening. For example, do you speak to yourself in disrespectful ways? Do you have a habit of tolerating disrespect from others and even covertly training them that it's okay to put you down? Are *you* the one who first spoke in a disrespectful way? These are the kinds of questions that can help you understand your part in the dynamic between you. If the answer is no to all of these questions, then ask yourself how you might respond in a nonvictimized way to what's happening. How can you use this as a teaching moment to share what it could look like to build respect between the two of you?

You see, the truth is . . . you can make someone wrong and go to all sorts of lengths to blame them and shame them for their bad or unconscious behavior . . . in fact, you can even get rid of that person entirely, but until you take full responsibility for how you have been an invitation for the abuse, you'll most likely

> Whenever you are pointing your finger at someone, notice that there are always three fingers pointing back at you.
>
> —Anonymous

attract another abusive person in spite of your best efforts to avoid re-creating that situation. So rather than just getting rid of this person, first try graduating yourself from the role you have played in this dynamic. Then do your best to align your relationship with new, healthier ground rules that are based upon an unconditional commitment to respect each other, even when you don't like what's happening.

The extent to which I am in full ownership of all that is occurring in my relationships is the extent that I am empowered to make improvements in those relationships. When I become spiritually lazy and buy into the first thought I have without examination, usually a "victim" thought (e.g., "So-and-So is inconsiderate" or "So-and-So is not doing what he *should* be doing"), then I have no power to effect change. Victim consciousness goes something like this: "It's not my job," "I couldn't help it," "It just happened," "It's your fault," and so on. When you find yourself justifying your poor behavior or when you notice that you are making excuses and blaming others for your choices, stop and ask yourself, "What am I unwilling to be responsible for in this situation?"

Although at times being 100 percent responsible for whatever's happening in any given moment may not seem "fair," doing so now will prepare you for the relationship you are calling into your life. This way, you will be ready to create a conscious, caring, committed love when he or she does appear. A relationship that's about growth and evolution, rather than the acting out of childhood hurts in ways that re-wound you both. I'm happy to report that Nicole and Nancy were able to escape the toxic cycle that they were in when they first came to see me, and evolve in ways that created greater happiness and health in their relationship.

Let go of your attachment to being right, and suddenly your mind is more open. You're able to benefit from the unique viewpoints of others, without being crippled by your own judgment.

—Ralph Marston

Taking responsibility for everything that happens in your life is not necessarily because you are responsible. We all know that things happen that are outside of our control, and that others sometimes say and do hurtful things. Yet it's a powerful and commanding way to live, and one that the Universe richly rewards. Because when you know that it's you that's calling the shots, you can begin aiming yourself more clearly to begin hitting the bull's-eye.

PRACTICE: LETTING GO OF BLAME

Take out your journal. Answer the following questions:

- Who am I making wrong and for what? *(For example, my best friend for not considering how her behavior is impacting me.)*

Now choose one person on this list and answer the following:

- What old belief about others may be coloring my perception of what's happening between us? *(For example, I'm assuming that others don't care about me.)*
- What might also be true, or what might be even more true than this belief? *(For example, Someone might care about my feelings and needs if I had the courage to share them clearly.)*
- Seeing this clearly, what is my part in this situation? *(For example, When I don't share my feelings and needs and assume someone should just know them, then I set people up to disappoint me.)*
- How could I begin showing up in ways that might foster well-being in this situation? *(For example, Take the risk to begin sharing my feelings and needs more authentically.)*
- What could I accept about this situation that would help me give up blaming and shaming? *(For example, Others cannot read my mind, and it's my job to broadcast what I need and what I feel.)*
- What can I appreciate about this situation? *(For example, My friend actually loves me and wants to take care of my feelings and needs.)*

Bonus: Practice in Action

Your task is to take the charge off "being wrong" today by admitting to yourself and others your culpability in each challenging situation.

You can do so without making it into a big deal. Just freely admit your responsibility in a situation to a family member, co-worker, friend, or acquaintance. You may need to apologize, offer to do something to rectify the situation, or ask someone what they need from you to make the situation right. If so, offer to do this, but do *not* beat yourself up or allow yourself to be shamed in any way.

Practice being 100 percent responsible for everything that happens to you today, without being overly responsible for the bad behavior of others. (If you have this tendency, then even see being overly responsible for the bad behavior of others as something to be responsible for!) Examine your role in all situations as intensely as you would ordinarily examine the role that others are playing.

Before bed tonight, write about what it was like for you to freely admit your mistakes and flaws to others and your experience of being 100 percent responsible for all that happened to you today.

Living the Questions

To arrive is to be in prison.

—Henri Matisse

Inside of your commitment to find your way to an unprecedented and unpredictable future, you must be open-minded, inquisitive, and curious. You must be more interested in finding really great questions than you are in getting concrete answers. In fact, inquiry must become your primary way of walking through the world.

I appreciate those who have all of the answers. They make me feel safe. As though someone, somewhere has it all under control. In the unpredictable world of modern-day dating and mating, where uncertainty and insecurity are the norm, knowing the answers to how this is all supposed to work provides a sense of comfort and direction. Having acknowledged that, I must admit my preference for "living the questions," as it's a much more powerful place from which to grow in wisdom, depth, self-awareness, and sound judgment—all necessary ingredients to making good decisions that can lead you to happy, healthy love.

A while back, I led a weekend *Calling in "The One"* Breakthrough Intensive. On the first day, thirty-nine-year-old Pamela had a hard time not interrupting me. She kept raising her hand to ask for specific instructions on how to get a man. She wanted to know when she should tell him that she wanted a serious relationship and exactly how she should tell him so he wouldn't be scared away. She wanted to know when she should sleep with him to ensure that (1) she wouldn't lose him by waiting too long, and (2) he wouldn't dump her because she was "too easy." She wanted to know if she should hide how financially successful she was so that she wouldn't in-

> If love is the answer,
> what is the question?
>
> —Uta West

timidate someone who might make less money than she did and, thereby, frighten him away. I couldn't answer these questions for her—not because I didn't have opinions about those things, but because they would not have been helpful to her. Because nowhere in those questions was Pamela addressing that she didn't believe that any man would actually ever love and take care of her. She wasn't addressing how difficult it was for her to simply be present and listen to others. Nor was she addressing the fact that she didn't trust people enough to let them get close to her. How did I understand that after knowing her for only a few hours? Because she didn't believe that I was going take care of her that weekend. She wasn't listening to the answers that I *was* giving her and she wasn't trusting that if she just let me run my workshop, she would get what she needed. When I tried to tell her these things, she got a headache and left early.

Standing for meaningful change will require you to be deeply engaged in the "right" kind of inquiry—one that will reveal to you your own nature, and access your own deeper knowing to help you fulfill your highest potentials in life and in love. Other than the natural, yet largely unconscious, process of evolution that we're all engaged in, the deliberate pursuit of self-awareness is our only real access to transformation. I mean, life does have a way of teaching all of us—even those of us who are the most reluctant of students. Yet, when we actually desire to grow ourselves beyond who we currently are, and take that on as one of the most important—if not *the* most important—task that we're here to accomplish, then inquiry becomes our greatest ally. For the catalyst of most life-altering changes are usually a few really good questions.

How do we know what distinguishes a "really good question"? These past few weeks, we've been inquiring about you and your life—your attitudes, beliefs, thoughts, feelings, choices, and actions—as a way to help you understand what is (or is not) happening in your love life. You learned in Week 2 to ask "a more beautiful question" to help you see yourself as the source of your habitually disappointing experiences in love more clearly. This has not been a matter of blame, but simply a matter of discovering your ability to change and finally access the power to alter a painful pattern.

Today, we want to explore how you can now use what we'll call "generative inquiry" to inspire forward movement, and provide the clarity you'll need to know how to weave the future you're standing for into the manifest world.

So, let's start by reviewing the questions you've been asking yourself in this process. Largely, they're open-ended questions. Open-ended questions are ones that invite reflection, as opposed to those that simply require you to answer with a yes or a no. They are also questions about you—your worldview, and how you show up inside of that, rather than about others or things you can't change. While it's helpful to understand the impact that your environment has had, or is now having on you, generative inquiry will awaken you to the new choices you can make, or the new actions you can take that can facilitate true change in your life. So, rather than ask yourself a question like "Why don't men like me?" as though men liking you or not is something static and fixed, you might instead ask something like "What's really likable about me, and how could I show this side of myself more easily to others?" Instead of asking a question like "How can I stop getting involved with these narcissistic people?" you might instead ask a question like "What would it feel like to be with someone who really cares about my feelings and needs, and what's the commitment I'd need to make to myself to accept nothing less?" Or instead of asking, "How much longer will I have to be alone in life?" try asking something like "By when do I want to be in the relationship that I'm calling into my life, and what would that require of me today?" You can almost feel the questions moving you forward, like the boost of a wave under a boogie board. It's a question that lifts you, and takes you somewhere. The question literally thrusts you forward into the future.

When looking for powerful questions that can catalyze rapid change in your life, try not to ask "why" questions, such as: "Why am I still single?" "Why don't men seem to like me?" or "Why can't I get a date for Saturday night?" "Why" questions tend to be shame-based and lead nowhere. Instead, ask more provocative and thoughtful questions such as "What am I looking forward to most when I'm in my relationship, and what can I do today to begin experiencing some of that right now?" or "What might make me even more magnetic to love today?"

As a follow-up to *The Road Less Traveled*, psychotherapist and author M. Scott Peck wrote *The Different Drum*. In it, he

> Wisdom begins in wonder.
>
> —Socrates

It's what you
learn after you
know it all that
counts.

—John Wooden

explained his theory on the four stages of spiritual development. These stages were profoundly helpful to me in understanding the value of ongoing inquiry as a way of life.

Stage One, the "chaotic, antisocial" stage, includes those of
us who are underdeveloped in our ability to love others much
beyond what they can do for us. People in this stage are un-
principled and governed exclusively by their own will, which
vacillates according to their current needs and desires. They have very little self-
awareness and even less interest in cultivating it. The questions people in Stage One
ask revolve around trying to figure out how to get what they want without having
to give up anything. (I know. You dated someone like that once. This explains so
much.)

Stage Two, the "formal, institutional" stage, is a leap in consciousness from
Stage One's "no rules apply to me" to "everything is about the rules." In this stage,
we are very concerned with right versus wrong and good versus evil. God is external from us and if we want to avoid being punished, we need to obey His dictates
to the best of our abilities. The only real inquiry here has to do with studying and
memorizing the rules. It is in this stage that we tend to have a rigid mindset and
think we have all the answers. Wanting to know the concrete rules of exactly what
to do to find your partner might fall into this category.

Those in Stage Three, the "skeptic, individual" stage, Dr. Peck describes as
"more spiritually developed" and yet, many times, not as religious. I think I can
safely say that this describes many of you who are reading this book. Often, we are
introduced to this stage through disappointment or disillusionment. Some in Stage
Three will even describe themselves as atheists or agnostics, because the religions
they grew up with don't quite fit any longer, yet they've not yet landed anywhere.
They are principled people who may be deeply involved in their communities and
with social causes. Those who are advanced in Stage Three
are usually seeking truth in some active way, which means
they're involved in asking questions meant to promote growth
and self-awareness. If they do so deeply enough, Dr. Peck believes that they enter into the final and most advanced stage,
Stage Four, which he calls the "mystical, communal" stage.

I know nothing
save the fact of
my ignorance.

—Socrates

Stage Four is characterized by mystery and a fascination with the interdependence of all things. People in this stage are not afraid to acknowledge the enormity of the unknown, nor do they feel compelled to reduce the mysteries of the universe down to palatable, known quantities. Sometimes, people in Stage Four will dedicate themselves to a religious order, but more often than not, they will develop their spirituality in more unconventional and individual ways. In Stage Four, people are able to tolerate the emptiness that comes with not having the answers. Living the questions is their daily practice.

Albert Einstein once said, "We cannot solve the world's problems at the same level at which they were created." I would say that the same is true on a personal level as well. We cannot solve our own problems at the same level of consciousness at which they were created. For the most part, we know what we know and we know what we don't know. But what about all those things that we don't even know we don't know? If we're ever going to move beyond where we are right now, we will have to venture into this territory as well.

I recall my daughter when she was a mere toddler. Her sense of wonder led her throughout the day, as she was swept up in the mystery of it all. Everything was a question and she was completely open and available to learning new things. This is why most spiritual paths encourage us to be as little children. What might we learn if we approached each day as though it held infinite opportunities for growth and expansion? As the future you're calling into your life still lies in the unimagined, it seems that curiosity and a sense of wonder might be in order for us as well. As in, "I wonder what it might look like, smell like, taste like, and feel like to be happily partnered in life. I'm curious about who I'd need to be today to compel this future to appear in my life."

When you seek to know all of the answers, then your life will be limited by what you already know. Yet when you seek to ask deep, provocative, and relevant questions, your life will be limited only by how much courage and willingness you display to show up outside of who you've known yourself to be before now.

> The only Beloved is the living mystery itself.
>
> —Kathleen Raine

PRACTICE: CREATING GENERATIVE QUESTIONS

Think about a situation or two in your life that disturbs or baffles you in some way. I now invite you to take out your journal and write down three questions for each one of these situations. Write open-ended questions that will help you deeply examine the issues that these problems represent. For example, "What can I let go of here that might generate greater love between myself and others?" or "What am I not yet seeing about the power I have to positively impact this situation?" or "What can I learn from this experience that will help me become a more loving person?"

After you've written your questions, take a few minutes to journal on each of them.

Bonus: Practice in Action

Today, I invite you to take an action to apply the wisdom you accessed in responding to the generative questions that you created. Allow the inquiry you engaged this morning to become a guiding light on how you show up today by being willing to apply what you learned.

Listening
with an Open Heart

How do I listen to others?
As if everyone were my Master
Speaking to me His
Cherished last words.

—Hafiz, translated by Daniel Ladinsky

When I was in my twenties, my girlfriend Price, who was my romantic interest at the time, was given a substantial financial gift by her elderly aunt, who was well over ninety. As her aunt handed Price a very generous check, she paused a moment to look deeply into her eyes. "Remember, love," she said with a quiet intensity, "the greatest gift you can ever give anyone is your complete and undivided attention. Never underestimate the importance of simply listening to others."

At first when Price shared this with me, I dismissed her aunt's words as the frivolous sentiments of an old woman who was preparing for death. But as the weeks went by, I became more and more impressed with the transformation I saw in Price, who, in an effort to honor her aunt, began slowing down and being more present with others. Suddenly, it seemed to me

> The greatest problem of communication is the illusion that it has been accomplished.
>
> —George Bernard Shaw

Shallow brooks
murmur most.

—Philip Sidney

that she was becoming more and more sought after and valued by others, as well as calmer and happier within herself. When I began noticing how much I myself was benefiting from her newfound, kinder way of being, I became a hardcore convert. Thus began my study of the art of listening.

The late humorist Erma Bombeck once said, "It seems rather incongruous that in a society of super sophisticated communication, we often suffer from a shortage of listeners." There are many things going on in the world right now that are profoundly affecting our ability to give our total and absolute attention to others.

This time in history has been called the Age of Distraction, the Age of Anxiety, and the Information Age. Regardless of the term we use, it's clear that we are being showered with ever-increasing demands for our attention. In a single day, most of us will take in more information than those who lived a hundred years ago did in the course of a decade. When you consider how often we are interrupted, how much we are expected to know, and how frequently we are pulled in different directions, it's understandable that we often turn off our listening abilities, and disengage from those around us, or reduce our interactions to mere transactions, rather than be present and truly relate to others.

We have to ask ourselves what happens to our sense of belonging and our overall experience of emotional well-being when we shut down and stop listening to one another. Each day, roughly 25 million Americans, most of them women, are taking doctor-prescribed pills meant to diminish feelings of loneliness, low self-esteem, and a lack of connection. While I've seen firsthand the helpful effects of medication, I can't help but wonder where all of this collective anxiety and sorrow is coming from. Rather than a pathology, perhaps it's the part of us that intuitively knows that we're meant to be living closer to one another than we currently are. Perhaps we need to listen to this tribal moan, as though it were feedback on how we're collectively doing.

Our distracted, transactional, and hurried ways of relating to one another are severely inadequate for the human heart. In our hasty attempt to push the river of our lives to get more, do more, and be more, we have profoundly underestimated our need for simple

The greatest compliment that was ever paid to me was when someone asked me what I thought, and attended to my answer.

—Henry David Thoreau

closeness and connection. In so doing, we have forgotten how delicious it is to slow down, look someone in the eye, and savor a good story. We have denied ourselves the opportunity to unburden our hearts by sharing the God's honest truth about who we really are, while sitting with someone who actually cares and wants to know. This is the longing for a soul mate—that one person in the world who inspires you to slow down enough to experience this exchange. But what if, as author Thomas Moore suggests in his book *Soul Mates,* we each have many "soul partners," as he calls them? What if every person you came in contact with today—co-workers, family members, neighbors, even the strangers you pass on the street—carried the possibility of a profound gift for you, and you for them, and your job was to give each of them enough of your attention to exchange these offerings?

> Blessed is the man who, having nothing to say, abstains from giving us wordy evidence of the fact.
>
> —George Eliot

On average, we decide within the first fifteen seconds whether or not we think someone is worth the time and effort it takes to listen to them. We walk around selectively closing ourselves off to many, if not most, of those we come into contact with. It's understandable, of course. In a world where we feel bombarded with instant messages and incessant marketing, it's easy to forget to just be present, without an agenda. To listen simply to discover who someone is, and who we might be together, rather than for what they might be able to do for us. We listen for leverage, for the chance to impress, how others are wrong or why we are right. Is it any wonder that so many of us are feeling lost and alone? Many of us are walking around feeling like we have to sell ourselves each time we want some simple human contact.

One of my favorite authors, Susan Cain, who wrote the wonderful book *Quiet: The Power of Introverts in a World That Can't Stop Talking*, reminds us, "Everyone shines, given the right lighting." In order to live soulful, meaningful lives of deep connection and belonging, we'll want to consciously choose to slow down, give up our hidden agendas, and develop the capacity to focus on others by making an effort to understand them. We'll need to cultivate curiosity about ways of thinking

> Listening is an attitude of the heart, a genuine desire to be with another which both attracts and heals.
>
> —L. J. Isham

> You can give another person a precious gift if you will allow him to talk without contaminating his speech with your own material.
>
> —Robert A. Johnson

that are different from our own. We'll want to open ourselves up to discover who others are and what they have to teach us. We'll need to learn to enjoy just being present, rather than being preoccupied with potential payoffs.

Attention is the currency of care. And authentic listening is the giving of our undivided attention to another without imposing our personal agendas, something that might take a little practice. It is the generous act of giving someone the space to be exactly who they are and exactly who they are not. Once you have mastered the ability to authentically listen with your whole body, absorbing even the rich subtleties in the unspoken, you will have discovered the key to intimacy. For truly, listening is love in action.

PRACTICE: NOTICING WHAT YOU'RE LISTENING FOR

Today I invite you to consider the possibility that when others speak to you, you are bringing covert agendas to the way you listen. By doing this, you are drastically diminishing the quality of your relationships and preventing others from bringing profound gifts of love and service to you. Go through the following list and identify those things that you think might be going on for you when you are attempting to listen:

- I'm judging the speaker.
- I'm judging myself.
- I'm thinking of how I should respond.
- I'm trying to make a good impression.
- I'm fixated on forcing a particular outcome.
- I'm on the defense.
- I'm making the speaker wrong.
- I'm making myself wrong.
- I'm gaining evidence for how I'm right.

- I'm busy trying to protect myself.
- I'm self-conscious about how I look.
- I'm trying to control the conversation to go a certain way.
- I'm trying to fix a perceived problem.

> O Divine Master, grant
> that I may not so much
> seek to be understood,
> as to understand.
>
> —St. Francis of Assisi

Using the list as a reference point, write in your journal for several minutes on the following question:

- What is going on within me when I am listening to others?

Bonus: Practice in Action

Today, have at least one conversation in which you consciously choose to slow down and give your complete and undivided attention to another person. Notice if you have any covert, personal agendas when that person is speaking to you. If you discover a covert agenda, try letting it go and simply bring yourself back to being present with the person who is speaking.

Go out of your way today to connect with those around you and look to discover the gift of each interaction.

Speaking Up

Ask, and it shall be given you.

—Jesus

There is no possibility of true relatedness when we are inauthentic in our speaking. Communication skills are never the goal, but rather the means—the goal itself is communion. How we give and receive information is simply our vehicle for getting there.

Sara, a high-powered executive in the entertainment business, was nearing forty when she met and married her husband, Peter. For the first few months all was wonderful. Six months into their marriage, Peter lost his job. Instead of looking aggressively for a new one, as Sara hoped he might, Peter took his time, enjoyed his days off, and allowed his wife's salary to cover the mortgage on their new home. Sara was upset over Peter's laid-back approach to finding work but she kept it to herself.

When Sara was a little girl, her mother, an immigrant from China, had a motto: "Be sweet, be pretty, be smart." Reflecting an old Chinese custom, Sara had learned to speak only when she had something nice and encouraging to say. Otherwise, she kept her mouth shut. She was never given permission to speak her truth in her family, nor had she seen her mother do so. This was becoming a rather severe handicap in her ability to create an authentic relationship with her new husband, who was a third-generation American and had no understanding of the subtleties of relationships with women raised with this old-world way of being.

Sara came to see me one day so that she could have a safe place to tell the truth. At that point, Peter had been unemployed for well over a year, and Sara was secretly contemplating a divorce. All this time, she'd never said one word to him to indicate her unhappiness. He thought their marriage was in great shape, and he frequently and good-naturedly bragged about the "low-maintenance" woman he had married. Little did he know.

Sara was operating out of an erroneous expectation she had of how a "good" wife might behave in the face of a challenge. Instead of becoming a good wife, however, she'd become a "should" wife who was covertly judging her husband and losing all respect for him, without offering him the possibility of doing anything differently. Her inauthenticity was threatening to destroy the very thing it was initially designed to protect. In the meantime, her love for him was waning. True empathy—the key ingredient to good communication—was present only in its most superficial form.

"You know, Sara," I began, "you really haven't created your marriage yet." She looked at me a little confused. After all, she and Peter had been married nearly two years by now. I continued, "Taking vows just provides the framework for a union, but that relationship does not automatically exist. You have to build it. All you have right now is a commitment to create a union but because you are withholding so much of yourself from your husband, you are failing to fulfill it." Sara got a tear in her eye and nodded her head, indicating that she understood what I was saying.

We had to work quickly to get her to begin expressing the authenticity of what she was feeling in a healthy way before she threw away the possibility of a good marriage. When she actually began to share bits and pieces of what she was feeling, she was surprised to find Peter quite responsive and attentive. To her great relief, in response to her concerns, Peter took on part-time work as a consultant while he more aggressively pursued his search for a full-time position.

When we speak words of truth, we are standing in the very center of our power. Saying no when you mean no, asking directly for what you want without regard for what others might think of you, asserting an opinion you suspect others will disagree with, or having the freedom to admit that you don't know something when you don't are all actions that cause us to be more authentically and fully who we are.

Many of us struggle with addictions to alcohol, food, cigarettes, or drugs precisely because truth was denied in our household when we were growing up. We had to numb what we knew to be true. We weren't allowed to speak of things

> The cruelest lies are
> often told in silence.
>
> —Robert Louis Stevenson

directly and so we stuffed our feelings, hid our pain, and tried to get with the program—all at the great cost of having an intact ability to know and assert our truth. The healing and recovery for all addictive behaviors includes learning to cultivate a discipline of telling the truth, first to oneself and then to others.

Everything we aspire to in life—success, fulfillment, and loving relationships—depends upon our ability to share ourselves with others by telling the truth about who we are, asking directly for what we need, and setting clear limits about what we do or do not want. It seems simple enough, but for many of us, it's not.

Consider Dominick, an intelligent, attractive, and successful actor in his mid-fifties who has never been married. Although Dominick came to me purporting to want a relationship, he in fact avoids them like the plague. Dominick is terrified to make requests or set boundaries because he fears that people won't like him. And so he complies with the demands made of him, and concedes to others even though he feels resentful and irritated. In order to do this, he has to dismiss his feelings as unimportant and rationalize his self-deprecating behavior. In the long run, it's just easier not to go out on a lot of dates or make too many friends.

There are several reasons why we don't assert ourselves in relationships, and most of them start with the "F" word—fear. There's the fear of rejection, the fear of abandonment, or the fear of being humiliated. There's the fear of being known and the fear of not being liked, even by perfect strangers. There's the fear of being vulnerable and defenseless, which of course reinforces itself, since you can never really know that it's safe to be flawed with another unless you actually take the risk of being vulnerable with them. Then there's the fear that we'll never have what we want anyway (so why bother trying) and the fear that if we do gather the courage to ask for what we want, we will surely do it wrong. And, of course, there is always the fear that if you take any risks at all in life, you will most certainly find out that your worst fantasies are actually true—that you really are inferior and destined to fail.

Although many of these fears could easily be laid to rest if only we would challenge them, many of us live our entire lives dancing around and interacting with them, without so much as questioning their validity. When you begin to consider what this costs us in aliveness and love, it's staggering. Sara could easily have gotten to the point where she threw away a potentially loving marriage to a good man who absolutely adores her and who would do anything to please her, *if she had not told him what she truly felt and needed.*

Lena, an attractive, professionally accomplished woman, was a recent Breakthrough Intensive participant. When called on, she spoke sadly and slowly. "I don't understand why it is, but every man that I am with ends up telling me exactly the same thing. 'I like you. I respect you. I enjoy being with you. But I do not love you.' They all leave me for this reason." Lena seemed baffled. She could not understand how each one of her relationships ended in exactly the same way. Yet, when we began to explore the specific ways in which she might be the cause of her experience, Lena had a breakthrough. "I never share my feelings with a man because I don't want to be vulnerable," she shared. "Ever since my mother died when I was a little girl, and my father made it clear to me that I had to be strong and never cry, I have been unwilling to let a man see how I truly feel." "Lena," I asked her, "do you understand the connection between your unwillingness to be vulnerable and the pattern of men not falling in love with you?" She looked confused. "It's like this," I continued. "People will usually like us for being nice. They will admire and respect us for having our act together. But they can love us only when we allow them to see our vulnerabilities and our flaws." She was shocked. She'd been trying for years to hide her feelings and her flaws in order to be loved and here I was telling her that she had to do exactly the opposite.

Lena was responding to all men as though they were her father, who she believed would love her only if she were emotionally self-contained and "strong." Even though it had been horribly isolating for her to not be allowed to openly grieve her mother's death, she also grew comfortable with withholding herself from others. She even came to rely upon her ability to shut down emotionally as the perfect way to protect herself from ever being as hurt as she was after her mother died and left her so alone.

Once Lena understood herself as the source of the pattern, the power of choice was restored. She could give up generalizing that all men would be like her father, and she could give up protecting herself from the possibility that someone else she dared to open her heart to might also die. The first new possibility—that the men she dated would probably be very different from her father—was not so difficult. It was the second that presented the greater challenge and one that she might have to work with for some time to come. But at least now she could give up being a victim of the pattern, and start to deal with her ambivalence about surrendering to love.

Until we risk telling the truth, we cannot have an authentic experience of love. We can have entanglements, we can be "involved," we can even be married, but we will not have the experience of love. For even if you *were* really loved by another person, how would you know if you didn't allow yourself to tell the raw, naked, vulnerable truth and risk the consequences of that? You would just believe that you were being loved for the false persona you were presenting. The gift of authentic communication, then, is a gift that you give to yourself.

A couple once came to see me to help them decide whether or not to break up. Although they loved each other very much, they seemed to be fighting more often than not. The man began telling me what he could no longer tolerate in his girl-friend. She sat there stunned as he complained for several minutes about her poor eating habits and his disappointment that she rarely cooked healthy and wholesome meals for the two of them. When he was finished, I turned to her and asked if he had ever made a request that she cook for him. Looking hurt and sad, she shook her head no. In their entire three years together, she had no idea that he wanted her to do this. Had he asked her, she assured us, she would have been happy to accom-modate his request.

The man had been engaged in a fantasy that if his girlfriend really loved him, she would know what he wanted without his having to tell her. But operating under the illusion that others *should just know* is magical thinking. While magical think-ing helped develop the qualities of wonder and imagination when we were children, adults who relate in this way are simply cultivating the qualities of passivity and resentment in their relationships. Clearly, the time for magical thinking has passed.

When we allow fear to dictate the quality of our communication, we will often engage in passive-aggressive behavior. We'll do things like come late to a party that we didn't really want to attend, burn a meal when we secretly would have preferred being taken out for dinner, or "have a headache" when it's time for bed after our partner has failed to live up to our covert expectations that afternoon.

Yet in spite of knowing all of this, some of us still have a hard time asking for what we want and need. Here's the key to making requests of others—both reason-able and unreasonable. As long as you have the space for someone to say no, you can ask them almost anything. If you have space for them to say no, they'll feel it and your request will be more palpable because they're free to make a true choice. Once you have mastered this form of nonattachment to getting what you want, then you'll be at liberty to ask anyone for anything at any time.

> Don't think of what's being said but of what's talking. Malice? Ignorance? Pride? Love?
>
> —Joseph Campbell

Speaking authentically also requires us to know our own truth. Before sharing our feelings, we must understand what they are. Therefore, speaking our truth demands of us a certain level of emotional literacy. When I was learning how to identify and express my feelings to others, I spent a lot of time journaling to try to sort through the many feelings and sensations that had, for so many years, remained unnamed within me. I had to own feelings and thoughts that were contrary to my image of myself as a "nice" person. I had to tell the truth, even at the risk of looking bad. There's no way around it. You can't be invested in looking good if you want to have an authentic experience of love.

A word of caution: Keep in mind that the goal of communication is communion. Before you "speak your truth," you would be wise to first make a concerted effort to understand the perspective of the other person and to clear yourself of the need to be right, make someone wrong, blame, punish, strategize, or get your way. Remember, we are listening and speaking in the service of creating loving, harmonious relationships. I have learned, sometimes through the regret of hurting another person, that before we speak our minds, we would do well to ask ourselves what exactly it is that we are committed to creating in our communication. Then speak in ways that are generative of that future.

PRACTICE: CLEARING YOUR COMMUNICATION BLOCKS

Take out your journal and write on the following questions. Don't censor yourself. Just write whatever comes to mind when you read the question.

- What's upsetting me that I've not yet expressed to the person I'm upset with?
  - What is this costing me and/or our relationship?
  - How might I share this upset in a way that could allow our connection to deepen?
- What vulnerabilities have I been withholding, and from whom?
  - What is this costing me and/or our relationship?
  - How might I share my vulnerabilities more authentically in a way that could allow our connection to deepen?
- What complaints have I been making lately about someone who matters to me?
  - What is this costing me and/or our relationship?
  - What request could I make of this person instead in a way that could allow our connection to deepen?
- Where have I been failing to ask for what I want and need from another?
  - What is this costing me and/or our relationship?
  - How might I share what I want or need more directly, in a way that could allow our connection to deepen?

Bonus: Practice in Action

Do at least one thing today that (1) reveals your true feelings to someone that you've been hiding or withholding from, or (2) transforms a complaint into a request, or (3) has you let go of magical thinking where you are hoping that someone can read your mind, and instead, ask more directly for what you want or need.

Becoming "The One"

To find the Beloved,
you must become the Beloved.

—Rumi

For the past few weeks, you've been actively seeking to become magnetic to happy, healthy love: waking up out of victimization, naming and challenging core beliefs, standing for a future that isn't going to happen unless you claim and cause it, learning to care for yourself more deeply, and consciously preparing yourself to receive love. All of this has been leading you to lean in and try on the "you" of your future, and begin living from this center in how you show up with others.

While many of us have been sitting on our therapist's couch for years to explore the traumatized self, few of us have so actively begun organizing our lives around the fulfilled, happy self of the future we're committed to manifesting. Doing so is clarifying the ways you'll now need to stretch and grow yourself in the direction of your dreams.

At this point of your journey, you are now actively identifying new ways of relating that are congruent with the deeper truth of your value and power, and you're taking risky, bold actions to start showing up in these new ways. Which is no small matter, because in all likelihood, you don't always feel confident about doing things like asserting your truth, making your feelings and needs known, or setting clear and healthy boundaries. In fact, it might irritate some of the people in your life for you to start asserting yourself in these ways. Not everyone likes it when they lose a doormat! Yet you must practice fidelity to the future you're standing for by starting to relate to others from the center of your power and your truth if you ever hope to graduate from old painful patterns.

Let me tell you why this matters so much. Your beliefs about yourself were formed in relationship with others, yes? People you loved and depended upon? The meaning you made about your relationships with others—that somehow, they don't care about you, or that they're better than you, or that they'll always leave you— was formed in response to what was or was not happening between yourself and others. Unfortunately, you've now had those beliefs validated more times than you can count. Before you understood yourself as the source of these beliefs, you took that mountain of evidence to mean that the beliefs were actually true. Yet now you know better. Now you know they're not actually true. In fact, you have ideas about what might be even more true than the conclusions you came to as a child, adolescent, or young adult. For instance, if you had the courage to share what you really feel and need, that others might actually care about you. That others are neither superior nor inferior to you, but that we're all evidence of Divine Love. Or that, in challenging moments between yourself and others, you have the power to show up in ways that can deepen love, rather than destroy it. You now understand that it's often a simple matter of identifying and learning a new skill that would allow this to happen. Like how you can set a healthy boundary in order to dismantle the wall you'd built, or how you can have healthy expectations that others treat you with respect.

Here's the thing . . . until you have the courage to actually start showing up in these new and empowering ways, others won't have the opportunity to show up differently, either. Until you take the risk of speaking up, stepping back, chiming in, or bowing out—showing up in ways that are new, foreign, and most likely way out of your comfort zone—then others won't have the chance to change their dance steps, either. And you'll not be able to bridge that wide gap between what you know, and your ability to actually live it.

When Hanna stepped into her power by declaring with her whole heart to her *Calling in "The One"* group that she was a woman who was worthy of being loved, she was hopeful that she could finally graduate from always being a booty call, to being someone's bride. Yet two days later, when someone she'd just met online called at midnight to ask if he could come over, she felt too anxious to say no. Her belief about others—that they liked her only because of what they could get from her—

felt more real to her than her Power Statement of being a woman who was worthy of being loved. She feared that if she didn't take the crumbs he was offering, she'd never see him again. Predictably, she never saw him again after that night anyway. It was the wake-up call she needed to finally change the steps of her dance routine. It wasn't long before another man she liked called late one night to ask her if she wanted to come over to his place. Certain that he'd never want to see her again if she didn't give him what he wanted, she chose to honor herself over taking care of him. She said no, and politely suggested he call earlier in the day and ask her out on a proper date if he wanted to spend time with her. Imagine her surprise when three days later he called to ask if she wanted to go to the movies the following weekend.

> Do not try to change people; they are only messengers telling you who you are. Revalue yourself and they will confirm the change.
>
> —Neville Goddard

The transformation of your core beliefs about others can happen only when you have the courage and the conviction to show up in new ways that are outside of who you've known yourself to be. Others are not who you've assumed them to be. Not all men will think you're a burden, like your big brother did when you were three. Not all women will love you only because of what you can do for them, like your narcissistic mother did as you were growing up. Here's what's actually true about how others feel about you: They're taking their cues from you. If you like yourself, they'll tend to like you. If you value yourself, they'll tend to value you. If you honor yourself, they'll tend to honor you, too. And to graduate forever from your False Love Identity, you'll need to take your transformation all the way home to being willing to show up in brand-new ways. Because that's when you'll see a newfound respect in the eyes of another. Or have the experience of your call being returned as soon as someone receives your message. You'll finally have the corrective experience of being given a seat of honor at the table, or of being the one that's chosen over all others.

All of your work on your beliefs up until now will stay theoretical in nature until you begin to make these new choices. Without the experience of others treating you in ways that validate the deeper truth of who you are—mirroring back to you your worthiness, your power, or your ability to keep yourself safe—you will eventually return to your old story, and to generating your life from that center. Your True

Love Identity will become a mere memory of something you woke up to for a minute, and wrote about in some journal way back when.

Do not let this happen! Transforming your love life will require that you actively begin taking bold actions to interrupt this well-worn path of how relationships go for you. You can't just talk about your core beliefs with a coach or a therapist and think that something will change. It won't. Life can change only through you. Through the different choices you make, and the different actions you take. Change cannot just happen to you. You have to have the courage to do things differently, so that others can begin to treat you differently. For it's when you see the truth of who you are reflected back to you in the eyes of another that you finally graduate forever from your old sense of self. Because, as I've said, beliefs are relational. They were formed in relationship, and they must evolve in relationship, too.

PRACTICE: IDENTIFYING NEW WAYS OF SHOWING UP WITH OTHERS

Take out your journal and write on the following:

1. **Review Your False Love Identity.** Write down that erroneous belief you formed about yourself as it relates to love. *For example, I am alone, I am invisible, I am not good enough, I am not wanted.*

2. **Name Your Belief About Others.** Your belief about yourself also has a corresponding belief about your relationship with others. *For example, I'm alone and everyone always leaves me, or I am invisible and no one cares about me, or I'm not good enough and others are better than I am, or I'm not wanted and everyone will always reject me.*

3. **Identify How You Show Up from That False Belief.** Become conscious of how you then show up with others inside of this assumption. *For example, Inside of a belief that others will always*

leave me, I avoid conflict like the plague or I always leave them first. Or inside of a belief that others don't care about me, I don't ever share my feelings or needs with them. Or inside of a belief that others are better than I am, I underpresent myself and over-give to try to prove my value. Or inside of assuming others will always reject me, I try too hard or I end up rejecting them first.

4. **Identify the New Ways of Relating from Power Center.** Standing in the truth, in what new ways could you begin to show up with others that could generate a different experience? *For example, I could engage conflict in a healthy way to give our relationship a chance to deepen. Or I could share my feelings to give people a chance to show they care about me. Or I could give a little and wait to see if someone is able to reciprocate before I give again. Or I could contain my energy more to give someone a chance to come toward me.*

Bonus: Practice in Action

Take a risk today to show up differently with others. Look for the opportunity to make a new choice and/or take a new action. Be grateful if your old pattern shows up, and see it as an opportunity to finally graduate.

Suggested Study Guide for Group Discussion

1. Who did you give up making wrong this week, and what were you able to see that is valid about their perspective?

2. What is it like for you to accept your life exactly as it is, and as it is not? What attachments have you given up in service to choosing to be happy?

3. What did you notice about your ability to be 100 percent responsible for the quality of your relationships and what has that opened up between yourself and others?

4. What were some of the generative questions you came up with and what did you discover in response to these questions?

5. What covert agendas do you bring to your conversations, and what has it been like to simply let them go?

6. What have you done differently in how you communicate with others this week?

7. What risks did you take to show up differently with others and what happened as a result?

Living Love Fulfilled

The more we are, the richer everything we experience is.
And those who want to have a deep love in their lives
must collect and save for it, and gather honey.

—Rainer Maria Rilke

As we move into our final week together, we continue cultivating the characteristics of love, celebrating all that is beautiful, good, and true in our lives today.

This week, we will:

- Increase your awareness of the magic, synchronicities, and signs you're receiving along the way to encourage and inspire you to stay the course
- Deepen the distinctions of forgiveness to keep your heart light and open to love
- Take on a practice of radical gratitude to shift you into a consciousness of "having" to generate joy and draw all good things toward you
- Begin making the profound and life-altering transformation from a *me*-centered life to a *we*-centered life

- Discover how to be unstoppable by learning to use all disappointments, obstacles, and delays as catalysts for your transformation
- And learn to hold the high watch to magically weave a future of deep happiness in love into the manifest world

Living an Enchanted Life

I think it pisses God off if you walk by the
color purple in a field somewhere and don't notice it.

—Alice Walker

Falling in love can be likened to an eruption of vibrant and radiant colors in a previously black and white world. The mundane is suddenly transformed into the magical, and the ordinary quickly morphs into the most meaningful moments of your life. The yearning to "call in" a beloved is the deep desire to be swept off our feet in these magical and mysterious ways. To see the world in the enchanted ways we imagine God might see it, as an endless swirl of possibilities and a field of limitless potentials. It is the radically invigorating experience of being fully and joyfully alive.

Yet for far too long, you've been on the outside looking in. Nose pressed up against the glass, and longing to be on the inside of this fabulous festival of laughter and light that we call a loving relationship. Waiting, waiting, waiting for someone— the "right one"—to finally appear and ask you to dance. Yet as the weeks, months, years pass you by, you begin losing heart, and hope, that it will ever happen for you.

Let me share with you a secret that poets, mystics, and magicians have known for longer than a thousand years: You need not be so long-suffering! For the portals of magic are everywhere. And in particular, they lie in wait within you. For you, dear reader, are the source of the magic you seek. And magic is exactly what you're needing right about now.

Committing to finding your way to the fulfillment of love isn't like deciding to build a house. You can't just draw up plans to make true love happen. Instead,

> Remember that the most beautiful things in the world are the most useless: peacocks and lilies for instance.
>
> —John Ruskin

you have to lean in and listen for the present possibilities, and for how life is guiding you to realize them. You must pay attention to the magic, synchronicities, and signs along the way and be open to following them, as though you were trailing gumdrops in an enchanted forest. As if you could catch the waves of potential that are present, and ride them to shore with complete trust that something magical is indeed afoot.

Synchronicity, that delightful kind of happenstance that reveals the deep and pervasive interconnectedness of all beings, fills us with a sense that we're on the right track, and that we're not alone to find our way home to love. Think about how many "how we met" stories are filled with this sense of magic and seemingly coincidental good fortune. As finding true love lies in the realm of synchronicity, magic, and miracles, you would be wise to begin paying attention to and even looking for the signs you'll start seeing once you open your eyes to look for them.

When my sweetheart Michael and I first met, we lived hundreds of miles apart. As we couldn't meet for tea, we would spend hours on the phone getting to know each other. We both enjoyed these conversations immensely. Yet it was not until one evening when he mentioned his favorite song that I understood how special our connection was. Out of the millions of songs in the Universe, the one he loved most, "My Sweet Lord" by George Harrison, was—drum roll, please—also my favorite song. In fact, I'd told my daughter just two days before while driving that "My Sweet Lord" was my favorite song. I mean, really. What are the odds?

Your task right now is to pay attention. To observe your body and acknowledge what it's telling you—to notice whether you feel burdened and heavy, or happy and inspired by the choices you're making. Like the childhood game of hot and cold, where you were given instructions of "cold" when you were on the wrong track and "hot" when you were on the right track, follow the hot energies present and see them as validation that you're moving in the right direction. Attend to your deeper knowing, and don't dismiss the synchronicities that happen as mere coincidence. If you begin listening to the subtle winds and whispers that Life is constantly offering, your hearing will become more acute. For some, it may be like learning a new language. Yet if you practice, you'll soon become more and more fluent.

Love lies in the mysteries. If you're feeling desperate for love, then you're likely anchored in scarcity, and disconnected from the magic of Life. You're trying to push Life to give you what you want from your head, and not partnering with Life to manifest the possibilities present from your heart. When we live in disconnection, nothing works. Life occurs as a sort of frustrating fragmentation where all the pieces don't quite fit, and all the dots don't quite connect. You'll become exhausted trying to fix the many problems that are present. Particularly the problem of how to find a needle in a haystack, or more accurately, how to find your beloved out of the nearly 11 million people who are currently on Match.com.

> *Lovers think they're looking for each other.*
> *But there's only one search:*
> *Wandering this world.*
>
> —Rumi

Your beloved is not a problem to be solved or an object to be acquired. They are not someone who matches your checklist of what you think you want. In fact, they may not look anything like you've been assuming they would. You must look for love with your inner eyes, more than your outer ones. For you're looking for someone to enter into the mysteries with you. Someone to co-create with. Someone to inspire, and to be inspired by. A person who meets you in the space where words need not be spoken. Go there now and begin weaving your magical web of enchantment today to prepare for your date with destiny.

If you're bored, then you're likely not listening to what Life is trying to tell you. Maybe you're talking yourself out of it, or dimming down what you sense to be true. Remember, navigating your way to your beloved will require you to depend more and more upon these alternative ways of knowing—where you are simply open to what lies in the unimagined and receptive to the energies of Life both surrounding and within you.

Stop waiting to meet "The One" before awakening to the beauty and magic of your life. If you're doing this, ask yourself, "If I am numbing myself, and letting myself go through life as though I'm sleepwalking, what have I to offer another?" Don't look for someone who can jump-start your dead batteries. If you do, you'll quickly drain the magic out of your initial falling-in-love experience, and drag

> Waking up this morning, I smile. Twenty-four brand new hours are before me. I vow to live fully in each moment and to look at all beings with eyes of compassion.
>
> —Thich Nhat Hanh

your new sweetheart down into your slumber with you. You know that couple. They used to live next door. Don't be like that. Nurture your imminent relationship even now, before your beloved has arrived, by learning to turn your love light on, and walking through the world as though you're grateful for each precious second that you get to be alive.

PRACTICE: WATCHING FOR SYNCHRONICITIES AND SIGNS

You'll want to increase your experience of synchronicities and signs that validate you're moving in the right direction. The way to grow anything is to place your attention on it. Therefore, I suggest you begin documenting the synchronicities and signs you're receiving each day in your journal.

You can begin by making a list today of all of the synchronicities and signs you've received on your journey thus far.

For example,

1. Meeting my friend who told me she had just read Calling in "The One" right after I made the decision that I was now ready for a relationship.

2. Going to the bookstore right after seeing her and finding the book on the shelf right next to one I'd gone into the store to get.

3. As soon as I started this process, my former boyfriend from three years ago calling out of the blue to apologize for treating me badly.

Bonus: Practice in Action

Do at least one thing today that enhances the experience of enchantment and magic in your life. For example, do something ordinary with extraordinary kindness and mindful attentiveness, or allow yourself to become enraptured by a beautiful sunset, or spend some time lovingly tending to an animal.

Generating Love

Make love your lasting legacy.

—Jeff Brown

Years before she was known as an esteemed political activist, Marianne Williamson was known throughout the world for her profoundly inspiring teachings on *A Course in Miracles*. I devotedly attended her lectures in Los Angeles for well over a decade. Once I met my then-husband Mark, I introduced the two of them and, for a time, he produced an internationally broadcast call-in talk radio show for her. One New Year's Eve, as I sat on a white leather couch in Mark's office, I listened intently as Marianne counseled Grace, a woman calling in from Sydney, Australia.

Grace sounded like an intelligent, thoughtful woman who, like many of us, was devoted to her career. While she was quite successful in business, she shared with Marianne that she often felt lonely and isolated from others during the hours she was not working. This, then, prompted her to devote more and more of her time to her work, and less time to tolerating the loneliness of her nonexistent social life.

Marianne listened as Grace admitted that her idea of creating love in her life was to watch Hollywood movies and wait passively for her knight in shining armor to come along. When that didn't happen, she felt deeply disappointed and became resigned about ever finding love. Marianne challenged her by comparing the drastic, extreme measures she was willing to go to to ensure her professional success to what little she did to create more love in her life. Grace acknowledged that she needed to become more proactive in cultivating greater care and connection in her everyday life.

If we made a commitment to develop our ability to love and be loved with the same level of focus and devotion that many of us give to our careers, most of us would become enlightened beings in no time. We have a tendency to think that enlightened teachers such as Jesus, Buddha, and Muhammad were simply born that way. Yet even these great masters toiled for years to cultivate their ability to give and receive love before ascending to their positions as spiritual leaders. None of us finds a shortcut to fulfillment.

> The heart is like a garden. It can grow compassion or fear, resentment or love. What seeds will you plant there?
>
> —Jack Kornfield

Love is a choice we make to expand beyond the limitations of self-concern. It is not something to get, as much as it is something we generate into the field between ourselves and others. Like Grace, many of us are waiting for a knight in shining armor to rescue us from our sorrow by bringing love to us, as though love were only to be found outside of ourselves. When it looks like our knight is not coming, we delve into depression, believing our lives to be void of love. The Universe is somehow withholding from us. We become frustrated and angry. How awful it is to be at the random mercy of fate that smiles upon some with the light of love yet frowns upon others by its absence. However, *A Course in Miracles* tells us that the only love missing in our lives is the love that we ourselves are not giving.

In *Not Just Stories*, author Rabbi Abraham Twerski writes of a woman who went to see noted Hasidic leader, the Maggid of Kozhnitz, to ask his blessing, so she and her husband could conceive a child. They'd been trying unsuccessfully for several years and were quite discouraged. The Maggid said to her, "My parents, too, were childless for many years. Then my mother sewed a coat for the Ba'al Shem Tov, and after that I was born." The woman excitedly replied, "I will gladly sew a coat for you, a beautiful coat!" But the Maggid gave her a sad smile and replied, "No, my dear woman. That will be of no avail. You see, my mother did not know this story."

When we're generous with our love, life tends to be generous with us in return. Yet often, we're so wrapped up with the form that love takes, that we miss the opportunities right there before us to experience and exchange it, shutting down the flow of love in the process. We're trying to get love to look a certain way—the ring on the finger, the white picket fence, or the two-point-five kids. When we do not get exactly what we want, we'll withhold even more. Like a two-year-old throwing

> The goal in life is to be a vehicle for something higher.
>
> —Joseph Campbell

a tantrum, we'll refuse to do it any other way, as if to say, "If I can't have love *this* way, then I won't have love at all." But love itself is not interested in form. It is interested only in you expanding beyond your expectations. If that one special person has not yet appeared, then the best you can do to prepare for their arrival is to keep the channels of love open. Spiritual teacher Eckhart Tolle reminds us, "Love is not selective, just as the light of the sun is not selective. It does not make one person special. It is not exclusive." If you say you want a loving relationship, then let's begin the love part today, with whoever and whatever is present in your life right now.

Remember those bumper stickers "What would Jesus do?" In allowing yourself to become a conduit for love, try asking yourself throughout the day, "What would love do now?" When you are willing to surrender yourself to the qualities of love—compassion, forgiveness, graciousness, and kindness—you'll not be left void. My friend, minister Mary Manin Morrissey, reminds us, "God can only do for us what He can do through us." It's foolish to ask God for a great love without being willing to become a great lover, just as it would be foolish to say that we wanted to become a great doctor without being willing to go to medical school.

Your first response to the thought of yielding to love over being petty may be resistance. Attacking thoughts that would justify an unloving response may flood your mind. If that happens, try not to take it personally. See if you can simply observe these thoughts and choose to move beyond them without acting them out. In this way, you make room for the possibility of love to move through you. Rather than clinging to being right, you can consider the possibility that the other person may indeed have a point. Rather than exposing someone's flaw, you might choose to graciously cover for them. Rather than punishing an offense, you might see it as a chance to practice forgiveness. In doing so, you may find your heart growing bigger and softer. You may notice that you feel more grounded and mature.

Many of us make the mistake of trying to expand our ability to love at the expense of ourselves. But a heart that is inappropriately open will cause a great deal of suffering. I used to believe that being a spiritual person meant that I had to keep my heart available to others, even if they were being disrespectful or unkind toward me. It took me a while to understand that, by doing this, I was displaying a lack of self-respect and self-worth. Love is never fulfilled at my expense, and being a loving person is not to be confused with being a doormat. Buddha said, "You can look the whole world over and never find anyone more deserving of love than yourself."

> If one wishes to know love, one must live love, in action.
>
> —Leo Buscaglia

PRACTICE: IDENTIFYING LOVE IN ACTION

Take out your journal.

First, write a list of four or five qualities that you believe define love. *For example, patience, empathy, kindness, or compassion.*

Second, write down three situations in your life that are irritating to you. *For example, I'm irritated that I'm being passed over for a promotion at work.*

Third, write down the names of those directly involved in these situations. Next to their name, write down what your judgments of them are. *For example, Bettie: for brownnosing the boss, being manipulative and greedy by taking a position that should have been mine.*

Finally, write a response to the following question:

What would love (or any other quality you listed such as compassion or kindness) do now?

Write on this question for each of these three situations. For example, I would acknowledge that Bettie has worked harder than I have these past few weeks and that I took an extended vacation at a crucial time, even though I knew it would cost me. Love would congratulate Bettie for her accomplishment, and offer my support of her new position. Love would see my envy as evidence that I too wish to advance in my career. Love would (1) begin to take actions consistent with that desire, such as get to work on time each day, (2) go out of my way to go above and beyond what is expected of me, and (3) let my superiors know that I am committed to advancing as well and ask for their guidance and support.

Bonus: Practice in Action

As you go through your day, each time you notice yourself irritated or upset, ask yourself:

What would love (or any other quality you listed such as compassion or kindness) do now?

Allow yourself to choose love over pettiness throughout the day. Stretch yourself to become the most loving version of yourself possible by doing that which you believe love would do in any given moment.

Expanding from "Me" to "We"

Though modern marriage is a tremendous laboratory,
its members are often utterly without preparation for the
partnership function. How much agony and remorse and
failure could have been avoided if there had been at least some
rudimentary learning before they entered the partnership.

—Carl Rogers

I'm always amazed at those who say they want a better marriage, yet have the stingy habit of keeping score. If I cook tonight, then it's your turn tomorrow. If we do this your way, then you owe me one. It's such a miserly way to try to love someone. The "me, me, me" mantra of our postmodern culture is profoundly impacting our ability to be happy in our intimate relationships. While we may yearn for solid, strong connections, many of us come to the table with little practice in being thoughtful and bighearted. Our schooling taught us to compete, more than to cooperate. To beat others, instead of helping them better themselves. To win debates, rather than acknowledge a good point you'd not yet considered. There are times, of course, when we spontaneously stand with and for each other. Like in the aftermath of tragedy. Suddenly, the walls come down and for a blessed brief moment, we are together in the way I imagine poet Walt Whitman meant when he wrote, "We were together. . . . I forget the rest." Yet, within a relatively short period

> To touch the
> soul of another
> human being is
> to walk on holy
> ground.
>
> —Stephen Covey

of time, we're predictably back to business as usual, two separate individuals duking it out and vying for power.

Modern-day mating has built into it an inherent conflict. Still defined by a sense of love and belonging to something larger than ourselves, as was so in past generations, contemporary unions also bring the hope of helping us become all we have the potential to be. This is particularly true in Western cultures where the values of self-actualization and individuation are more highly valued than the ideals of sacrifice and duty. In our never-ending quest for personal development, you're more likely to have taken a class on self-assertiveness than on selflessness. Yet if we wish to be truly happy in love—in a way that can deepen over time—then we must learn to nourish the field between ourselves and others, as much as we aspire to nourish ourselves.

I once saw a couple for close to a year who nearly broke my heart. Their marriage was a war zone. Yet for the sake of their children, they faithfully came back week after week, in the hope that they could mature themselves faster than they destroyed what little love was left between them. It was a race against the clock. The main problem they wrestled with was the way they conceptualized their union. Because they had no model for a healthy marriage, they saw it more as a "whoever dominates and screams the loudest, gets to have their way" type of arrangement. Either he won or she won, but someone always lost. Their conversations were all about the struggle for control, as there was really room for only one of them in their relationship. It didn't even occur to them to explore the needs and wants of their partner with genuine care and interest, then treat each other's needs as though they were their own.

They tried to accommodate this new idea. Switch gears. Switch hats. Switch hearts. But it's so much harder to change a dynamic once it's firmly in place, and has been reinforced time and time again. You, however, get to prepare now so that you and your beloved won't have to struggle, no matter what modeling you had or did not have. You can do this by taking on practices to help grow your capacity for mutuality, reciprocity, and healthy interdependence. By learning to nurture what my brilliant friend, contemporary spiritual teacher Patricia Albere, calls the "we" space between yourself and others. Start to mindfully develop your ability to stay present and available to the connection. Grow your capacity for authentic care. That is, care that—unlike codependence—is wholesomely motivated and offered as a gesture of true generosity of spirit. Leaning in to cultivate the qualities of empathy and compassion. Learning to expand your sense of identity to be inclusive of those you love. You can and should do this right now, with whoever is in your life that matters to you.

Some of us fear moving toward being a "we" because we have a more fragile sense of self. In response, we can create all sorts of love-avoidant painful push-pull drama-traumas that destabilize a relationship and prevent the growth of healthy interdependence, to try to keep ourselves safe. Ultimately, we fear being overpowered by a codependent acute awareness of the needs of the other, before we even have a good grasp on our own. It's the age-old "how much of me do I have to lose to be loved by you?" dilemma, which is fueled by an unhealthy assumption that I have to give someone everything they want to keep them from leaving me. Leaving means not just physical leaving, but the withdrawal of someone's love and approval. Yet this codependent way of navigating a relationship creates the opposite of safety. Because (1) you've given so much of yourself away that you're a shell of your former self, and have no core to come home to, and (2) you've trained someone to completely disrespect and disregard you. So much so that it's actually easy to eventually leave you. This is not the "we" we are talking about. Remember, the foundation for happy, healthy love is that you are safe to set limits, to say no, and to define yourself as autonomous and unique from another. The happiest long-term partnerships are formed between two people who have worked to develop a firm and resilient sense of identity within themselves. Put simply, you have to be a strong "me" in order to form a strong "we." Healthy "we-ness" always enhances and strengthens the individuality of who you are. It provides support that enables you to be more fully yourself in the world.

We talk so much about our crazy dysfunctional families. I constantly hear about people's narcissistic sister, alcoholic brother, bipolar aunt, abusive father, or codependent mother. Sometimes I ask my students if they know what a functional family looks like, so they have something to emulate. Most do not. So, I think it's important to talk about what the goal is here. Functional families allow for the individuality of each member. People are free to express their needs, their wants, and their feelings, because those expressions are met with acceptance, consideration, and love. They are then taken into account in all subsequent decision-making. True

> Love is the extremely
> difficult realization
> that something other
> than oneself is real.
> Love, and so art
> and morals, is the
> discovery of reality.
>
> —Iris Murdoch

"we-ness" allows each person to be a fully formed "me," with likes, dislikes, beliefs, attitudes, and opinions that may be unique to them. In true community, there's a spirit of inclusiveness and expansion, where there's room for everyone. We don't all have to agree; we can just agree to disagree. We make space for all of it, with an underlying foundation of respect and appreciation for our differences. In this atmosphere, you and your partner can both feel safe. You can both feel secure enough to admit your mistakes, and hopefully, to reach out with sincere humility to make amends when necessary. You can both feel supported enough to take risks in life, knowing that if you fail, you will still be loved. And that if you succeed, you will be celebrated. You want to actively be engaged in preparing yourself now to co-create this happy family. To be someone who is capable of creating this level of goodwill and well-being with another, then sustain it over time.

If you're doing this course in the way it was designed, you should be feeling a little on the hot seat right about now. I hope you're feeling compelled to grow and develop yourself with a sense of urgency. You have sent out the signal, and you are faithfully doing your part. You must act as if your beloved is on their way right now, and could arrive at any moment. Prepare! Do not just pray for love. Pray to be ready when your beloved appears.

PRACTICE: BEING PRESENT AND AVAILABLE TO LOVE MEDITATION

Many of us are guarded with others. In trying to protect ourselves from the possibility of being hurt, we've put up walls. We painstakingly present ourselves in carefully measured ways meant to impress or influence others to see us in the ways we wish to be seen. Yet these masked ways of relating are only organic when we are somatically centered in a false self, such as "I'm not good enough," "I'm alone," or "I'm not lovable."

Today, I invite you to connect with others from the deeper truth of your own inherent worthiness and power. What might emerge is a true availability to connect with others outside of ego—yours and theirs.

Read the following meditation through two times, then do it with eyes closed, as best you can from memory.

CONNECT WITH YOUR POWER CENTER.

Before relating to anyone else today, take some time to cultivate a conscious connection with the "true you." The part of you that is not your body, your story, or even your accomplishments. Drop down deeper and wider to locate the truth of your inherent worthiness, power, goodness, intelligence, and belonging. Experience yourself as you imagine the Universe experiences you, through the eyes of unwavering love, gratitude, joy, and grace.

IMAGINE YOUR BOUNDARIES AS STRONG YET FLUID.

Staying anchored in this larger perspective of who you are, imagine drawing a solid, strong, yet fluid, clear, and unbreakable bubble of light around yourself. See this bubble of light as a safe and happy place to be. Notice that the bubble is resilient and sturdy, yet also adaptable and flexible. Notice that you are the one in charge of your bubble, and that it does whatever is needed to keep you healthy, well, and safe.

IMAGINE OTHERS HONORING YOUR BOUNDARIES.

Allow yourself to imagine that others whom you care about, and want to be close to, are able to stand before you. One by one, imagine each person standing on the outside of your strong yet fluid bubble boundary. See that each of these people also has a strong yet fluid boundary bubble around themselves, too.

See yourself drawing in each person, one at a time, to be closer to you. Notice your bubble boundaries gracefully pulling inward to accommodate your desire to be closer to each other.

> What is love? It is that powerful attraction towards all that we . . . hope beyond ourselves.
>
> —Percy Bysshe Shelley

Now imagine expanding your bubble boundaries outward for one of you to say no, set a limit, tell a truth that may disappoint the other, or simply to bring your attention back home to yourself.

Imagine you both graciously going with the flow and accommodating whatever one of you needs or desires, knowing you are both safe to take care of yourselves—without fear of losing your connection, or of having the boundaries between you disappear.

IMAGINE BEING DEEPLY CONNECTED WITH OTHERS FROM A FOUNDATION OF BEING CONNECTED TO YOURSELF.

In your mind's eye, practice this experience of being deeply connected with others from a foundation of being deeply connected to, and honoring of, yourself. Feel a beautiful "we" space between you growing, as you make yourself available to simply be present and connect from a place of health and well-being within.

This is what it feels like to have healthy boundaries that can replace any walls that may be keeping love at bay. As you go through your day today, try taking this meditation with you. As you do, simply hold space for greater connection, clarity, and care to naturally emerge between yourself and others in organic and healthy ways.

Bonus: Practice in Action

Become a student of happy, healthy love by finding a resource to start studying what relationships look like when they are healthy and well. There are a wealth of resources available to you both online and in bookstores. Buy a book, watch a video, or sign up for a weekend workshop. Get moving on making your relationship your happy, safe space.

Forgiving Yourself and Others

Jesus said we should forgive seventy times seven times . . . I think [He] was trying to tell us that deep wounds require more than just one pass through forgiveness before they can be truly healed.

—Karla McLaren

Those of us who aspire to live a nonvictimized, empowered life sometimes assume we must quickly forgive any harm done us, whether or not we think our offender deserves it. Yet when Jesus suggested we "forgive seventy times seven times," He was reminding us that not all anger can be so easily released. And in fact, not all anger should be so easily discarded, for anger might actually be what's required for us to have a true breakthrough.

We get angry for a reason. We've been violated. Our boundaries have been broken. Our integrity's been compromised, or our good character attacked. While it's admirable to try to push the river toward an easy resolution, sometimes forgiveness needs to be coaxed or courted to ensure that we're not confusing it with its counterfeits—repression, spiritual bypass, or denial. True forgiveness is an emotional expansion of the heart that must be arrived at honestly and organically.

There is such a thing as letting go too soon. If you're

> I had often fantasized about running into my ex and his wife. In those fantasies, I was running over them with a truck.
>
> —Sarah Jessica Parker
> in *Sex and the City*

being violated, then anger is likely the right response. Forgiveness should occur only once your boundaries have been firmly reestablished and your personal safety restored. I once had a woman come to a *Calling in "The One"* Breakthrough Intensive. She spoke with deep shame about her feelings of resentment due to an inability to forgive her former husband for all the horrible things he'd done. Upon exploration, we discovered that her former husband was actually still perpetrating abusive actions against her—in the present. He lied consistently about his activities with their children, didn't pay his child support on time, if at all, and bad-mouthed her to their three young daughters constantly. I instructed the woman *not* to forgive this man until she was able to secure better boundaries with him, whether by setting clear rules directly with him and securing his agreement to adhere to them, or by doing so through the courts. At the time, she needed her anger to help mobilize her into taking much-needed action.

Many of us judge ourselves for being unspiritual when we feel anger. We fear we have only two options in response. Either we can lash out, and risk doing great damage to ourselves and others in the process; or we can minimize or swallow our anger, often concealing our feelings even to ourselves. Neither option is helpful. Many of us have lost friendships or relationships with people who mattered to us because we behaved unwisely in response to feeling anger, and many an illness has been ascribed to the latter, including depression and cancer. However, anger is a warning, much like physical pain. If you put your hand on a hot flame, it hurts. That pain screams at you to move your hand. NOW. Anger is similar. The healthy response to rage is to take the fury of it and point it in the direction of much-needed positive change.

Anger needs to move. It's the force of transformation, and if you let it go too soon, you will lose your momentum. If you can listen to what your anger is trying to tell you, you'll hear that anger is requiring, even demanding, an action from you. To do something to reclaim your rights. To fix a wrong. To secure a boundary. To restore integrity. When anger takes over your body, you'll want to welcome it. Hold it from a deeper center. Listen for the change that it's requiring you to make. Like gold, the proactive, positive message of anger must be searched for and mined. Breathe deep and ask yourself, "How am I giving my power away?" "What right

> Thou hast permission at all times to say "NO," to change thy mind, and to express thy true feelings.
>
> —Catherine Cardinal

do I need to reclaim?" "What personal boundary do I now need to set?" "What amends do I need to make to myself?"

Why is this conversation an important one for you to engage in at this point in the course? Because without learning how to have an empowered relationship with your feelings of anger—allowing these feelings to inform you of what you'll need to do to keep your relationships healthy and strong—then you'll likely have a hard time trusting yourself to form an intimate partnership, or keeping love healthy once you find it. Anger can tell you when and how to say no, how to set healthy limits, negotiate on your own behalf, or tell the truth even when it's the hard thing to do. If you have a history of being with narcissists; or if you've habitually had issues with being a doormat, or giving more than your fair share; or if you're often with people who betray, use, or abuse you in some way, learning how to manage feelings of anger wisely will be the number one skill you'll want to acquire. If you're in a disempowered relationship with your own feelings of frustration, irritation, or rage, then you'll likely create drama/traumas out of someone's bad behavior. Yet if you're in an empowered relationship with anger, you'll be able to use those feelings to access the power you'll need to move the relationship to higher ground.

If you focus your anger outwardly, as though it's only others who must do things differently, without also examining what you yourself need to change, then you'll miss the growth opportunity that anger has brought to you. The woman whose former husband was abusive to her admitted to us that she'd always been a doormat for someone—her father, her older brother, then a series of boyfriends who treated her poorly. One bully after another seemed to somehow find his way into her bed. Was it that *they* had to change? No. She herself was the one who needed to change. She had to start standing up for herself in life and insist that people treat her better.

Years ago, when I was in private practice, my client Howard would complain, week after week, of intense feelings of rage toward his former girlfriend with whom he was desperately trying to maintain a friendship. The terms of the friendship, however, seemed to address her needs without addressing his. Since she rejected him, he was the one who'd done most of

> Forgiveness is not an emotion. It is a decision made by your whole self after your true emotional work has been done.
>
> —Karla McLaren

the work to try to adjust to the new direction of the relationship. She remained emotionally and financially dependent upon Howard, expecting him to continue caring for her, even though she'd already started dating another man. He was trying. She called him to talk about her insecurities with the other man until he became furious and would blow up at her. He then apologized the next day and tried to be there for her again, out of some ideal that this was the "loving, spiritual" thing to do. She again began talking about her problems with her new boyfriend, and he again became angry, although this time he managed to keep it to himself. However, after their phone conversation, Howard promptly went out and had a car accident. This is a clear example of someone who was not using their anger to inform them of how to renegotiate their boundaries and need for personal safety.

If you feel angry, then there's work to be done. While your anger will predictably point you to someone else as the reason you're mad, if you dig below the surface, you'll often discover that the person you're most angry with is yourself. For letting it happen. For not listening to your intuition. For not standing up for yourself. For making choices out of the weakest part of yourself. When this happens, you'll want to soften into the feelings beneath the anger. Disappointment. Frustration. Sorrow or despair. These are appropriate feelings to have in the aftermath of disregarding and disrespecting yourself.

I had a student once who was furious with herself for letting her abusive former boyfriend back into her bed one night. She was horrified to think he might judge her as someone he could so easily use and then discard. She desperately wanted to call him (since he wasn't calling her) and tell him that she wasn't normally "that kind of woman." Given that he'd already displayed his lack of regard for her by predictably disappearing after "getting the goods," I suggested that she focus instead on restoring her own regard for herself. She needed to be with her feelings of shame and embarrassment about giving herself to someone who had consistently demonstrated that he had so little regard for her welfare. By doing so, she had an opportunity to channel her pain into the action of making a deeper commitment to herself—one that caused her to develop strong boundaries that honored her need for safety and connection before she opened up emotionally and sexually again.

> The most beautiful thing that [a person] can do is to forgive a wrong.
>
> —Rabbi Eleazar of Worms

Self-forgiveness begins with allowing yourself

to feel what you feel after betraying yourself in these ways, and again, by asking, "What needs to change?" For Howard, what needed to change was that he had to accept the loss of the relationship and stop overgiving in the hopes that she'd change her mind. And he needed to promise himself to never ever again overgive at his own expense. For

> The stupid neither forgive nor forget; the naïve forgive and forget; the wise forgive but do not forget.
>
> —Thomas Szasz

my student with the abusive former boyfriend, she needed to honor her need for emotional safety before getting naked with someone—particularly someone who was so clearly self-serving and unwilling to extend care to her.

Anger begs action. Action to restore a sense of safety, and reestablish or establish (for the first time) a healthy boundary. When you learn to relate to your anger in this constructive way, you will have discovered how to make an ally of your anger and channel its force for good.

PRACTICE: CHANNELING ANGER FOR GOOD

Take out your journal.

WHO ARE YOU ANGRY WITH?

Write a list of three to five people you feel angry with or resentful toward and why. You may include yourself on this list.

IDENTIFY EMPOWERED ACTIONS IN RESPONSE TO ANGER.

Now, one person at a time, go through the following questions:

What boundary violation and/or loss of personal safety did you suffer that is causing you to feel angry? If it was someone else who violated your boundaries, how might you have allowed or even colluded with their bad behavior?

What action is your anger wanting you to take to restore balance, well-being, and integrity to this situation?

Anyone can become angry–that is easy. But to be angry with the right person, to the right degree, at the right time, for the right purpose, and in the right way–that is not easy.

—Aristotle

What amends will you now commit to making moving forward?

NOTICE WHO YOU'RE NOW READY TO FORGIVE, IF ANYONE.

Now that you've learned your lessons and resolved to make much-needed change, whom can you forgive and for what?

Bonus: Practice in Action

Take at least one action today that firmly establishes your boundaries and/or restores personal safety to your life.

As a result of taking this action, if forgiveness is now an option, then forgive someone you've been holding resentment toward.

Being Grateful for It All

The greatest discovery of my generation is that a human being
can alter his life by altering his attitudes of mind.

—William James

Several years ago, I was captivated by a romantic relationship that alternated passionately between feelings of euphoria and deep despair. As the despair took over and began to dominate the relationship, I became more and more despondent. Unable to excavate myself from a destructive situation, I was terribly upset and confused. Not only had I lost respect for my then-boyfriend, but my inability to end the relationship was causing me to fast lose respect for myself as well. I began berating myself for what appeared to be a weakness of character on my part. Finally, not knowing what else to do, I surrendered. "I must need to be here," I told myself, and I gave up resisting my predicament. I began to chant over and over in my mind, "Thank you, God, for this relationship. Thank you, God, for this pain that is sitting on my chest and causing my heart to break open. Thank you, God, for using this man to teach me to be a more loving and compassionate person." Miraculously, after just a few minutes of repeating this prayer to myself silently, my heart began to lighten. Although I still saw no way out of the impossible situation I was in, a sense of peace washed over me. Encouraged, I began this practice each time I'd get knotted up into an emotional pretzel (which was often). Each time, I was able to alleviate the emotional agony I felt. Eventually the relationship worked its way out of the state we were in, and we were able to part ways in a kind and respectful fashion.

Sometimes the value of a relationship (even a miserable one) is that it provides

> To be upset over what you don't have is to waste what you do have.
>
> —Ken Keyes Jr.

an opportunity for you to grow and mature in ways that you might not have done otherwise. There were many lessons I learned from this challenging encounter, and the extraordinary power of gratitude to transform us was one of them. In his book *The Power of Now*, Eckhart Tolle says, "Your task is not to search for love but to find a portal through which love can enter." Gratitude is such a portal.

When we think of gratitude, many of us think of turkey and pumpkin pies, notes written in haste, sweet, superficial lists made up of life's little blessings, or childlike utterances of "God is great, God is good." That is *not* the gratitude that I am talking about. While all expressions of gratitude are beautiful, I'm talking about gratitude as a kind of alchemy that transforms our very experience of life. I'm talking about gratitude that moves the heart from contraction to expansion, from broken to whole.

Out of my experience with my former boyfriend, I began to understand the power of giving thanks. I decided to do an experiment. Every day for thirty days, I set my alarm clock a half hour earlier than usual. I woke up, grabbed my morning cup of coffee, took out my pen and notebook, and wrote five full pages of things that I was grateful for. Not as a list, mind you, but as though I were writing a journal entry. "Dear God: Thank you for the beautiful hardwood floors throughout my apartment. Thank you for how sweet and loving my cat, Clover, is to me each and every day. Thank you for my health. Thank you for this quiet time . . ." Pretty soon I'd run out of things to thank God for that I actually felt glad to have. I'd have to start stretching myself. "Thank you that my neighbor downstairs has finally stopped drinking, so I don't have to worry about him burning the building down with his cigarettes. Thank you that my crazy narcissistic boss quit last month so I don't have to deal with her anymore." But pretty soon I'd run out of those things to say as well. That's when I *really* had to stretch. "Okay, God, well, thank you for the fact that I'm broke again because I appreciate the opportunity to once again practice having faith. Thank you that I have no date on Saturday night, giving me the opportunity to push past my self-conscious feelings of social inadequacy and go to the movies alone. Thank you that I gained five pounds with my period because I get to love my body even when I don't necessarily like its shape . . ." You get the gist. I had to dig pretty deep.

Now, this is the miracle. During that thirty-day period, I began to feel a pervasive sense of joy. This sense of joy was completely unattached to whether or not my life was going the way I wanted it to. I simply began to feel blissful most of the time. I was truly happy just to be alive.

Let the beauty you love be what you do.
There are thousands of ways we kneel and kiss the earth.

—Rumi

What I learned about gratitude is this. When we give thanks for *everything* in our lives, specifically and exactly for *the way they are,* regardless of our preference for them to be different, *our lives become lit up with joy.* And when we are lit up with joy, we become an absolute magnet for the blessings of life, including love.

Our minds are generally overwhelmed with what we *don't* have, and we're usually upset about that to some degree. "I don't have enough love." "I don't have enough money." "I'm not having enough sex." "I don't have enough time." That's understandable. After all, when you have a toothache, you aren't thinking, "Well, gee, I'm awfully glad that my feet feel fine and that my hands don't hurt." No. You think about the agony your tooth is in. Yet the danger of our preoccupation with the lack in our lives is that we are creative beings, and whatever we give our attention to is what we create more of. Our constant attentiveness to our unhappiness does *not* create abundance—it just creates more unhappiness.

Gratitude shifts our perception from what we *don't* have to what we *do.* In shifting our focus this way, we increase our sense of abundance. In turn, this attracts more abundance. Perhaps that is what Jesus was pointing to when he said, "To him who has, more shall be given." Gratitude is an inner map that instructs the Universe to give us more. Just as depression is an inner map that says, "You will never have what you want no matter how hard you try. It's hopeless. You should just give up"; and anxiety says,

Giving up on the idea that we *simply have to* find a soulmate may be a necessary prerequisite to actually finding one. For one thing, it amounts to a decision to dissociate ourselves from our . . . insatiable neediness and entitlement, and to be grateful for what life has given us already.

—Carolyn G. Miller

> The measure of mental health is the disposition to find good everywhere.
>
> —Ralph Waldo Emerson

"Life is terrifying and dangerous. Better be careful, hedge your bets, and don't get your hopes up. Be attached to something specific, but don't dare believe that you'll actually get it," so does gratitude affirm, "Good things are always coming to me. Look, there's another one right now. Life is good to me even when it doesn't appear to be so at first glance. I know that love belongs to me because I have constant evidence of its beautiful presence in my life."

I love the parable of Jesus feeding the multitude. His first action was to give thanks. He then broke bread. And as the story goes, that affirmation of abundance turned five loaves of bread and two fish into enough food to feed thousands. Jesus understood the power of gratitude to create an abundant life, filled with all that's needed in any given moment. When he admonished us to "consider the lilies of the field, how they grow," he was beseeching us to give up worrying so much about what we don't have and to fill our minds instead with what we *do*. Our constant worrying and fretting about life must have seemed as foolish to Him as if the lilies of the field were all huddled around, whispering words of fear to one another: "What if there is no more rain? What if the sun doesn't shine tomorrow? What if there is an earthquake and we become uprooted from our soil? Oh, what will become of us then?"

As life is constantly redefining itself according to our consciousness, gratitude is the absolute best way to attract all that is good and lovely and wonderful into our lives. It begins with something both simple and profound—giving thanks for exactly the way things are and exactly the way that they are not in your life right now.

PRACTICE: WRITE A MORE RIGOROUS GRATITUDE LIST

Take out your journal. In journal style, write five full pages of things that you are grateful for. Stretch to look for the silver linings. Look to be grateful for the ways you are growing, for the lessons you're learning, for the wisdom you've gained. Be rigorous. While five pages may seem like a lot to ask, the ability to shift your mindset from one of "lack" to one of "abundance" is worth the time and effort.

Bonus: Practice in Action

Today, I invite you to take on the practice of being grateful for everything exactly as it is, and exactly as it is not. Throughout the day, regardless of whether or not you like what's happening, say a prayer of thanks that things are just the way they are.

At least once today, express your gratitude to someone. Tell this person exactly why you are grateful for their presence in your life. Be very specific. *For example, "I always feel like I can talk to you without being judged," "You always try your best to take my complaints seriously," "You inspire me to be a better person."*

Becoming Unstoppable

. . . you must not be afraid. You need to have sufficient
courage to make mistakes. Disappointments, defeat, and despair
are the tools God uses to show us the way.

—Paulo Coelho

Dating is not for the faint of heart. It can be hard to put yourself out there. You're taking a risk to let down your guard, and show your hand to near strangers. It's even more discouraging when things don't work out after getting your hopes up. Learning to relate to disappointments, obstacles, setbacks, and delays in an empowered way is crucial to this journey. Particularly now, as you're about to graduate from the structure of our daily time together.

I will warn you. Disappointment is the number one trigger for a false center to kick in. If we were playing Monopoly, disappointment would be your "Go directly to jail, Do not pass Go, Do not collect $200" card. It can send you straight back to the emotional center of your old story, imprisoning you in your default false meaning that goes something like, "See, I'll always be alone," or "No one will ever want me," or "I am too much," or somehow "I'm just not good enough." When this happens, you must remember that you have the key to unlock your prison cell right there in your back pocket. It's called your Power

> The temptation when the path to success gets too bumpy is to leap back into the comfort zone. Don't. Keep pushing forward, always forward. The comfort zone is the land of dreams and wishes. Success is the land of results, where all those dreams come true.
>
> —Mark Burnett

Statements. Those assertions of truth that you crafted when you first identified the story you came up with about yourself in response to the disappointments and hurts of your youth.

In these moments, you must remind yourself that your feelings are not facts. In these moments, you must remember to ask the part of you that is discouraged and hurting, "How old are you, angel?" In these moments, you must recall a deeper truth, and lovingly, firmly, steadfastly push back against the certainty of these false beliefs to correct these misperceptions.

Some things don't happen because it's just not in our best interest, even if we think otherwise. And sometimes we pull in people who duplicate our old patterns just for the opportunity to (1) respond differently or (2) interpret what's happening differently. Life must evolve through us and not just to us, from the different choices we make, the different actions we take, and the different ways we decide to make meaning of our experience. This is what it is to turn the river in a new direction.

My friend, mentalist Gerard Senehi, bends objects with his mind. I wouldn't believe it except for the fact that he's done this right before my eyes. He literally pulled a fork out of my kitchen drawer, held it pointing upward toward the ceiling while holding it from the bottom, and focused on it for about three minutes. I watched it bend over. Right in front of me. Not just a slight bend, but a full-on bend where the top of the fork was now facing the ground, even though the bottom of it was still there in his hand, pointed toward the sky.

Gerard has done this all around the world, performing on *The Ellen DeGeneres Show* and the *Today* show, as well as at the White House for the Clintons. He loves reminding people that we have the power to transform anything we've been assuming is fixed and unmovable. His life's work is to open up an awareness of unlimited potential, and awaken us to a sense that anything is possible. I sometimes think of this mind-blowing moment in my kitchen as a metaphor for *Calling in "The One."* Because now it's your turn to bend steel. You can do this by focusing your efforts on relating to all obstacles and delays as opportunities to graduate forever from your old painful patterns in love.

Normally we relate to disappointments, setback,

> You will have wonderful surges forward. Then there must be a time of consolidating before the next forward surge. Accept this as part of the process and never become downhearted.
>
> —Eileen Caddy

Ever tried. Ever failed.
No matter. Try again.
Fail again. Fail better.

—Samuel Beckett

and delays as an indication that something is wrong, or as validation that our old, sad story is true. Yet much of your progress will happen in these moments when things are not going your way. This is where you get to show your stuff by applying what you've learned in this course. This is where you get to go deeper by valuing wisdom over getting what you want, when you want it. Or by affirming the goodness of Life, even when the risks you've had the courage to take appear to be for naught.

To love is to risk. There's no way around it. If you're one to shy away from failure in life, or if you play only the games you're sure you'll win, then you're probably living a life that's way too small and far too boring. Taking a risk means there's no sure way to predict whether you will win (by getting what you want), or lose (by not getting what you want). A risk with an assured outcome is not a risk. That is simply you playing it safe in life. Until you embrace failure, loss, and disappointment as part of a life well lived, then you will likely have a life that doesn't really light you up or inspire you very much.

You've taken a stand and upped the ante. It's exciting. You are finally committed to creating a love life that is worthy of you. Yet don't be naïve in thinking it's all downhill from here. The great psychologist Joseph Campbell once warned us, "You can't make an omelet without breaking eggs. Destruction before creation." Remember that the first thing that happens when making a big commitment is the breaking down of everything that doesn't support that commitment. If you are really committed, you may experience an even greater number of disappointments and delays in service to showing you what now needs to change. The old unhealthy ways of keeping yourself safe will begin to backfire. The ways you've been covertly lying to yourself will be exposed. The ways that others have secretly been out of integrity with you will be revealed. Whatever happens, bless it all. Choose to see it as an answered prayer. In this way, you'll make empowered meaning of your experience, and become unstoppable in your commitment to change the story of how love goes for you.

The game you are in is not so much getting someone to propose to you by a certain date, as it is being ready and available to be proposed to by then. As such, your attention needs to be focused on showing up true to the future you're standing for, regardless of what's actually happening. If someone treats you poorly, then you take it as an opportunity to refuse to allow yourself to be defined by someone else's bad behavior. If someone is rude to you, you take it as an opportunity to practice speaking up and setting a boundary. If someone hurts your heart, you relate to it as the chance to change your old pattern of putting up a wall, and instead make the choice to reach out to try to clear the air between you. Life can do for you only what it can do through you, and this is what it looks like to bend the steel of an old well-worn pattern.

> Progress always involves risk; you can't steal second base and keep your foot on first.
>
> —Frederick Wilcox

It's time to leave behind your old ways of doing things, in service to the life you are creating. In order to activate a future of love fulfilled, you may now need to start saying yes to things you might have said no to in the past. You may have to give up judging and finding fault with everyone you go out with and start looking for the good in others. You may have to tolerate the discomfort of not being in control and take the risk to let someone else take the lead. You may even have to give up the paralysis that comes from allowing your fear of making a mistake to stop you. Remember, if it weren't for mistakes, most people on the planet wouldn't even be alive right now. There is a big difference between playing full out in life by taking a risk that may or may not pan out, and plowing straight ahead even though you know, in your heart, that what you're doing is a mistake. The latter is motivated by neediness and displays a lack of belief in yourself and others. The former is where all things worth having in life begin. Don't let your fear of making a mistake dictate your chances for happiness in love. Remind yourself that at least one good thing came out of every mistake you've ever made, and stop letting fear limit your life.

There is surely evidence in our world of why we should remain closed and defended with one another. Ask a widow or widower to share from their heart what it was like to lose their beloved, and you may begin to understand. Falling in love is one of the most vulnerable experiences that one can have in life. None of us can know for sure what's coming next. I say, all the more reason to have a positive relationship with disappointments, obstacles, and delays. So that we are no longer limited by what we fear might happen, but instead, expanded by our courage to be unstoppable in standing for what could.

PRACTICE: MAKING EMPOWERED
MEANING OF DISAPPOINTMENTS

To be unstoppable on your journey to the fulfillment of love, please engage in the following exercise to help you make empowered meaning of any disappointments, obstacles, setbacks, and delays you might experience along the way.

To practice, think of a recent disappointment you experienced, and allow yourself to connect with the emotions associated with what happened.

1. **Become Aware of Where You Feel the Emotions of the Disappointment in Your Body.** Notice where you are feeling the emotions about the disappointment in your body. From a deeper, wider center within you, extend a sense of presence and support to the part of you experiencing those emotions. Welcome in the difficult feelings, naming them one at a time. *For example, I can see I'm feeling sad, frightened, angry, hurt, dismayed, resigned, rejected, etc.*

2. **Notice the Automatic Meaning You Are Making of the Disappointment.** Notice the automatic interpretation you are making of the situation. What is the "I am/I am not" story present? Or the automatic old belief about your relationship with others, or about your relationship with Life that is being triggered? *For example, I am not wanted, I am alone, no one cares about me, Life doesn't support me, I can never have what I want, etc.*

3. **Notice How Old This Part of You Is.** How old is the part of you that is inside of that meaning?

4. **Connect with a Deeper, Wider Center Within.** Open your eyes and shake it out. Take a deep breath and consciously connect with a deeper, wider center within you that is outside of the emo-

tions you are feeling and able to see your situation from a larger perspective. Anchor into the part of you able to access a deeper truth. The part of you that is aware of your worthiness, resilience, strength, power, value, and resourcefulness. From this center, extend a sense of care and support to the part of you feeling the emotions associated with your disappointment.

5. **Lovingly Tell Yourself What's Really True.** Kindly but firmly remind yourself of the intention that you've set, and help yourself see why this breakdown might actually be a good thing. Identify the opportunity for growth inherent in the disappointment. *For example, This is a great opportunity to speak my truth, even if others don't want to hear it. Or this is a wonderful chance to love myself even when someone else is not loving me in the ways I'd hoped for.*

   See if you can make more empowered meaning of the disappointment, reassuring yourself that you are on the right path. Help yourself remember that everyone experiences disappointments, setbacks, and delays sometimes, and that these experiences are a natural part of a life well lived.

6. **Create a Power Statement About the Disappointment.** Create a Power Statement that helps you make empowered meaning of the disappointment, and which deconstructs any false beliefs that are being triggered in this experience. *For example, "All that's happening is I'm being given the chance to make a different choice and finally do right by myself." Or, "Life is protecting me by revealing who others really are, and what their motivations have been, so I can make wise and informed choices about how much of myself to invest in our relationship."*

Bonus: Practice in Action

At some point today, take a risk that is based upon the empowering meaning you are making of a difficult situation. *For example, in response to someone demonstrating a lack of commitment to you, cancel an obligation you've made to them that would, in fact, be overgiving. Or in response to someone not asking you out, pick up the phone and call them to ask them out.* Remind yourself you've got nothing to lose. Even if someone doesn't respond in the way you'd hoped they would, you will have stood for yourself and the future you're committed to creating. And that's a win, no matter what.

Holding the High Watch

When love isn't in our lives, it's on the way. If you know that a
special guest is coming at five o'clock, do you spend the day
messing up the home? Of course not. You prepare. And that is
what we should do for love.

—Marianne Williamson

There are several challenges with the practice of writing a long and detailed
list of what we want in a mate, making sure to include everything, for fear
that any omission will haunt us when "The One" arrives without that particular quality. As in, ugh, how could I have forgotten to write "financially solvent"
on my list? Or how could I have failed to remember to include a good sense of
humor? Or that they like to dance? Or that they don't snore? Or that they have the
same taste in furniture as I do? Or that they don't talk incessantly in the morning?
Yikes. What was I thinking?

It's also a challenge for some of us to even think of those things we'll need to be
happy in love, because we've never actually been happy in love. We literally have no
reference point for what we are standing to create. So, our lists are sometimes limited by what we don't even know that we don't yet know. Who knew, for example,
that it feels so good to be woken up each day with a soft and loving back rub? Or
that you absolutely melt when someone brushes your hair? Or that you really, really
needed someone who cared so much that they'd memorize that song your grandmother used to sing to you when you were little, just so they could sing it to you
when you were sick? These are just things you can't anticipate putting onto a list.

So, our lists are limited by what we already know, and by our own inability to anticipate what we'll need in order to feel happy and safe enough to become the best we can be. Because ultimately, that's what this is all about, isn't it? Creating a solid and count-on-able foundation for well-being and health in order to become the person you were born to become, and fulfill the unique potential that you and you alone possess? We often think that the desire to find a loving relationship is incidental to the larger goals of realizing our life's purpose or actualizing our spiritual growth. It's not. Loving relationships are the solid ground we stand upon to provide the support we need to live our most magnificent lives. No one becomes themselves by themselves. We need the love and support of others to make our greatest creative contributions to this world. It's not a mistake that I didn't write a bestselling book until I had Mark in my life. Nor is it a mistake that I released my first album as a jazz singer-songwriter, *Lucky in Love*, that went to #1 on iTunes and made the *Billboard* charts after I partnered with Michael, who is a brilliant producer of the arts. Before I created the *Calling in "The One"* process, I believed that getting married would take something away from me. I struggled alone for years thinking it was dangerous to my creativity to get too involved with someone, based upon toxic codependent patterns that I'd acted out for years. Little did I know that healthy relationships actually enhance our ability to realize our dreams and actualize our potential. I now know that this is true for you, too.

So, now that I've awakened you to your need for love, and convinced you that you can't possibly know exactly what "The One" will look like before they arrive, where do you go from here? Given we are about to lose this precious structure of our daily time together, how can you keep possibility alive and ensure you stay the course until you've manifested your intention for a deeply satisfying relationship? By staying close to love. By staying generative of care, compassion, and kindness between yourself and others. To give your love for no reason other than because it's the more beautiful way to live. To refuse to let your life be used up by the complaint that Life isn't giving you what you want when you want it, and instead choose to be one of those rare and beautiful beings who seeks to make life better for others, in any and all of the ways you can.

Take all of those qualities that you know that you want in a mate—happy, spiritual, self-aware, and kind—and place your full attention on becoming that person. If you fail to do this, then if and when someone arrives who possesses all these qualities, you could actually feel intimidated and run away! You might beg them to come back in a year or two to give you time to catch up. This is why we begin with you.

Look, here's the thing. No one writes a list of what they want in a mate that includes attributes like unsuccessful, out of shape, humorless, and victimized. Of course you want someone who is amazing. Someone who is winning at life, making a difference for others, who treats themselves and others lovingly, and is fully engaged in contributing their unique gifts in the ways that their soul is coded to do. But you know who winds up with these amazing people? Other amazing people! Contrary to popular opinion, not all the good ones are taken. They are, however, holding out for someone as wonderful as they have grown themselves to be.

Holding the high watch for love is the ability to see the possibilities surrounding you, and live into them as though they were real. "How long must one remain in the dark?" asks author Florence Scovel Shinn. "Until one can see in the dark," she cleverly answers. Holding the high watch is such a mystical sight. It's not so much standing for what you will *have*, as much as it is standing for who you will *be* in life: a grateful and happily partnered person who is cherished, respected, and adored by "The One" that you yourself have chosen to love. Many of us have this backward. We want to *have* love so we can *do* loving things so we can *be* loving. But the opposite is true. We need to activate the expansion of our hearts to *be* love and, from there, we must *do* loving things, so that we can then generate the experience of *having* more love in our lives. Rather than have, do, be—which is how most of us are trying to create our lives—it's actually be, do, then, finally, have.

As a teenager, I fell in love with the Old Testament. Not your typical reading material, I suppose, for a young person, but the deprivation of my childhood home created in me a hunger for truth, which I'm now quite grateful for. In the book of 2 Kings, there's a story that always stayed with me. It's about three kings who were wandering in the desert without any hope of finding water for their thirsty men and horses. The prophet Elisha was called on to help them. When Elisha prayed for water, God answered, "Thus saith the Lord, ye shall not see wind, neither shall ye see rain; yet make this valley full of ditches." And not long after, the story goes, "... it came to pass ... [that] the country was filled with water." Sometimes, we just have to dig ditches before the blessed rains can come to finally quench our thirst.

> By night on my bed I sought him whom my soul loveth.
>
> —Song of Solomon 3:1

So, get busy digging your ditches. Clean out your closets, both literally and met-aphorically. Put some daisies on your dining table and rose petals on your bed. Sur-render yourself completely to learning the ways of love. Give up being right. Take on listening more deeply and try sharing what you've been given with others. Choose to share a room with a stranger while on a meditation retreat. Volunteer to be the one who cleans up the kitchen after a meeting. And spend time delightfully playing with an animal who desperately needs your attention and love. Allow your commit-ment to love another person in this lifetime to inform all of the choices you make, and all of the actions you take. If you hope to make a baby in your body once you find true love, then start eating healthy now. If you want to purchase a beautiful home with your beloved, then start a savings account now. Plan for that future and weave it into the manifest world each and every day. Surrender to it fully, recogniz-ing how surrender differs from giving up or being resigned to your fate. This is the difference. Surrendering is like floating on the water. You relax, allowing the water to fully carry your weight, knowing that you are completely supported and safe to simply let go and enjoy the ride.

Resignation, on the other hand, is like sinking. You do not feel safe or certain that things are okay. When you feel this way, try going back to your Power Statements, and gently, firmly remind yourself that you are indeed powerful and that Life is already supporting you to manifest love. How do I know? Well, you are here, are you not? Life has brought us together and you have been receptive enough to read this far, yes? You have faithfully declared your intention, and you've backed it up with action to clear away the cobwebs and open yourself to love. All there is left to do now is to make the decision to keep expanding your ability to give and receive its grace.

New York Times wedding columnist Lois Smith Brady once wrote, "Whenever anyone asks me about love . . . I always say wait for that feeling, wait, wait, wait. Wait with the patience of a Buddhist fly fisherman." Now, I've never met a Bud-dhist fly fisherman but I imagine that this is someone who is not in reaction to the externals—the weather, the force of the current, the temperature of the water, or the amount of time they've been standing there waiting for a nibble. I imagine that they are able to patiently, unflinchingly, and unwaveringly stand in their commit-ment to catch that blessed fish. So too you. As the farmer who has planted his crops does not go out to his garden and tug on his plants in an effort to force them to grow, you now wait. You till the earth and keep watering your garden. Yours is an active waiting, not a passive one, knowing that 99 percent of all creation takes place beneath the soil. I'm here with you. We stand ready and alert. We know that the miracle is coming, and we receive that miracle now. And together we say yes, yes, yes, and yes.

> Remember.
> What is yours
> will come to you.
>
> —Ralph Blum

PRACTICE: MAKING YOUR LIST

Okay, *now* it's time to make "The List."

Take out your journal. Write down those qualities that you are looking for in a life partner. Do this now.

When you are finished, read through your list. Narrow it down to your top five qualities by circling those things that are the most important to you. These are your top five essentials. The qualities this person *must* have for you to move forward. Do this now.

Next, close your eyes and put your hand over your heart. Promise yourself to pursue only those who appear to have these qualities, and to refrain from dating those who don't.

Now go through your list again. For each of your top five essential qualities, I invite you to make a promise to yourself to do your best to develop and cultivate these qualities within yourself. For example, "Spiritual" becomes "I promise to prioritize my spiritual growth each and every day." "Has a sense of humor" might become "I promise to see the humor in every situation, to learn to poke fun at myself, and to have fun each and every day." "Intelligent" might become "I promise to be an avid reader and a lifelong learner and do all that I can to develop my mind each and every day".

Bonus: Practice in Action

Create a Power Statement that you can memorize and that affirms your ability to attract your beloved into your life. Read through the following Power Statements to see if any of these resonate for you as true. Feel free to create one of your own.

- Thank you, Universe, for bringing me a great and lasting love.
- I am worthy of the love that I am calling into my life.
- I have the power to learn how to keep love safe, and I open to receive happy, healthy love now.
- I open my heart to give and receive love, and I breathe the love of my beloved into my heart now.
- I know my beloved is on their way to me right now. Thank you, thank you, thank you.
- I am grateful that Life is right now in motion to magically, joyfully bring my beloved and me together.

My heart has burned with passion
and has searched forever
for this wondrous beauty
that I now behold.

—Rumi

Allow this Power Statement to become your mantra, speaking it to yourself over and over again and writing it often in your journal. Allow yourself to feel the joy and gratitude for the anticipated arrival of your beloved each time you recite your Power Statement. When in doubt, discouragement, or fear, return again to your Power Statement. Let it become the sacred song of your heart and soul. Sing it often and sing it loud.

And I join with you now, holding the high watch with you and for you, knowing that as you have asked, so shall you be answered.

Suggested Study Guide for Group Discussion

1. Share the synchronicities and signs you have received along the way that validate you are moving in the right direction.

2. Share how you define love, and how you choose to respond with love to a difficult situation you experienced this week. What opened up as a result?

3. In preparing yourself for intimate love, how have you grown your ability to set healthy boundaries this week?

4. Who in your life has been difficult to forgive, and why? What changes can you make or have you made this week to help move you in that direction?

5. In writing out five pages of things you're grateful for, what did you discover about the power of a shift in your perspective?

6. What disappointments did you endure this week and how have you made empowered meaning of those challenges?

7. Share the top five qualities you are looking for in a partner, as well as the Power Statement you created to help you stay generative of this future.

Note: On your final meeting together, I suggest you go around the room and acknowledge each member of your group as a way to create closure. One person at a time is invited to be on the "hot seat" as other members express their appreciation, admiration, love, and support for that person.

Postscript

The end is where we start from.

—T. S. Eliot

I f you have taken this course seriously, as I imagine you have, then you have probably hit a few bumps in the road. Transformation is never an easy path. As Shakespeare once said, "The course of true love never did run smooth." Quite likely, one of the more challenging aspects of this time may have been the disruption you experienced in your social circle. Not everyone will be happy with the changes you've made. They won't be all right with you no longer being willing to suffer silently through the subtle mistreatments that they've been getting away with for years. By now, I imagine you've pissed off at least one person who mattered, and I just want you to know how okay that is.

When we grow, we force those in our lives to grow as well—and they don't always like it. As a matter of fact, they sometimes resent us for it and even choose to leave our lives. Let them. Because the alternative—betraying yourself by reverting back to old, toxic ways of being—is no longer an option. Besides, diminishing yourself by dimming down your power has never really helped anyone anyway. You never want to give your power away to someone with a lesser consciousness than you. In the end, it will keep all of you playing too small. While it's sad when people choose to leave our lives because we are choosing to rise, it's their choice to make. And frankly, it's one we'd be wise to respect. As my friend and spiritual teacher Jeff Brown says, "Out with the old. In with the true." Although people may rant and rave that you have abandoned or disappointed them, the truth is, the best you can possibly do for anyone is to get healthy yourself, and model for them that true transformation is possible.

No doubt many of you began this course in order to attain a particular goal—that of love realized in your life. Indeed, *all* of us are working in some way to realize love, those of us who are in committed partnerships, as well as those of us who are not. Love is not a goal as much as it is a journey. It isn't suddenly realized simply because you have your beloved in your life. Love is a *verb*, not a noun. It's not something tangible. You can't put it in your safe-deposit box. Love exists to the extent that you give it away. It is as old as the last encounter you had, even in the most ancient of your relationships. Love will always require of us more than we initially intended to give, for it will take no less than everything we've got. Love rarely behaves itself, complying with our preconceived notions, our lists of demands, and our constant desires that it show up a certain way. Rather it insists that we rise to the summit of what it is to be human, constantly stretching ourselves beyond what we had previously believed to be our limitations. Love is a 24/7 job. It will never be contained in a particular form of a particular relationship on a particular time schedule. The fulfillment of love is not to be found in the future. The fulfillment of love is always to be found right now.

In my work over the years I have come to see that people are divided into two categories. Those who want love in their lives and will faithfully do the work to actualize love; and those who want love in their lives but won't. Those who *will* do the work understand love as a creative action that they are free to choose in any given moment. Those who *won't* do the work tend to see love as an object to acquire or as a place to hide out. I pray with all my heart that I have enticed you toward the former. For that is the fulfillment of my purpose in life—to ever expand my capacity to give and receive love with all those who cross my path, and to help others do the same. You, dear reader, are the fulfillment of love for me. And now I beseech you to please pay it forward.

Two roads diverged in a wood, and I—
I took the one less traveled by.
And that has made all the difference.

—Robert Frost

References

Adrienne, Carol. *The Purpose of Your Life*. New York: William Morrow and Company, 1998.

Albere, Patricia. *Evolutionary Relationships*. Independence, Va: Oracle Institute Press, 2017.

Anand, Margot. *The Art of Sexual Magic*. New York: G. P. Putnam's Sons, 1995.

Brooks, David. "The Nuclear Family Was a Mistake." *The Atlantic*, March 2020, https://www.the atlantic.com/magazine/archive/2020/03/the-nuclear-family-was-a-mistake/605536/.

Cain, Susan. *Quiet: The Power of Introverts in a World That Can't Stop Talking*. New York: Broadway Books, 2013.

Capacchione, Lucia. *Living with Feeling*. New York: Jeremy P. Tarcher/Putnam, 2001.

Chödrön, Pema. *When Things Fall Apart*. Boston: Shambhala Publications, Inc., 1997.

Chopra, Deepak, ed. *The Love Poems of Rumi*. New York: Harmony Books, 1998.

Dalai Lama, His Holiness The. *Ethics for the New Millennium*. New York: Berkley Publishing Group, 1999.

Dalai Lama, His Holiness The, and Howard Cutler. *The Art of Happiness*. New York: Penguin Putnam, Inc., 1998.

Dweck, Carol. *Mindset: The New Psychology of Success*. New York: Ballantine Books; 2007.

Fetters, Ashley, and Kaitlyn Tiffany. "The 'Dating Market' Is Getting Worse." *The Atlantic*, February 2020, https://www.theatlantic.com/family/archive/2020/02/modern-dating-odds-economy-apps-tinder-math/606982/.

Forward, Susan. *Emotional Blackmail*. New York: HarperCollins Publishers, Inc., 1998.

Frankl, Viktor. *Man's Search for Meaning*. New York: Pocket Books, 1959.

Gawain, Shakti. *Creative Visualization*. New York: Bantam Books, 1978.

Gibran, Kahlil. *The Prophet*. New York: Alfred A. Knopf, 1962.

Goleman, Daniel. *Emotional Intelligence*. New York: Bantam Books, 1995.

Hafiz, translations by Daniel Ladinsky. *The Gift*. New York: Penguin Books, 1999.

Hollis, James. *The Middle Passage*. Toronto: Inner City Books, 1993.

James, William. *The Varieties of Religious Experience*. New York: Macmillan Publishing Co., Inc., 1961.

Markus, Hazel, and Paula Nurius. "Possible Selves." *American Psychologist* (1986), https://doi.org/10.1037/0003-066X.41.9.954.

Masterson, James F. *Search for the Real Self: Unmasking the Personality Disorders of Our Age*. New York: Simon & Schuster, 1990.

McLaren, Karla. *Emotional Genius*. Columbia, Calif.: Laughing Tree Press, 2001.

Miller, Carolyn Godschild. *Soulmates*. Tiburon, Calif.: H J Kramer, 2000.

Moore, Thomas. *Care of the Soul*. New York: HarperCollins Publishers, Inc., 1992.

———. *Soul Mates*. New York: HarperCollins Publishers, Inc., 1994.

Muller, Wayne. *Sabbath: Finding Rest, Renewal and Delight in Our Busy Lives*. New York: Bantam Books, 2000.

Myss, Caroline. *Why People Don't Heal and How They Can*. New York: Three Rivers Press, 1997.

———. *Sacred Contracts*. New York: Harmony Books, 2001.

Peck, M. Scott. *The Different Drum*. New York: Simon & Schuster, 1987.

Rosenberg, Joan. *90 Seconds to a Life You Love: How to Master Your Difficult Feelings to Cultivate Lasting Confidence, Resilience, and Authenticity*. New York: Little, Brown Spark, 2019.

Rumi, translated by Coleman Barks. *The Illuminated Rumi*. New York: Broadway Books, 1997.

Schiffmann, Erich. *Yoga: The Spirit and Practice of Moving into Stillness*. New York: Pocket Books, 1996.

Schucman, Helen. *A Course in Miracles*. Glen Ellen, Calif.: Foundation for Inner Peace, 1975.

Shafir, Rebecca Z. *The Zen of Listening*. Wheaton, Ill.: Quest Books, 2000.

Shinn, Florence Scovel. *The Game of Life and How to Play It*. Marina Del Rey: DeVorss & Company, 1925.

Tolle, Eckhart. *The Power of Now*. Novato, Calif.: New World Library, 1999.

Vanzant, Iyanla. *In the Meantime*. New York: Simon & Schuster, 1998.

Walsch, Neale Donald. *Conversations with God, Book I*. New York: G. P. Putnam's Sons, 1995.

Whitney, J., and D. F. Chang. "Inner Tradition Made Visible: The Interpersonal Benefits and Effects of Meditation Practice on Close Relationships." *Current Psychology* (2020), https://doi.org/10.1007/s12144-020-00738-9.

Williamson, Marianne. *Enchanted Love*. New York: Simon & Schuster, 1999.

———. *A Return to Love*. New York: HarperCollins, 1992.

Zweig, Connie, and Jeremiah Abrams, eds. *Meeting the Shadow*. New York: Jeremy P. Tarcher/Putnam, 1991.

Don't just pray for true love.

Pray to be ready when it finally arrives!

Happy, healthy love is not just about meeting the right person.

Great relationships are about having the development necessary to navigate the normal ups and downs that all relationships go through in ways that can help to continually deepen your bond and sustain healthy intimacy, warmth, and goodwill over time between yourself and your beloved.

About the Author

Katherine Woodward Thomas is a licensed marriage and family therapist, and the *New York Times* bestselling author of *Conscious Uncoupling*: *5 Steps to Living Happily Even After.* Katherine trains and certifies people as Certified *Calling in "The One"* Coaches and Certified *Conscious Uncoupling* Coaches. She's also a *Billboard* charting, #1 iTunes jazz artist with her album, *Lucky in Love*, which was co-written and co-produced with the Brothers Koren and released in 2019.